Media Firms:
Structures, Operations
and Performance

Edited by
Robert G. Picard

Turku School of Economics
and Business Administration, Finland

D1614657

LAWRENCE ERLBAUM ASSOCIATES, PUBLISHERS

2002   Mahwah, New Jersey   London

Lawrence Erlbaum Associates, Inc., Publishers
10 Industrial Avenue
Mahwah, New Jersey 07430

Cover Design by Kathryn Houghtaling Lacey

Library of Congress Cataloging-in-Publication Data

World Media Economics Conference (5th : 2002 : Turku, Finland)
  Media firms : structures, operations and performance / Robert G. Picard, editor.
    p.   cm.
  Conference held May, 2002.
  Includes bibliographical references and index.
  ISBN 0-8058-4165-2 (alk. paper)
    1. Mass media–Economic aspects–Congresses. 2. Corporations–Congresses.
  I. Picard, Robert G. II. Title.

P96.E25 W67 2002
338.4'730223–dc21

                                                    2002019390

Printed in the United States of America
10 9 8 7 6 5 4 3 2 1

Contents

\1,2

Chapter 1
The Centrality of Media Firms

Robert G. Picard
Turku School of Economics and Business Administration

Media firms are central to questions involving media economics, yet limited research in the field has actually focused on the company level since scholarly inquiry in the field began to flourish three decades ago. The literature of media economics is replete with studies at the industry level and with theoretical examinations of companies and their behaviour, but only a small portion explores media from the perspective of real firms and real choices.

This narrowness has perhaps resulted from an overreliance on industrial organisation studies focused on industry structures, national market analyses, and local market studies that asked broader questions about consumer and advertiser demand, industry performance, and competition issues. It has also been influenced by the fact that much research has concentrated on identifying conditions that exist in media industries and markets and providing evidence about the structures and forces at work in media and communications industries.

These approaches have been appropriate because the research of past years has been building a foundation of understanding of media economics and media as business entities, and much research was intended to provide evidence of industry conditions for policy purposes.

The dominant approaches, however, are limited and do not effectively explain how and why individual media companies behave as they do and how their choices and decisions create or respond to the conditions and forces found in the industry. Increasing interest in questions about these issues is a consequence of the foundations laid by industry- and market-oriented research of past decades and the interest they have generated in understanding company options and choices.

Questions about individual companies are important because they provide a clear picture of market dynamics and the pressures that lead company executives to make economic choices and choices about the ways their companies will be structured, the activities they will undertake, and the performance that is subsequently produced. They also help explain why certain market structures emerge and why media and communications industries exist in various forms and produce different results.

Analyses at the market or industry levels, then, provide collective pictures of media but through their focus on the overall situation miss the pressures, constraints, and choices faced by individual firms. Analyses at the company level reveal how managers wrestling with these factors pursue different responses, how internal differences in company cultures and traditions, organisations, and resources produce different choices, and why there is such a wide range of performance among firms.

COMPANY STUDIES EXPLORE DIFFERENCES IN FIRMS

Companies are central to media economics study because they individually raise capital, create facilities, employ personnel, create media products and services, sell them in the market, and grow or wither. Together, these companies create the media and communications industries, which have some common interests and issues, but they operate individually, facing individual economic and managerial challenges, making individual choices, and pursuing individual strategies.

The theory of the firm asserts that the primary goals of commercial firms are maximising profit and company value (Williamson & Winter, 1993; Demsetz, 1997). These goals and the pursuit of these goals have been explored and developed by economists during the past three centuries (An excellent collection of classic works in the development of the theory of the firm is found in Putterman & Kroszner, 1996).

A weak understanding of the theory of the firm has led numerous media observers who do not take a company perspective to make sweeping generalisations about how media companies operate, without discriminating between companies that make very different choices in pursuing profit and company values. These ignore many of the complexities of company organisation and governance (Jenson, 2001), assume a simplicity in firm structure, operation, and performance, and present a deterministic view of the ability of managers to fully control firms and their performance.

At a very basic level, firms differ widely in the ways they balance the desires to produce profit and to increase company value. Companies rarely attempt to pursue both simultaneously with equal vigour. Decisions of which to pursue more strongly at a given time are driven by company goals, resources, operational needs, and environmental factors. A company may place an emphasis on short-term profit, for example, and do little or nothing to enhance overall company value. Conversely, a company's managers may seek to increase value by sacrificing profit in the short term.

Companies thus differ in terms of their goals, in the expectations of owners, managers, and employees, and in the means by which choices are made internally. These issues are at the basis of what has been called a behavioural theory of the firm (March & Cyert, 1992).

How company executives make choices and guide company behaviour is also affected by wide differences among companies that are often ignored when industry-level analyses are made. These differences are critical, however, and constrain or direct the choices made for companies and the ways that they are structured and operate. At the broadest level, issues of size, ownership, and location produce important differences among companies.

Large and small firms—whether measured by income or number of employees—pursue different missions and goals, have different organisational structures, operate with different levels of resources, face different opportunities and threats, and encounter different sets of economic and financial pressures. As a result, one has to take size into consideration when attempting to understand company choices.

Similarly, the type of ownership makes a difference. Privately owned and publicly owned companies typically encounter different types of goals and pressures from their owners, have different financial resources available, and are able to undertake different levels of business risk.

Geographic location creates significant differences among firms. Metropolitan and small town media, for example, face unique levels of competition, operate differently, typically receive most of their income from separate sources, and encounter varying levels of performance expectations from their owners.

In the end, however, one cannot be deterministic about companies based solely on factors such as size, ownership, or location. The philosophies, strategies, and goals of owners and managers produce widely differing choices among media firms of similar size, ownership, and geography.

These factors result in media firms choosing different patterns of diversification, selecting different business models for products or services in the same medium, and pursuing divergent approaches to company growth (Penrose, 1995). The factors lead to companies creating individual modes of horizontal and vertical integration, implementing separate levels of specialisation, and coordinating and cooperating with others firms to varying degrees. These choices are compelled and constrained by economic factors (Besanko, Dranove, & Shanley, 1999; Baye, 1999) and a variety of internal and market factors (Jenster & Hussey, 2001).

The results of the range of choices made by companies and their success in the market produce differences in the ability of firms to generate wealth, to respond to market changes, and to sustain themselves. This occurs because some media firms operate with lower costs and higher efficiency than others and because some firms produce low-cost products for large numbers of consumers, whereas others produce high-cost products for small numbers of consumers. It occurs because some produce more successful products and services than others and because some enterprises choose to regularly reinvest profits in their firms while others choose to remove profits from the company.

Media firms differ widely in their abilities to generate the resources they need, and the organisation of the firms and their behaviour is in great part dictated by their need to gain and utilise resources from outside the company. No company is independent of such pressures, and each is dependent and interdependent on outsiders for capital, supplies, and revenue to varying degrees.

As a result of environmental factors and the range of choices that are made within firms, no two companies are alike. Media firms are social organisations, and most involve complex structures that govern an array of activities that must be organised and controlled in order to produce their communication products and services and implement the business models that support those activities.

Firms are also important because their existence (especially in telecommunications, broadcasting and cablecasting), industry structures, ownership, and operations are directly tied to issues of policy decisions and regulation. This state intervention is an important economic force affecting media firms worldwide and often results from activities and initiatives of firms themselves.

A FOCUS ON MEDIA AND COMMUNICATION FIRMS

This book presents studies applying the company-level approach to media and communications firms. It explores differences among missions, strategies, organisational choices, and other business decisions. It reviews economic factors and pressures on media and communications companies and seeks to improve understanding of how these affect market and company structures, operations, and performance of firms.

The chapters were selected from papers on the theme of media firms presented at the 5th World Media Economics Conference held in Finland in May, 2002, hosted by the Turku School of Economics and Business Administration and *The Journal of Media Economics*.

The chapters, by leading scholars worldwide, address questions about how the introduction of new products and services has changed the dynamics of markets and industry structures, how strategic choices and business strategies have affected the ability of firms to compete and have altered industry, market, and company structures and performance, and how various economics and business analysis methods can be used to understand the activities and performance of media and communications companies.

Terje Gaustad presents a model for analysing the production and distribution activities of media firms and how transaction costs influence the structure and governance of companies and industries.

Allan Brown discusses the introduction of digital television in Australia and how leading media firms influenced policy decisions implementing this new form of broadcasting. He explores the impact of these processes on the television market, industry structures, and media companies.

How the number, types, and strategies of professional information providers are affecting that industry is explored by Richard van der Wurff. He reveals how prices, product differentiation, and innovation are influenced by the structural changes.

Angel Arrese and Mercedes Medina investigate how the development of new media opportunities changed the competitive environment of financial news and information providers and the strategies that have emerged as major players have responded to the new economic environment.

How the appearance of free daily newspapers has affected the industry, markets, and traditional publishers is studied by Piet Bakker. He reviews the strategies of market industry and the responses of existing publishers, and he suggests models of short- and long-term effects from the introduction of these competing publications.

Marina Pavlikova reveals the strategies and forces behind the development of the Internet in Russia, showing how economic forces, business concerns, and the interests of major media companies have influenced the scale and scope of Runet content.

Alan Albarran and Terry Moellinger explore the world's leading media firms, reviewing differences in how they developed, the types of products and services they provide, how they have structured themselves, and how they perform.

The forces and strategies that lead newspaper firms to internationalise their activities are explored by Jan Helgesen. He explores the economic and business reasons behind newspaper companies' choices to transform themselves into international entities, the methods that are used, and their implications for companies and the industry.

Li-Chuan Mai studies how differences in ownership, size, company structure, and costs and price strategies have affected satellite television firms in

Taiwan and the implications of these findings for traditional strategic analysis methods.

David Goff focuses on the development and strategies of four major European telecommunications companies, showing how their choices have been influenced by their economic environments and technological changes and how these strategies have altered their environments, potential, and performance.

Aldo van Weezel explores how issues of journalistic quality and productivity require managerial attention as competition increases. He reviews methods for monitoring these factors and how company managers in Chile view the need to do so.

The requirements of human capital for cross-media publishing are explored by Tasos Politis, who discusses how workflow changes created by digitalisation and cross-media activities affect companies and their employees. He then studies the Greek publishing market to determine the extent to which they are able to compete in cross-media publishing.

Finally, Mikko Grönlund focuses on issues of customer satisfaction in the graphic arts industry, discussing its influences on customer choices of firms, relationships with firms, and the financial performance of those firms. Using data from the Finnish industry, he examines the factors that influence demand and perceptions of firms and how these should influence strategic choices of firms.

The studies collected in this book provide an overview of economic and related managerial issues affecting the structures of markets in which firms compete, the operations of media and communications firms, and their financial performance. It thus expands the discussion of economic issues traditionally associated with the field because of the narrowed focus of earlier books in media economics, and it is hoped that it will induce additional avenues of inquiry regarding such issues.

REFERENCES

Baye, Michael R. (1999) *Managerial economics and business strategy*, 3rd ed. New York: McGraw-Hill.

Besanko, David, David Dranove, and Mark Shanley, eds. (1999) *Economics of strategy*, 2nd ed. New York: John Wiley and Sons.

Demsetz, Harold (1997) *The economics of the business firm: Seven critical commentaries*. Cambridge: Cambridge University Press.

Jenson, Michael C. (2001) *The theory of the firm: Governance, residual claims, and organizational forms*. Cambridge, Mass.: Harvard University Press.

Jenster, Per, and David E. Hussey. (2001) *Company analysis: Determining strategic capability*. New York: John Wiley and Sons.

March, James G., and Richard M. Cyert. (1992) *A behavioral theory of the firm*. Oxford: Blackwell Publishers.

Penrose, E. T. (1995) *The theory of the growth of the firm*, 3rd ed. Oxford: Oxford University Press, 1995.

Puttermand, Louis, and Randall S. Kroszner, eds. (1996) *The economic nature of the firm: A reader*. Cambridge: Cambridge University Press.

Williamson, Oliver E., and Sidney G. Winter, eds. (1993) *The nature of the firm: Origins, evolution and development*. Oxford: Oxford University Press.

Chapter 2
Joint Product Analysis in the Media and Entertainment Industries: Joint Value Creation in the Norwegian Film Sector

Terje Gaustad
Norwegian School of Management BI

The process of creating and making media and entertainment products available to consumers usually relies on interaction and cooperation between two or more companies or business entities. In the media economic literature, such interfirm relations issues have so far only drawn modest interest despite the increasing attention it is receiving from scholars rooted in different branches of business studies. In the marketing literature, Webster noted already in 1992 that the (re)emergence of cooperation among firms is a fundamental reshaping of the field (Webster, 1992); strategy scholars Brandenburger and Nalebuff (1997) observe that firms rarely create value in isolation, particularly in advanced economies; and within the general framework of interfirm relations specialty fields have emerged studying such issues as foreign market entry and channel structure (Ghosh & John, 1999). An important contribution to the media economic literature is given by Caves (2000), who adopts a similar approach to media industry studies. Drawing on analytical resources of industrial economics and contract theory, he explains some starkly different approaches to contracting found in the creative industries, where artistic inputs are combined with "humdrum" inputs in the process of creating joint products.

Examples of crucial interfirm relations on which the supply of media and entertainment products depend are plentiful. In the motion picture industry, producers are dependent on distributors to market and circulate their products to audiences in different territories and media. In the publishing sector authors are dependent on publishers, but may also rely on other gatekeepers or middlemen such as literary agents, and in the music industry an intricate bundle of transactions involving composers, lyricists, musicians, managers, music publishers, record companies and others is required to get popular musical products on the market (Caves, 2000).

When two or more companies or business entities located at different levels in a products' value-added chain collaborate to create joint products, their success—and thus the joint value of their inputs and efforts—is dependent on the *crucial transactions* between the parties. The structure within which these transactions are organised may play a significant part in the success or failure of any media and entertainment product's performance, and the possibility to organise the transactions in a desired structure may prove critical in establishing a climate that encourages production and distribution of specific types of media products.

Drawing primarily on New Institutional Economics, and then particularly on transaction cost reasoning (Williamson, 1985) and its extension into transaction and governance value analysis (Zajac & Olson, 1993; Ghosh & John, 1999), this chapter proposes a mode of analysis for media and entertainment production where focus is set on these crucial transactions and the joint product created by the transaction parties. It is argued that understanding the basic economic properties of such joint products and the structure of the crucial transactions is essential for implementing a supply-side treatment of media and entertainment products into a broader economic analysis of media and entertainment markets.

The empirical focus of this chapter is on the motion picture sector, and data is drawn from a Norwegian pilot study of production–distribution relations. However, reference is also made to three other media and entertainment industries: music, publishing and television sports. Limiting the references to four sectors or industries does not imply that the analytical framework of joint product analysis is restricted to these. On the contrary, it should be applicable to almost any media or entertainment industry and even to creative production in the—for traditional economists—"outlandish" areas of the art world (Frey, 2000). The limitation to the four sectors selected here is primarily a practical one enabling the author to draw on the same coherent empirical references throughout the chapter.

First the motion picture industry is discussed in a joint product view. Transaction attributes and some key economic properties of significance to these attributes are then identified and analysed, before findings from the Norwegian pilot study are presented and discussed. Finally, turning to music, publishing and television sports, I briefly identify joint product transactions for each, the output of each transaction partner and the partner's joint product, and discuss structures of the joint product transactions in a transaction cost perspective.

CRUCIAL TRANSACTIONS AND JOINT PRODUCTS
IN THE MOTION PICTURE SECTOR

Identifying crucial transactions for joint product analysis starts with detecting transactions between parties at different levels in a vertical value-added chain that together produce some joint product. One may argue that any two parties in a value-added chain do produce a joint product, and that a joint product analysis could be applied to any product. Such analysis is, however, most valuable in those cases where each transaction partner is dependent on the other to a non-trivial degree, and when the value of each party's output is tied to the value of the joint product. Such transactions are frequently referred to as *non-standard transactions* and in this chapter the label *crucial transactions* will be used for transactions where the value of each party's output is heavily dependent on the value of the joint product.

In the motion picture industry joint product relationships exist between producers and distributors. Table 2.1 shows the output associated with each vertical sector in this industry. The product columns specify both the output of the particular sector and the cumulative output produced up to each stage. For the first stage, the production sector, where the first copy of the actual movie is assembled—combining cast, crew, direction, music and so forth before recording and editing the performance—the product is the film itself or the *first copy movie* materialised in the film negative and the bundle of contracts that follows it. The distribution sector adds marketing and circulation by licensing copies of the movie to different media in the exhibition sector. The cumulative product of the film itself and these distribution efforts may best be described as the movie's *image*, as this term is used by Boorstin (1992). A movie's image is the audience's pre-consumption perception of the movie, which determines its attractiveness. The image is dependent on production factors such as star cast and director, technical quality, exotic locations, etc. and distribution elements such as advertising intensity, the width of the release, etc. Finally, in the exhibition sector, presentation of the movie to the audience is added through cinemas, different formats of home video, and through television or online broadcasting. The cumulative product at this final stage is the audience's movie experience, and that is what the audience consumes.

The focus of this chapter is on the cumulative product of the production and distribution sectors, since investments made in these two sectors are primarily tied to each specific movie project—the investments are transaction specific. Investments in the exhibition sector, on the other hand, are mostly transaction non-specific since they are usually not tied to any specific movie. Investments into, for example, sound, picture and comfortable seats for a first-class cinema presentation benefits all movies shown in the theatre, and the added value is thus not limited to any specific movie. For such investments an exhibitor is therefore not dependent on any one distributor beyond a non-trivial degree.

Table 2.1. Product and cumulative product by sector (motion picture industry)

Vertical Sector	Product	Cumulative Product
Production	Film Negative (first copy)	First Copy Movie
Distribution	Awareness / Circulation	The Movie's Image
Exhibition	Presentation	The Movie Experience

Transaction Cost Analyses of Joint Products and Crucial Transactions

For the parties to joint product transactions, the value of each party's output is dependent on the value of the joint product. The parties therefore have strong incentives to devise joint value maximising exchanges, and by minimising the transaction costs they get closer to the desired goal of joint value maximisation. Since transaction cost analysis (TCA) offers powerful analytical tools for aligning cost-minimising governance structures with transaction attributes, it provides important guidance to transaction partners on how to maximise joint value.

Transaction cost economics holds that the degree to which transactions along the value-added chain are governed by fully vertically integrated structures (such as organisations), semi-integrated structures (such as joint ventures) or left as market transactions (where the parties have an arms-length buyer–seller relationship) is largely determined by three key transaction attributes: *asset specificity, uncertainty* and *frequency* (Williamson, 1985). A major strength of TCA is its ability to determine cost minimising—and thus joint value maximising—transaction governance modes based on exactly these three key attributes.

Transaction Specific Investments (Asset Specificity) in Motion Pictures

Transaction specific investments or asset specificity is the principal dimension with which transaction cost economics explains transaction governance structure, and is also the main focus of the joint production transaction cost analysis in this chapter. The level of asset specificity refers to the level of transaction specific investments undertaken by the transaction parties. If the assets, which are created or acquired through producer or distributor's investments, are redeployable outside the context of the transaction they reduce asset specificity; if not, they increase asset specificity.

In the motion picture industry, production companies do not require much in the form of endurable assets and can even be managed on a one-off project basis. Most investments in the production sector are thus allocated directly to specific movie projects, and since they therefore cannot easily be reallocated to other movie projects they are transaction specific and create asset specificity. Distribution companies, however, require substantial investments in an endurable overhead to administer their network of main, district, and international offices (Corts, 1999). These are transaction nonspecific distribution assets—not tied to any specific movie transactions. The distribution companies' marketing investments (advertising, publicity, etc.) as well as the print copying and distribution for specific movies are, however, transaction specific distribution costs. These are sunk and nonsalvageable. Advertising investments sunk into one movie cannot be redeployed to another. Such transaction specific distribution investments are investments into a specific movie's image, and correspond best with what Williamson (1991) labels *brand name capital*. Producer's asset specificity therefore tends always to be high, while distributor's transaction specific investments may vary from slight to significant.

Transaction cost theory holds that markets are favoured as governance structure where asset specificity is slight due to lower governance costs and potential scale economy benefits. Accordingly, one would expect a shared variance between low distribution investments in particular movies and market-based production–distribution transactions since distributors would seek market-based governance structures when they only intend to put in small specific investments. In such cases of low asset specificity, the distribution company spends little on advertising and promoting the movie, but rather just feeds the film into its distribution or circulation system, utilising the existing network. For movies handled in this manner distribution costs are nonspecific and the distribution resources allocated to the movie—mainly the use of overhead—can easily be redeployed to other movies.

Where asset specificity is substantial, hierarchy or internal organisation is the preferred governance structure. A transaction party that undertakes significant transaction-specific investments will seek to safeguard this transaction through more integrated structures and higher control-mode contracting. Since these investments are nonsalvageable outside the context of the transaction, they create "lock-in" problems that makes market governance structures hazardous (Williamson, 1985). One would thus expect that distribution companies that are prepared to invest substantially into marketing and distribution of a specific movie will seek integrated structures or high control-mode contracting for the production–distribution transaction.

Key Economic Properties of Transaction Specific Investment in the Movie Industry

Transaction specific investments in the movie industry, and the other media and entertainment sectors discussed in this chapter, share some key economic properties that need to be taken into consideration to fully understand the implications of the asset specificity they create.

First, products created in these industries usually have strong public good characteristics that create significant scale economies. They are typically *marketable public goods*, which means that they are non-rival but excludable (Adams & McCormick, 1993). Most media and entertainment joint products, including movies, fit this category, as one person's consumption of the product does not reduce the amount of it that may be consumed by others, and since it is feasible to exclude non-paying customers from consuming it. A person who refuses to pay is not let into a cinema and is not given a home video cassette. A television channel that refuses to pay a license fee is not given the right to broadcast a movie. Unlike pure public goods, marketable public goods are well suited for commercial trade since the free-rider problem is solved by the excludability.

Since the joint product created by producer and distributor is a marketable public good, more paying consumers means obtaining lower per-consumer costs without reducing the utility each consumer gains from consuming the product. The marginal returns on both producer and distributor's investments are thus increasing with sales, and even with declining prices for additional consumers through price discrimination schemes producer and distributor earn marginal profits and increase total profits as long as each new paying consumer pays a price above the marginal distribution cost, which is low for most media and close to zero for electronic media.

Furthermore, transaction specific production and distribution investments are, to some degree, interchangeable. In the absence of transaction costs the value of a joint product (JPV) will be determined by the sum of production and distribution investments:

$$JPV = \Sigma\, I_P + \Sigma\, I_D \tag{1}$$

Media economic research carried out on the motion picture industry confirms that there is a positive correlation between both production and distribution investments and performance. This research has been carried out in within two branches. First, extensive regression analyses carried out by Litman and others have established a positive relationship between both production and distribution investment variables and market performance (Litman, 1983, 1998; Litman & Kohl, 1989; Wyatt, 1991; and Sochay, 1994). Another branch of research carried out to explain the American dominance in the international market for audiovisual products also gives empirical support to the proposition of a positive relationship between production investments and market performance (Wildman & Siwek, 1988, 1993; Waterman & Rogers, 1994; Dupagne & Waterman, 1997; and Jayakar & Waterman, 1999). There is no reason to believe that this is different for other media and entertainment joint products.

This means that the same joint product value can be achieved with different combinations of production and distribution investments. The contribution of investments into superstar actors (a production sector element) in the motion picture industry illustrates this effect. As argued by Houcken (1999), such investments consist of both a production cost element (*performance value*) and a distribution cost element (*brand value*): An actor that is paid $20 million for a role in a movie could likely be substituted—for artistic or performance purposes—by another highly talented but less known or less popular actor charging $5 million. The $15 million premium for the superstar is thus an investment made for that star's brand value, which contributes substantially to the value of the movie's image (the actor's face and name on posters and in other advertising; publicity centred around the actor's participation in the movie; etc.). Reallocating the $15 million brand value premium from the production budget to the marketing budget by settling with a less known actor but hiking the general advertising intensity would in principle result in the same joint product value.

Finally, as noted by Caves (2000), creative products, such as the media and entertainment joint products discussed here, tend to have multiplicative production functions. For a normal production function it is assumed that the inputs are substitutable, so that, for example, two units of labour and one unit of capital may give the same output as four units of labour and no capital. In *multiplicative production functions*, however, every input must be present and must perform at or above some threshold level of proficiency if any commercially valuable output is to result.

Production functions may be multiplicative within the production and distribution sectors. A motion picture produced without a good cinematographer will not be of much value despite the high quality all other cast and crew members may represent, and a great marketing campaign is of little value if the movie it promotes does not play in theatres. More important for the joint product analysis is a multiplicative production function between the production and distribution sectors. This implies that if either producer or distributor only performs close to a minimum threshold level, the value of the joint product would be marginal even if the other party's performance and input should be considerable. A large number multiplied by zero is still zero.

It should be noted here that performing above a threshold level may not necessarily equal investing financially above a threshold level. A highly talented creative performance may, to a large extent, substitute financial input. The movie "The Blair Witch Project", for example, was produced on a shoestring budget that normally would have been deemed below a threshold level for an American theatrical release, but due to its remarkably clever concept its production elements were still performing well above any such threshold level.

It follows from these economic properties (the public good characteristics, the interchangeable nature of production and distribution investments, and the multiplicative production function) that both production and distribution investments are both *selfish and cooperative* in nature. Transaction specific investments are said to be selfish if they only benefit the investor, but not the transaction partner. If they benefit only the transaction partner but not the investor they are cooperative. Finally, if they benefit both the investor and the transaction partner they are both selfish and cooperative (Che & Hausch, 1999). In the transaction relationship between producer and distributor, production investments increase the joint product's value and may also increase the distributor's marginal return on investment, and such investments therefore clearly benefit both producer and distributor. Distribution investments have the same effect. The interdependence between producer and distributor is therefore significantly strengthened.

The multiplicative production function increases the interdependence between producer and distributor even more. Not only is the marginal return of one party's investments dependent on the other party's investment level, but also, if the other party's investments fall close to or below this threshold level, hardly any valuable output will result and the marginal return approaches zero.

Effects of Uncertainty and Frequency on Crucial Joint Product Transactions

Although the focus of the transaction cost analysis in this chapter is on transaction specific investments, the effects of the other two main transaction attributes, uncertainty and frequency, need to be discussed.

Will a new movie become a box-office success or not? Industry practitioners like to say "nobody knows",[1] and causal estimates suggest that

---

[1] William Goldman's much-quoted observation about the motion picture industry (quoted in Caves, 2000).

roughly one out of ten movies earns substantial profits, three will break even, and six will end up with a deficit (Wyatt, 1994). Furthermore, for most media and entertainment goods, pretesting has proven largely ineffective because the product's success can seldom be explained even ex post by the satisfaction of some pre-existing needs (Caves, 2000). Uncertainty is therefore generally high, making transaction specific investment into media and entertainment joint products a high-risk venture.

Transaction cost economics holds that uncertainty is important for transactions that involve transaction specific investments. The risk that follows from such investments makes it more imperative to organise the transaction under a governance structure that has the capacity to "work things out" (Williamson, 1985). Where the specific investments are substantial, the high risk and uncertainty provide additional incentives for integrated transactions or high-control mode contracting.

Theatrical motion pictures usually represent large projects relative to the size of the production companies carrying out the production and the frequency of productions therefore tend to be low. Accordingly, the frequency of transactions between a producer and distributor is also relatively low. In general, low frequency of transactions discourages hierarchical governance structures, since the governance costs associated with these will be more difficult to recoup from transaction cost savings. Producers with a high production rate are thus more likely to operate under integrated production–distribution structures than those with a low production frequency. The frequency should, however, be adjusted for size since larger transactions more easily can justify the costs of an organisational (or semi-organisational) structure than smaller transactions (Williamson, 1985). High-budgeted movies would therefore provide stronger incentives for production–distribution integration and high-control mode contracting than lower budgeted projects.

PRODUCTION–DISTRIBUTION RELATIONS IN NORWEGIAN FILM

A pilot study of production–distribution relations in the Norwegian feature film sector was carried out in the spring and summer of 2001. The study collected information about all Norwegian theatrical feature films that were first-time released domestically in 2000. In addition to collecting various written documentation about the films (including production and marketing budgets, business and marketing plans, etc.), one representative of both the producer and distributor of each movie was interviewed about the production–distribution interaction. This data was supplemented by information from the Norwegian Film Institute.

The study was an exploratory pilot study, and the main purpose here is not to draw decisive conclusions about production–distribution relations and joint product creation in the Norwegian film sector, but to illustrate how joint product transaction cost analysis may contribute to explaining certain problematic features the film sector is struggling to overcome. The study and its findings should therefore be seen in a context of discovery rather than a context of justification.

The Norwegian production sector is not untypical for most European countries. It is populated with a number of smaller companies, most with one or two permanent employees, which try to produce a feature film at least every second year. The distribution sector is dominated by foreign-controlled companies (owned by North American, Swedish or Danish corporations), but a couple of independent Norwegian distributors do handle a significant number of films every year, from which a box-office hit occasionally emerges (Aas, 2000). The Norwegian film sector is maybe most notably different from that of its neighbouring countries, Sweden and Denmark, in that it lacks a fully integrated corporation handling production, distribution and exhibition (Grønnestad, 1999).

From some practitioners in the Norwegian film sector it has been argued with increasing strength over the last few years that most Norwegian films are not given proper marketing and distribution for domestic release and that this is one of the main reasons why they tend underperform compared to foreign movies (Svingen, 2000). If this is true, it means—in a joint product transaction cost framework—that the distribution sector is underperforming or underinvesting, and that the joint product value thus suffers even when the production sector performs well. Focus was thus set on the distributors' participation in the joint product creation, both through involvement in the collaboration and through transaction specific investments.

A total of nine Norwegian films had their first theatrical release in 2000. Even though all used market forms of contracting for the production–distribution relationship, there were some significant differences in the collaboration that took place under these contracts. One therefore finds nuances within the market based transactions, and some approach resemblance of semi-integrated structures even if formal contracting is market based. First, there were differences with regards to when the parties entered into a contract and started collaborating. With the exceptions of two movies this happened at an early stage, either during development or pre-production of the movies. Entering into a formal relationship at an early stage did not, however, always mean close collaboration between producers and distributors. Of the projects where producer and distributor had contracted already at the development stage, their actual collaboration and interaction ranged from very intense to almost non-existent.

The combination of early contracting and low to average intensity in the collaboration may seem surprising, as one would expect that both early involvement and close collaboration would be part of a more integrated production–distribution relationship. However, much of the explanation lies in the requirements for public production funding, where the producer is required to submit an intentional agreement with a theatrical distributor. To obtain production financing the producer is thus forced to contact a distributor, regardless of his or her intention or wish to collaborate with the distribution partner or vice versa.

The most integrated production–distribution relationship was found in film number 3—a project where the producer had formal marketing training, marketing experience from the film sector and very specific ideas about how the film should be released and promoted (Table 2.2). The producer took incentive to involve the distributor in the process, which the distributor welcomed. The collaboration between the parties was close throughout the process.

Table 2.2. Summary of findings from Norwegian pilot study

Film #	Intensity of collaboration	Time of contracting (Stage)	Distribution budget as percentage of total budget
1	Average	Pre-Production	19%
2	Average	Pre-Production	8%
3	High	Development	19%
4	Average	Development	6%
5	Average	Post-Production	5%
6	Average	Pre-Production	10%
7	Low	Development	22%
8	Average	Pre-Production	4%
9	Low	Post-Production	13%

The most important finding was that the distributors' transaction specific investments were low or non-existent. Even though the resources invested into marketing and distributing the movies could represent up to 22 percent of a movie's total production and distribution costs, this did not necessarily reflect that there was any transaction specific investment from the distributor. The explanation for this phenomenon is also found in the public support system, where all funding—also monies intended for marketing and distribution of the movie—is paid out to the producer. The producer thus controls the distribution and marketing budget and usually has the final say also in marketing and distribution matters. This resembles the rent-a-distributor type of contracting found in North America and other territories (Cones, 1997) where the distributor's role is more that of a service provider than a production partner (for the joint product).

This was also reflected from respondents who said that the producer was in charge of the overall production and distribution project since "he controls the money". In some cases the distributor's role was also described as "being a pure distributor", basically meaning that the distributor feeds the movie into its network, licensing it to cinemas and other outlets.

The control of the distribution function is thus very much left to the producer, and typically, in those cases where the largest shares of the total costs were spent on marketing and distribution the producers seemed very conscious about reaching a large audience. However, this was not always the case since more commercially oriented incentives like these could suffer in a trade-off with more artistically driven incentives of producing "a better movie". In the latter cases, the marketing budget under the producer's control could take the function of a contingency budget for production cost overruns and increases. As a result, the distributor would be left with very limited resources for the release of the movie, leading to distribution sector underperformance from which the movie's joint value would suffer. This obviously becomes a serious problem if the distributor is pushed to perform close to a minimum threshold level for the multiplicative production function between production and distribution. In such cases one risks to lose much of the joint product value due to reallocations from marketing and distribution to production.

Discussion of Norwegian Findings

Due to the sector's heavy reliance on public funding and support it cannot be approached with the expectations that producers and distributors will act according to market logic. A microanalytical approach is thus necessary to uncover the workings and logic of the heavily regulated market. However, joint product analysis of even this complex data shows that this approach is able to identify likely sources of inefficiencies.

The Norwegian public funding system provides support for both production and marketing/distribution, but it is set up so that the producer controls both transaction specific production and distribution investments. Contributing both, the producer has strong incentives to seek contracting forms with the distributor that leave the producer in control. Since no producer has a high enough turnover or frequency of production to justify a distribution subsidiary, they are likely to seek higher control modes of market contracting. This, however, may discourage distributors from contributing through transaction specific investments, and with little or no transaction specific investments at stake a distributor's incentive to maximise joint value is significantly reduced.

Had the public funding for marketing and distribution been channelled through the distributor it would have significantly increased the distributor's transaction specific investments in the movie. This would have given the distributor incentives to seek higher control mode contracting and to get involved not only in the marketing and distribution efforts of the movie, but— due to the effects of the particular economic properties of these specific investments—also in production issues. Under this alternative system, both producer and distributor would have strong incentives to devise a joint value maximising exchange between themselves, and this would likely result in a more efficient use of resources with lower transaction costs and better performing products.

Finally, it is important to note that these arguments on value creation only are valid if the parties are able to claim the value created. As noted by Ghosh and John (1999), firms remain self-interested, so they will implement the activities associated with the larger joint value if and only if they can claim a share of the increased value resulting from such activities. For a change in the public funding system to be efficient this must be taken into consideration.

Joint Products and Crucial Transactions in Music, Publishing and Television Sports

The framework of joint product analysis that is presented and applied above is not limited to the motion picture industry. Transaction cost analysis is widely used for numerous industries (Williamson, 1999), and since the key economic properties of the transaction specific investments are similar for many other media and entertainment products, the particular form of analysis presented above could prove as valuable for other media and entertainment sectors as for the film sector. It is beyond the scope of this chapter to go into any detailed analysis of other sectors, but to illustrate other applications crucial transactions and joint products similar to those discussed under the treatment of the film sector are identified for the following industries: music, publishing and television sports.

Music

In the music industry the relationship between the musical artists and their producer on the one side and the record companies and music publishers on the other side resembles the production–distribution relationship from the motion picture industry. We may define the artists and technicians required to produce the master copy of a musical product as the production sector, and the record company and music publishers that promote the products and collect revenues as the distribution sector.

The output of the production sector is the master recording while marketing and circulation is added in the distribution sector, creating a joint product that may be best described as *the album's image*. Even if the term "album" is used here, "album image" is applicable to any released musical recorded product including albums, singles, EPs distributed on CD, vinyl, or as digital data files. In creating valuable products for music consumers the distribution sector may play an even more important part in the music industry than in the motion picture industry since new artists or new albums that will be given broad release require extensive marketing campaigns involving substantial investments. The music outlets, such as record stores, radio stations, music television channels, and now also online sales, represents the parallel to the exhibition sector in the motion picture industry, and their output is not considered part of the joint product to be analysed here.

Publishing

In the publishing industry the transaction between author and publisher resembles the production–distribution transactions discussed previously. Here the "production sector" is represented by the author or authors, who produce the master copy of the manuscript, maybe in collaboration with an editor appointed by the publisher. The publishers offer promotion and circulation of the books, creating a joint product—*the publication's image*. Again, outlets such as bookstores, book clubs, etc. parallel the exhibition sector, which is not part of the crucial transaction.

Television Sports

For television sports the crucial joint product transaction is the one between the sports organisation and the television station or channel that broadcast the sports event. This is slightly different from the preceding three cases, since the sports organisations do not produce a first copy or master copy of the program. The sports organisation's production is limited to the underlying property, the sports event itself, while the television channel or station undertakes the audiovisual production either through an in-house unit or an independent production unit contracted for the specific job. This is the most common structure for the production of television sports, but other structures has been used, where for example the sports organisation in fact has also carried out the audiovisual production by contracting an independent audiovisual production company. However, the joint product relationship is similar. The sports organisation, or the production sector in the terminology used above, creates a sporting event that is marketed and distributed, as well as audiovisually produced, by the TV channel or station (the distributor in our terminology). The value of the joint product— the sports program—is highly dependent on each transaction party's input.

The differences in the joint product for TV sports and the other three sectors are quickly evident in the comparison shown in Table 2.3.

Table 2.3. "Production" and "distribution" sectors and their joint product for motion pictures, music, publishing, and television sports

Industry	Production	Distribution	Joint Product
Motion Picture	Production	Distribution	The Movie's Image
Music	Artists/Producer	Music Publishers / Record Companies	The Album's Image
Publishing	Author	Publisher	The Publication's Image
Television Sports	Sports Organisation	Television Channel	Sports Program

CONCLUDING REMARKS

The transaction cost joint product model outlined here offers a framework for analysing crucial transactions between different levels in a vertical value-added chain and the joint products created by the transaction parties. It is rooted in transaction cost theory but emphasises joint value creation through joint value maximising exchanges (Zajac & Olsen, 1993; Ghosh & John, 1999). Due to its careful treatment of the key economic properties of transaction specific investments typically found in the media and entertainment industries, the model offers specific guidance for these industries—particularly on aligning transaction governance structure with the sought-after balance of transaction specific investments between the parties.

The model may, for example, help explain why a freelance writer for newspapers or magazines may be comfortable with writing articles "on spec" while an author embarking on a three-volume series on the history of the popular music industry probably will require some advance or guarantee from a publisher. It also explains why a movie producer may be able and willing to produce a low budget feature film without a distribution agreement up front, while he probably would not want nor manage to produce a big-budget blockbuster without a distribution agreement up front that probably also would put a lot of creative control in the hands of the distributor. For a sports organisation seeking more prominent television coverage it will provide guidance to why and how the organisation may have to treat better coverage as a trade-off against granting their television partner more control over the final sports program in terms of timing, content and appearance.

The model may furthermore be useful for regulators seeking to encourage the production of certain media and entertainment products, or even arts. The model may suggest that the problem does not lie in the production sector of products one seek to promote but in the distribution sector or in the transaction structure between the two sectors. As illustrated in the Norwegian study presented here, it may even lie in the transaction partners' lacking regulatory possibility to devise joint value maximising exchanges.

As with all new models the one outlined in this chapter is not well tried empirically. Further empirical applications may therefore reveal weaknesses and provide a basis for improvements.

REFERENCES

Aas, N.K. (2000) *Film og video, MedieNorge 1999: Fakta om norske massemedier*, Bergen: Fagbokforlaget.

Adams, R.D. and McCormick, K. (1993) Research note: The traditional distinction between public and private goods needs to be expanded, not abandoned, *Journal of Theoretical Politics*, vol. 5, no. 1, p. 109 – 116.

Boorstin, D.J. (1992) *The image: a guide to pseudo-events in America*, (25th anniversary ed.), New York: Vintage Books.

Brandenburger, A.M. and Nalebuff, B.J. (1997) the added-value theory of business, *Strategy and Business*, vol. 9, no. 4, 4-6.

Caves, R.E. (2000) *Creative industries: Contracts between art and commerce*, Cambridge, MA: Harvard University Press.

Che, Y.K. and Hausch, D.B. (1999) Cooperative investments and the value of contracting, *The American Economic Review*, vol. 89, no. 1, pp. 125-147.

Cones, J.W. (1997) *The feature film distribution deal: a critical analysis of the single most important film industry agreement*, Carbondale, IL: Southern Illinois University Press.

Corts, K.S. (1999) The strategic effects of vertical market structure: Common agency and divisionalization in the u.s. motion picture industry, working paper revised September 1999, Harvard Business School.

Dupagne, M. and Waterman, D. (1997) Determinants of us television fiction imports in Western Europe, *Journal of Broadcasting and Electronic Media*, vol. 42, no. 2, p.208-220.

Frey, B.S. (2000) *Arts & economics: Analysis & cultural policy*, Berlin: Springer-Verlag.

Ghosh, M. and John, G. (1999) Governance value analysis and marketing strategy, *Journal of Marketing*, vol. 63 (Special Issue 1999), 131-145

Grønnestad, D. (1999) Myten om kommunaliseringens konsekvenser for norsk Filmproduksjon, *Norsk Medietidsskrift*, no. 2, 1999: 63-79

Houcken, R. (1999) The international feature film industry: National advantage and international strategies for European film companies. Doctoral dissertation, University of St. Gallen, Switzerland.

Jayakar, K. and Waterman, D. (1999) The economics of American movie exports: An empirical analysis. Paper presented at AEJMC, August 1999 (Draft revised April 1999).

Litman, B. (1983) Predicting success of theatrical movies: An empirical study in *Journal of Popular Culture*, vol. 16, no. 4, p. 159-175.

Litman, B. (1998) *The motion picture mega-industry*. Needham Heights, MA: Allyn & Bacon.

Litman, B. and Kohl, L.S. (1989) Predicting financial success of motion pictures: The '80s experience. *The Journal of Media Economics*, no. 2, p. 35-50.

Sochay, S. (1994) Predicting the performance of motion pictures. *The Journal of Media Economics*, vol. 7, no. 4, p. 1-20.

Svingen, A. (2000) *Med filmvisjoner på menyen*, Visjoner 2000.

Waterman, D. and Rogers, E. (1994) The economic effects of television program production and trade in the Far East Asia, *Journal of Communication*, vol. 44, no. 3.

Webster, F.E. (1992) The changing role of marketing in the corporation, *Journal of Marketing*, vol. 56, no. 4, 1-17.

Wildman, S. and Siwek, S. (1988) *International trade in films and television Programs*. Balliger.

Wildman, S. and Siwek, S. (1993) The economics of trade in recorded media products in a multilingual world: Implications for national media policies in Noam, E and Millonzi, J (ed.) *The international market in film and television programs*. Norwood, NJ: Ablex Publishing.

Williamson, O.E. (1985) *The economic institutions of capitalism*. New York: Free Press.

Williamson, O.E. (1991) Comparative economic organisation: The analysis of discrete structural alternatives, *Administrative Science Quarterly*, vol. 36, p. 269-296.

Williamson, O.E. (1999) *The economics of transaction costs*. Edward Elgar Publishing, UK

Wyatt, J. (1991) High concept, product differentiation, and the contemporary US film industry in B. Austin, *Current research in film: Audiences, economics, and law*, vol. 5, Norwood, NJ: Ablex

Wyatt, J. (1994) High concept: *Movies and marketing in Hollywood*. Austin, TX: University of Texas Press.

Zajac, E.J. and Olsen, C.P. (1993) From transaction cost to transaction value analysis: Implications for the study of interorganizational strategies, *Journal of Management Studies*, vol. 30, no. 1, 131-145.

Chapter 3
From Analogue to Digital Television Broadcasting:
A Case Study of Australia and Australian Firm Experiences

Allan Brown
Griffith University

The transition from analogue to digital transmission is perhaps the major development in broadcasting since the commencement of television. Australia was a relatively early adopter of digital for terrestrial television broadcasting, with digital transmissions commencing there on 1 January 2001.

The technological advantages of digital over analogue television broadcasting are well known. Digital generally provides improved sound and image reception, including the elimination or reduction of interference and "ghosting". Digital facilitates "multichannelling", which is the transmission of more than one discrete stream of programming over a single television channel. With digital, broadcasters may transmit "enhanced programming", that is, additional or alternative content relating to a broadcast program (for example, information concerning a player or a choice of camera angles during a sports telecast). Digital television reception equipment allows the transmitted signal to be displayed in a 16:9 aspect ratio, rather than the conventional 4:3, and a hard disk built into a set-top box (STB) or integrated digital receiver may be used for the local storage of video or other information for later viewing. A back channel or return path communication, usually provided through a modem connected to a telephone line, enables interactive services or "datacasting".

From an industry structure viewpoint, however, the most important feature of digital transmission is that it is much more economical than analogue in the use of the broadcasting spectrum. In Australia, analogue transmissions are broadcast over 7 megahertz (MHz) channels, usually separated by 7 MHz "buffer" channels. Separate local translator channels are also used for "shadow" areas. The hillier the terrain, the more local translators are required. With digital, the spectrum used for buffers between analogue signals and for shadow infill is either not required or is greatly reduced. The greater Sydney area, for example, currently requires almost all of the 55 standard 7 MHz channels available to transmit the signals of its six television services. As few as five channels would be necessary to achieve a similar coverage with digital (Productivity Commission, 2000: 223–24). Digital transmission thus greatly increases the channel carrying capacity of the spectrum and provides scope for new players, more competition and additional services.

The transition to digital provides a significant challenge to governments and broadcasting regulators worldwide. Incumbent operators, especially commercial broadcasters, benefiting from the old regime of limited competition, can be expected to attempt to influence decision making so as to protect their positions. Without a successful conversion to digital and a subsequent switch-off of the analogue system, however, the key benefits of digital television will not be fully realised.

This chapter presents a case study of the digital television transition process in Australia. The next section briefly describes the range of television broadcasting firms operating in Australia. Then follows an outline and critique of the digital television policy of the Australian government. The following section examines the experience of Australian digital terrestrial television broadcasting one year after its introduction. The issue of datacasting in Australia is then discussed, and concluding comments are provided.

AUSTRALIAN TELEVISION FIRMS

Television broadcasting began in Australia in 1956. Most commercial free-to-air (FTA) television stations in Australia are owned and operated by one of the six networks. The predominant firms, both financially and in terms of audience share, are the three main commercial networks—Seven, Nine and Ten. They each own and operate stations in the three largest cities, Sydney, Melbourne and Brisbane, as well as in other metropolitan and regional markets. For the 1997–98 financial year the three major commercial networks collectively enjoyed a very high level of earnings (before interest and tax) as a percentage of revenues of 23.4% (Productivity Commission, 2000: Table 2.8).

The Australian television broadcasting firms are listed in Table 3.1.

Subscription broadcasting is a relatively recent addition to the Australian television system. It commenced in 1995, and by 2001 the penetration rate had reached around 17 per cent of Australian households. Three major providers of pay TV operate in Australia—Foxtel, Optus and Austar—although there are a number of smaller subscription services. Foxtel is owned 50% by Telstra, the major telecommunications carrier, 25% by the Nine Network, and 25% by

Rupert Murdoch's News Corporation. Although no pay TV operator has yet made a profit in Australia, the industry is generally expected to start trading profitably in the near future (Productivity Commission, 2000: 102).

Table 3. 1. Australian Television Broadcasting Firms

Advertiser supported	Seven Network
	Nine Network
	Network Ten
	TWT Holdings
	Prime Network
	Southern Cross
Subscriber supported	Foxtel
	Optus Television
	Austar
Taxpayer funded	Australian Broadcasting Corporation
	Special Broadcasting Service
Non-profit	Channel 31

Note: as at December 1999
Source: Productivity Commission, 2000: Chapter 2

Australia has two taxpayer funded, public service broadcasting FTA networks, the Australian Broadcasting Corporation (ABC) and the Special Broadcasting Service (SBS), both of which provide television and radio services. The ABC was established in 1932. Unlike a number of European public broadcasters, the ABC has always occupied a minority position in Australian broadcasting, in terms of finance, number of stations and size of audience. The SBS was established as the second arm of public broadcasting in 1975 as part of the government's policy of "multiculturalism". SBS television commenced broadcasting in 1980. ABC-TV typically obtains audience ratings of between 12% and 14%, significantly less than those of the commercial networks, while the average rating performance for SBS-TV is only around 2% to 4% (Brown & Althaus, 1996).

Community television commenced operations in 1994. Although community radio is well developed in Australia, there are only seven community television services—all known as Channel 31—five in metropolitan cities and two in large regional centres. It broadcasts mainly local programming, and accounts for a negligible proportion of the aggregate television audience.

GOVERNMENT DIGITAL POLICY

Digital television broadcasting in Australia is governed by the Television Broadcasting Services (Digital Conversion) Act 1998. This legislation was enacted following an enquiry by a Specialist Group on Digital Terrestrial Television Broadcasting that was established in 1993 by the broadcasting regulatory body, the Australian Broadcasting Authority (ABA). The legislation is strongly based on the final report of the Specialist Group, which was completed in early 1997 and endorsed later the same year by the ABA (Given, 1998). The 1998 Act was subsequently supplemented by the Broadcasting Services Amendment (Digital Television and Datacasting) Bill 2000.

The main elements of the conversion of television to digital in Australia are as follows:

- Digital television broadcasting is based on the European DVB set of technical standards.
- Digital terrestrial transmission commenced in state capital cities on 1 January 2001, and all other areas are to have digital broadcasting by 1 January 2004.
- Existing FTA broadcasters receive a "loan" of an additional 7 MHz of spectrum without charge until 31 December 2008, which can be extended on an area basis by regulation. At the end of analogue transmission broadcasters must return the spectrum currently used for their analogue services.
- The spectrum on loan is to facilitate simulcasting of programs by broadcasters during the transition period in three formats—analogue, standard definition (SDTV) and high definition (HDTV).
- There is a mandatory transmission quota of a minimum of 20 hours per week for material produced in HDTV, which is to be achieved by broadcasters within two years of the start of digital transmissions in an area.
- Multichannelling is permitted for the ABC and SBS, but prohibited for commercial broadcasters. Types of programming which compete directly with that of the commercial broadcasters, such as sports, movies, sitcoms, drama and national news, are not allowed on ABC and SBS multichannelling.
- All FTA broadcasters are allowed to provide enhancements to their digital programs provided they are directly linked to those programs—

for example, additional camera angles and statistics about a player in sports telecasts.
- The provision of subscription broadcasting services by current FTA broadcasters is prohibited.
- No new commercial FTA television licenses are to be granted in any area before 2007.
- There are stringent restrictions on interactive services (see below).
- The target switch-off date for analogue transmissions is 31 December 2008, but is subject to extension.

Although the government announced in 1998 that it planned to provide for the community sector to participate in digital television broadcasting, by the end of 2001 no spectrum had been allocated to community television broadcasters for digital transmissions.

Since its announcement, the government's digital television policy has been widely criticised, not least by the government's own microeconomic research body, the Productivity Commission, in its 2000 report on the broadcasting industry. There are several strands to that criticism:

- The free loan of 7 MHz channels to FTA broadcasters
- mandatory HDTV transmissions
- The lack of legislated analogue switch-off date
- The prohibition on new commercial broadcasters

Each of these is discussed in turn.

Free Loan of 7 MHz Channels to FTA Broadcasters

This part of the digital policy is based on the United States model, where each existing licensee receives a free loan of one standard 6 MHz television channel, and is required to simulcast its programs in analogue and digital for the duration of the transition period (Pepper & Levy, 1999). There are two separate aspects to this part of the decision.

The spectrum allocation is without charge. This contrasts with the normal method used in Australia since 1992 of allocating broadcasting spectrum by a price-based mechanism (auctions). Some believe the decision not to charge broadcasters for the additional spectrum has cost the government "several billion dollars" in foregone revenue (Encel, 2001: 39). The government argues that the free allocation of spectrum to the incumbent broadcasters is "in recognition of the high conversion and operating costs of digital" the current broadcasters will incur (Alston, 2000). There is some validity to this argument, considering that the decision to convert to digital was not made voluntarily by the industry but was imposed by the government. The commercial FTA broadcasters in particular would seem to have little to gain and much to lose from digital conversion, and would presumably prefer to retain analogue indefinitely. A less defensible part of this decision, however, is that the government naively accepted the broadcasters' claimed costs of digital conversion without scrutiny.

The allocation is for 7 MHz of spectrum. This is the crucial part of the digital decision and the major defect in the government's policy. The granting of 7 MHz of spectrum to each current FTA operator (except the community broadcasters) was to accommodate mandatory HDTV transmission (see below). An alternative approach would have been to allocate the FTA broadcasters only, say, 2 MHz of spectrum, sufficient for them to provide simulcasting in SDTV rather than HDTV. This would have left considerable spectrum capacity for new services and additional players, and radically changed the structure of the industry in the digital era. But this was the very outcome the commercial networks were keen to avert.

Mandatory HDTV Transmissions

This idea was advocated by the commercial FTA representatives on the Specialist Group, and adopted by the Specialist Group, the ABA, and subsequently the government. In announcing the government's digital policy the Minister justified mandating HDTV transmissions in the following terms:

> The Government agreed with the FTA broadcasters that HDTV can offer a significantly better viewing experience, and will therefore be an important component of the digital television system. Also, if free to air broadcasters do not have the capacity to provide HDTV, they could be placed at a disadvantage if [subscription] cable and satellite services start providing HDTV. As the broadcasters have been loaned enough spectrum to broadcast in HDTV—much more than they would need if they were to broadcast in SDTV—it is only fair that they should face a legal requirement to broadcast in HDTV (Alston, 1999: 8).

As the Productivity Commission points out (2000: 253), both the "significantly better viewing experience" and the capacity for FTA broadcasters to compete with cable and satellite operators could be attained by permitting but not mandating high definition (the U.S. approach). Furthermore, the government's "fairness" reason lacks logic: 7 MHz of spectrum can be used for a wide range of purposes, but only HDTV transmission has been mandated.

The main problem with making HDTV mandatory for broadcasters stems from the fact that the higher the resolution of the digital image the greater the amount of spectrum required for its transmission. For example, one high definition signal (in the "1080i" format which refers to a picture of 1080 horizontal lines with interlaced scanning) occupies almost an entire 7 MHz of spectrum, which could otherwise be used for the transmission of up to four SDTV signals. There is, therefore, a trade-off between using a 7 MHz channel for a single HDTV program, and using it to transmit a greater number of programs and/or services with smaller spectrum requirements. Requiring broadcasters to transmit HDTV programs thus restricts their capacity to provide multichannelling, enhanced programming and interactive services. Making the provision of HDTV programming mandatory also adds to the equipment costs of broadcasters, and the production costs of program producers and advertisers.

Lack of Legislated Analogue Switch-Off Date

Although the digital legislation sets 31 December 2008 as the target switch-off date for analogue television broadcasting, it does not stipulate a definite date to end analogue transmissions. Moreover, the legislation does not nominate criteria to be used to decide when switch-off should take place. Instead, it provides for extension of the simulcasting of analogue and digital. The statutory eight years to 2008, therefore, is a minimum period.

It can reasonably be expected that the government will not switch off analogue transmission unless and until a significant proportion of television viewers has digital reception equipment. It would be politically unfeasible to deny a sizeable number of people reception of FTA television broadcasts. It is notable that the U.S. Congress has directed that analogue switch-off not occur in that country until at least 85% of households have access to digital television signals (Pepper & Levy, 1999).

The decision to make the transmission of HDTV mandatory, together with the proh ition on multichannelling by the FTA commercial broadcasters, are likely to severely limit the incentives for viewers to invest in new digital reception equipment. As one commentator has questioned: "How can any government justify asking people to expend large amounts, merely to enjoy more or less what they already enjoy on sets that are performing to their satisfaction?" (Encel, 2001: 44).

Another factor likely to inhibit sales of digital receivers concerns the size of screens. Matsushita advises that to enjoy the full benefits of HDTV screens will need to be at least 90cm diagonal. The company points out further that 72% of analogue receivers sold in Australia in 1997 had screen sizes of less than 61 cm, and that there is little perceivable difference in the picture quality of a digital receiver with a screen size of less than 61cm compared to an equivalent sized analogue receiver with good reception (Productivity Commission, 2000: 247). This suggests that HDTV is inappropriate for casual television viewing, and suited more for the specialised "home cinema" viewing experience.

A slow consumer take-up of digital receivers will almost certainly prolong the simulcast period and delay analogue switch-off. This is recognised by the Productivity Commission (2000: 235): "if the policy remains unchanged, it appears highly likely that the analogue simulcasting period will be extended until digital equipment has been very widely adopted". The lack of a definite, legislated date for analogue switch-off also creates uncertainty in the minds of equipment manufacturers, retailers and consumers. There is also a substantial opportunity cost in retaining large portions of spectrum for analogue television broadcasting. Its use for simulcasting prevents it from being auctioned and used for other purposes.

Prohibition on New Commercial Broadcasters

As mentioned earlier, a major feature of digital is its capacity to allow the entry of new broadcasters. Nevertheless, one of the provisions for the transition to digital in Australia involves the prohibition on new players until at least 2007. The government's justification for this restriction is "to ensure the commercial FTAs' commitment to quality is retained, and to take into account the expensive transition to digital television" (Alston, 1998: 21). This aspect of the digital decision has been widely criticised (Productivity Commission, 2000; Encel, 2001; Papandrea, 2001), but perhaps no more strongly than in an editorial by Australia's major business newspaper: "Where else in the economy, least of all in information technology, would such a government protection racket be tolerated? What happened to consumer choice and media diversity?" (*Australian Financial Review*, 1998: 18). Although the government's digital decision prohibits the licensing of any new commercial FTA broadcasters before 2007, the ban on new licenses will in fact stay in place as long as there is simulcasting of programs, because no spectrum will become available for the entry of new competitors until analogue is switched off.

The decisions to grant spectrum to broadcasters without charge and to ban the issue of new commercial television licenses were contrary to the advice of the government's own major departments, namely, Prime Minister & Cabinet, Treasury and Finance (Lewis, 1999).

The commercial networks benefit from the free grant of spectrum and the prohibition on new competitors, but especially from mandatory HDTV and the indefinite date for analogue switch-off. The HDTV requirement places control of almost all of the broadcasting spectrum in the hands of the existing broadcasters, and the lack of a legislated date for the end of simulcasting allows this control to be extended. Although one of the government's policy objectives is to complete the transition to digital by 2008, there is nothing in its decision to ensure that this will be achieved.

The government's policy fails to recognise that the incumbent commercial broadcasters have a strong incentive to continue analogue simulcasting, despite its costs. The longer they retain control of the broadcasting spectrum, the longer the entry of new competitors is delayed. The digital decision also favours the pay TV broadcasters who benefit from the ban on new FTA licenses and the restriction on multichannelling by the commercial FTA networks. These decisions limit to three the number of commercial television signals, at least until 2007, and thus contain the extent of competition to pay TV from FTA broadcasting.

DIGITAL TELEVISION BROADCASTING: THE FIRST YEAR

A year after the commencement of digital terrestrial television transmissions in Australia the overwhelming majority of viewers were unaffected by the transition process, and most were probably unaware it was happening.

Taking advantage of permission to multichannel, the public service broadcasters are providing or planning to provide new digital television channels. ABC Kids commenced in September 2001. Targeted at young children, it is on air 6am-6pm, and broadcasts in SDTV format. A new ABC youth channel, FLY, started in November 2001. It broadcasts 6 pm-11pm, also in SDTV. SBS has announced that in 2002 it will launch a digital television channel for teenagers from multicultural backgrounds. Although these new public service channels have become available under the digital legislation, the small number of households with digital receivers (see below) provides them with insufficient audiences. To address this problem both the ABC and SBS have negotiated with the pay TV operators to carry their new "digital" channels.

The contribution of the commercial FTA broadcasters in the first year of digital transmissions was modest. Network Ten commenced a six-hour-a-day HDTV demonstration service, and provided alternative camera angles ("multiview events") in some of its major sports telecasts. The Nine Network's digital transmissions were confined to an on-screen program guide, available to viewers in the Sydney area only. The Seven Network had yet to participate in digital broadcasting (DBA, 2001).

It was mentioned in the previous section that the timing of the analogue switch-off is likely to be determined by the proportion of viewers with digital reception equipment. The viewer take-up of digital television receivers during the first year is not encouraging in this regard. Twelve months after the commencement of digital transmissions there were no integrated digital receivers commercially available. When they do become available the prices of receivers will depend on their specifications, display capabilities and other facilities, but are predicted to vary between A$5000 (US$2500) for an SDTV receiver and A$20,000 (US$10,000) for a top-of-the-range HDTV set. In December 2001 there were four brands of SDTV digital STBs available at around A$700 (US$350), and one HDTV at around A$900 (US$450).

Verified sales figures for STBs in Australia are not publicly available, although industry sources estimate the number sold in 2001 to be somewhat less than 10,000 (Alex Encel, personal correspondence, 18 October 2001). This represents approximately one STB for every 1,000 analogue television receivers in Australia. It is common for new technical products to experience slow adoption rates for the initial period after their launch on the market, to be followed by a sales take-off as "positive feedback" among consumers takes effect (Shapiro & Varian, 1999). The Australian government will be relying on this type of consumer adoption dynamics to vindicate its digital television policy.

DATACASTING

A contributing factor to the very low level of digital STB sales has been the false start of the government's datacasting strategy. *Datacasting* is a term used in Australia to refer to interactive services that utilise the broadcasting spectrum. Datacasting allows interactive services similar to those available on the Internet to appear on the television screen. The government has legislated for a new class of license for users of the spectrum by distinguishing between the programs and services that can be provided by datacasters and those provided by broadcasters. According to Bourne (2000), no other country has drawn this distinction.

The types of programs and services that datacasters are allowed to provide include information programs, interactive home shopping, banking and bill paying, web pages, email, interactive games and educational services. Types of programs prohibited to datacasters include drama, current affairs, sports, music, lifestyle, children's, comedy, documentaries, "reality" television, quiz programs and game shows. The Minister explains that:

> … datacasting is different to television broadcasting. So it would not be right for datacasters to be able to show the same kinds of programs that we are used to seeing on television… Otherwise, people

might use datacasting as a 'back door' way of getting into broadcasting (Alston, 1999: 12–13).

Spectrum not used for broadcasting has been set aside by the government for datacasting. It was intended to offer two 10-year datacasting licenses in each of eight geographic service areas, and the required spectrum was to be allocated by auction in May 2001. (Incumbent FTA broadcasters were also to be allowed to use any of their spare spectrum for datacasting and were to be charged a fee for doing so.) It transpired, however, that most of the firms that originally registered to participate in the auction decided that the restrictions imposed undermined the commercial viability of datacasting, and withdrew from the process. The government cancelled the datacasting auction two weeks before it was scheduled to commence. It is expected to review its datacasting policy in 2002.

CONCLUSION

Australia's experience to date with the transition from analogue to digital terrestrial television broadcasting represents the triumph of sectional private interests over the general public interest. The existing commercial television firms, led by the metropolitan networks, recognised the threat posed by digital transmission to their high profits. They devised a strategy to both minimise and delay the adverse effects upon their profits of the transition to digital, and persuaded the government to adopt that strategy. Acting against the advice of its own major departments, a compliant government adopted the strategy of the commercial television networks as its digital policy.

The foundation of the network strategy, and the fundamental defect in the government's digital policy, is to make HDTV transmissions mandatory for terrestrial FTA broadcasters. This was despite the fact that no other country has done likewise, and that in the United States HDTV has so far been unsuccessful. It seems unlikely that many viewers will invest in digital reception equipment until it gives them access to new programming, services and broadcasters, which digital technology makes possible. The current digital policy of the Australian government, however, explicitly restricts the capacity for these potential improvements to the television broadcasting system. It is ironical that digital technology facilitates a large expansion in the number of television broadcasters, but the Australian government has legislated to prevent any increase in the number of players in the industry.

Over the next few years the key features of the government's digital legislative framework will be reviewed: the range of services allowable as datacasting (2002); the mandatory HDTV quotas (2003); and the prohibitions on new commercial FTA licenses (2006). It seems likely that the definition of datacasting services will be broadened to revive the auction process for datacasting licenses. At this stage it is too early to predict with confidence the outcome of the other reviews. A continuation of the very low take-up by viewers of digital reception equipment will put pressure on the government to revise its digital policies. Against this pressure, however, will be intense lobbying by the commercial television firms for continued protection from the forces of competition inherent in digital transmissions.

REFERENCES

Alston, R. (1998). Government's digital television bill passes Senate. Media Release 130/98, 3 July, Parliament House, Canberra.

Alston, R. (1999). Digital broadcasting and datacasting. Fact sheet, 21 December, Parliament House, Canberra.

Alston, R. (2000). Success of digital TV will rely on consumer choice. Media Release 062/00, 30 June, Parliament House, Canberra.

Australian Financial Review (The). (1998). Information age mockery. 25 March, 18.

Bourne, V. (2000). Digital television. *Australian Law Librarian*, 8, 205-213.

Brown, A. & Althaus, C. (1996). Public service broadcasting in Australia. *The Journal of Media Economics*, 9, 31-46.

DBA (Digital Broadcasting Australia). (2001). *DBA Information Bulletin*, October, www.dba.org.au.

Encel, A. (2001). Australia's digital television saga. *National Observer*, 48, 39-44.

Given, J. (1998). Being digital: Australia's television choice. *Media and Arts Law Review*, 3, 38-51.

Lewis, S. (1999). Ganging up on digital TV. *The Australian Financial Review*. 12 August, 18.

Papandrea, F. (2001). Digital television policy: A squandered opportunity. *Agenda*, 8, 65-78.

Pepper, R. & Levy, J. (1999). Convergence: Public benefits and policy challenges. In C. T. Marsden & S. G. Verhulst (Eds.), *Convergence in European digital TV regulation* (pp. 21-36). London: Blackstone.

Productivity Commission (2000). Broadcasting. Report no. 11, Canberra: AusInfo.

Shapiro, C. & Varian, H.R. (1999*). Information rules: A strategic guide to the network economy*. Boston: Harvard Business School Press.

The author acknowledges Alex Encel for his helpful comment on an earlier version of this manuscript.

Chapter 4
Competition, Innovation and Performance of Professional Information Providers

Richard van der Wurff
University of Amsterdam

Professional information is an indispensable resource in today's economy and tomorrow's information society. It encompasses information that skilled workers "must have" or "need to know" to carry out their professional tasks efficiently and effectively. As such, it is a valuable driver of competitive success and innovation in many industries and other segments of society. Equal access to diverse and high-quality professional information services consequently is an important condition for balanced, equitable and progressive political, social and economic development.

This chapter discusses how digitisation changes the number, type and strategies of professional information providers and consequently affects prices and diversity of professional information. The focus on digitisation follows both from observable trends in the sector and from ongoing and unresolved debates on the pros and cons of digitisation and other "information society" phenomena (such as e-commerce, disintermediation and customisation). The professional information industry is one of the few sectors in which these phenomena can be observed empirically on a relatively large scale and for a relatively long period of time. Given the growing role and importance of professional information and the remaining uncertainties about the social and economic consequences of "the information society", it is important to assess how digitisation affects performance of professional information markets.

The study focuses on developments in professional information publishing in The Netherlands in the 1990s, partly because The Netherlands is home country to three of the largest professional information providers in the world and partly because each has a relatively well developed digital strategy. This market and these players are introduced in Section 2. Section 3 presents a general and tentative overview of trends in The Netherlands in the 1990s, on the basis of 16 interviews with publishers and a review of expert literature.[1] Subsequently, Sections 4 and 5 investigate publishing strategies and performance of the Dutch agricultural (print and online) information market. This market changed considerably in the 1990s. Previously state-owned or -funded content producers (such as agricultural research institutes and extension agencies) were privatised, new players entered the market, and competition became more intense. At the same time, information intensity of farming increased, and individual and societal agricultural information needs changed (Leeuwis, 2000; Meulenberg, 1995; Vergouwen, 1992). The agricultural information market therefore offers an interesting case to study. Finally, Section 6 presents conclusions and discusses the implications for professional information market performance.

OVERVIEW OF THE DUTCH
PROFESSIONAL INFORMATION MARKET

The Netherlands has a flourishing professional information industry. It encompasses about 1,000 medium- and small-sized publishers, as well as three of the largest professional information publishers in the world (Reed-Elsevier, VNU and Wolters Kluwer). Small, medium-sized and large publishers together produced, per year in the mid- to late 1990s, approximately 3,700 scientific books (of which 2,300 in Dutch and 1,400 in English), 1,300 scientific journals (mostly in English), and about 1,800 trade journals (mostly in Dutch) (Bakker & Scholten, 1997; Stichting Speurwerk, 1999; Van Ankeren, Bakker, Crombags & Hendriks, 1996; R. Barnard, personal communication, June 2000).

Market Segmentation and High Subscription Income

This professional information market in The Netherlands is strongly segmented into a range of niche markets; and each niche is dominated by one or a few information providers. For example, Misset, which is now part of Elsevier Business Information, controlled 38% of the annual circulation of agricultural trade journals in the mid-1990s (Van Ankeren et al., 1996). Likewise, Wolters

---

[1] These interviews were conducted by Piet Bakker and the author in April 1999 in the context of a study for the Group of Trade and Scientific Publishers of the Dutch Publishers Association (reported in Van der Wurff et al., 1999). The co-operation of the Group and participating publishers is gratefully acknowledged. The views expressed in this article are the author's and do not necessarily reflect those of the Group or individual publishers.

Kluwer almost monopolises the legal and fiscal information markets (SDU bestrijdt..., 1997). Other scientific and trade information markets, too, tend to be dominated by a few players with reported market shares of 25% to 60%.

Another characteristic of the Dutch professional information industry is that it relies to a relatively large extent (60%, according to the Media Group, 2000) on subscription, rather than advertising, income. This strong reliance on subscription income builds upon and at the same time reinforces the observed tendencies towards market segmentation and limited competition. On the one hand, strong reliance on subscription income makes that publishers want to prevent subscription price competition. The best way to accomplish this goal is by offering a differentiated product (Porter, 1985)—a strategy that of course contributes to market segmentation. Product differentiation and market segmentation, on the other hand, are especially profitable when professionals, rather than advertisers, pay for information products. Professional information users generally are willing to pay a premium price for specific and exclusive need-to-know information. Advertisers, in contrast, are much less tempted to pay higher prices for specific products, because they can also use more general services to reach the same or a larger group at lower costs. In sum, the more publishers depend on advertising income and the less they depend on subscription income, the less they will be tempted and able to develop and market differentiated products for small niche markets. We come back to this issue at the end of the next section.

DIGITISATION OF
PROFESSIONAL INFORMATION PUBLISHING

Digitisation, the emergence of electronic publishing, affects market relations in the professional information industry in two ways. Most visibly, digitisation implies the provision of electronic products and services, next to or instead of print publications. Less visibly, but at least as significant, digitisation involves technological (or process) changes that in turn bring about changes in cost structures, competitive relations, and the vertical organisation of the information industry's value chain. We discuss these changes below.

Digitisation Changes Cost Structures and Stimulates New Entry

Firstly, digitisation reduces publishing costs (Hayes, 1998) and thereby enables providers to serve increasingly smaller niche audiences. The minimum edition for a semi-scientific book in the Dutch language, for example, now lies at about a hundred copies (Manager of a small scientific Dutch publisher, personal communication, April 1999). Average circulation of trade publications, that are included in the *Handboek van de Nederlandse Pers en Publiciteit* (Trade Book of Dutch Press and Publicity; 1994 & 2000), declined from 31,000 in 1994 to 11,000 in 2000. Digitisation, therefore, reinforces the already strong tendency towards market segmentation in the professional information industry.

Digitisation does not reduce all publishing costs in similar amounts. It reduces, in particular, information reproduction and distribution costs (ABN AMRO, 1998; Shapiro & Varian, 1999). One consequence is that information market entry barriers become lower for non-publishing players that possess valuable information. These players can easily use low-cost digital technologies to start distributing their information to audiences. Some publishers consider it a serious threat that advertisers—and other players for which publishing is not a core business—make good use of these opportunities and enter professional information markets. Such a combined process of disintermediation and commodification could destroy hitherto profitable professional information markets. Dutch publishers, for example, note that the Dutch taxation office destroyed the market for personal fiscal software by distributing a free tax return disc; and that governmental and other organisations increasingly provide legal information "for free" on the web.

Numerous examples for other countries can be added from the information trade literature. These examples all contribute to a picture in which traditional publishers face more intense competition by non-traditional information providers. These non-traditional providers enter the market to provide information to their audiences—not to make money, but to draw attention to their messages and/or core products. They include (former) advertisers and other attention-seekers that provide marketing or PR information directly "for free" to prospective buyers. They include researchers, government organisations and other original content producers that provide information directly to target groups. And they include libraries, information professionals and other groups of users that digitally share expensive information resources. All those players put a downward pressure on information prices. At the same time, they build upon their improved power position to demand a better deal from publishers.

Publishers' Strategies

According to Dutch professional information publishers, the core strategy with which these threats can best be minimised, if not averted, is by further improving quality and accessibility of content. As independent intermediaries between content producers, information users and advertisers, publishers supposedly add value by checking and selecting information. Hence, they should be able to outperform any other player by providing customised, high-quality access to high-quality content from multiple and diverse information sources. Expert reviews of "free" and "fee-based" information on the web confirm that professionals are indeed willing to pay for high quality services that offer better access, more advanced search options, more in-depth analysis, and more complete information (Gordon-Murnane, 1999; Lennon, 1999; Liebman, 1998; Raeder, 1997). Product differentiation strategies, moreover, have the advantage that they reinforce publishers' ties with end-users. At the same time, product differentiation requires that publishers develop exclusive relationships with preferred content producers, and that they acquire more complete (copyright) control over content. Whereas digitisation reinforces the power position of users vis-à-vis publishers and contributes at first to disintermediation, publishers' product differentiation strategies therefore amount to an attempt to regain control in the publishing value chain.

Remarkably, only a limited number of professional information publishers explicitly uses digital technologies and/or offers electronic services as part of their product differentiation strategies. This number includes, of course, the three major professional information publishers. As can regularly be read in financial-economic expert publications, Reed-Elsevier, VNU and Wolters Kluwer invest large sums of money in digitisation and Internet strategies. Their aim is to create a number of portals, where individual professionals can find all relevant information and other electronic services that they need (ABN AMRO, 1998; Reed Elsevier, s.a.; VNU, s.a.; Wolters Kluwer, s.a.).

Next to these major players, we find a few medium-sized and small publishers that not only have similar high expectations of the potential of electronic services, but also the willingness and opportunity to spend financial and human resources on the development and implementation of their digital strategies. Compared with the major publishers that invest heavily on their own digital strategies, these medium-sized and small publishers spend less and co-operate more strongly with other publishers and third parties.

Many small publishers, however, find the costs and associated risks of going digital still too high. They lack, for example, the resources to employ a dedicated electronic services editor with technical expertise; or to develop a CD-ROM version of a print publication. These players choose to reinforce their quality strategies in print publications. Building upon close personal contacts with content producers and information buyers, they maintain their position in their niches and await to see the experiences of their more adventurous and resourceful competitors.

Online Activities and Publications

The number of Internet services that is provided by publishers of print publications in The Netherlands therefore increases relatively slowly. In the mid-1990s, only a few publishers (15, according to Neyssen, 1995) and a few professional trade journals (49, as counted by Van Ankeren et al., 1996) are present on the Internet. In 2000, more than 2000 publishers had a web site. Nevertheless, of the 4,018 trade and scientific publications listed in the Handboek (2000), only 633 had their own Internet site (16%). These numbers are very small compared with the 400,000 to 500,000 domain names that were operational in 2000 (SIDN, 2001). Of course, only an unknown percentage of these domains competes directly with publishers on professional information markets. Nevertheless, available anecdotal evidence suggests that non-traditional providers, rather than professional information providers, play a major role on the Internet. For example, we find no publishers among the providers of the ten most popular Dutch financial information sites (Multiscope, 2000).

Strategic Groups on Professional Information Markets

Provisionally, we conclude that digitisation strengthens competition between traditional publishers and new, non-traditional providers. Traditional publishers aim to improve their competitive position by reinforcing their product differentiation strategies. They aim to offer relatively high quality information products to professional information users, for which they also charge relatively high prices. Non-traditional providers are original content producers and attention seekers that make use of digital opportunities to enter professional information markets. They primarily distribute information that they already possess. Consequently, their information offer is less diverse than what traditional publishers offer; but also much cheaper.

Within the group of traditional publishers, we further distinguish between publishers that operate (primarily) on information markets and publishers that operate (primarily) on attention markets. As argued above, product differentiation strategies are more feasible on information markets than on attention markets. We therefore expect the most explicit product differentiation or (mass) customisation strategies, as well as the highest information prices, on information markets. Publishers on attention markets, in contrast, have fewer opportunities to target niches. They rather provide relatively diverse and multiple source products at relatively low prices that can attract relatively large groups of professionals (Van der Wurff, 2001).

Within the group of non-traditional providers we make a similar distinction between providers that provide information for marketing purposes, and providers that provide information for educational purposes. The former group includes (former) advertisers that now aim to develop more direct relations with their buyers. They resemble publishers on attention markets, in the sense that both types of players provide information to create audiences. The latter group, in contrast, includes (former) content producers that find it more attractive to provide their information directly to end-users. These players resemble publishers on information markets; their main activity is to inform professionals. Consequently, they provide information of higher quality and perhaps also more heterogeneity than the former group. We investigate these expectations in the next section.

THE AGRICULTURAL PRINT INFORMATION MARKET

The Netherlands has a highly productive, innovative, and internationally competitive agricultural industry that also is increasingly information intensive. Farmers regularly need up-to-date information on cultivation methods, disease prevention and treatment, product characteristics, innovations (new crop variants, new equipment), management techniques, market trends (including prices), regulatory developments, relevant news items, and average production results (e.g., average milk production per cow) to evaluate their own work.

Agricultural Trade Journals

Part of this information is provided by agricultural trade journals. We define an agricultural trade journal as a print publication in the Dutch language, that appears between 4 and 52 times a year, at regular intervals, and that provides information relevant to professional farming activities. At the beginning of the 1990s, farmers on average received six trade journals and spent three hours a week reading them (Vergouwen, 1992: 32). These journals are provided by traditional publishers, by attention seekers (commercial suppliers and agricultural traders), and original content producers (research, extension and governmental organisations).

Within the group of journals provided by traditional publishers, we further distinguish between journals that depend to a relatively large extent on advertising revenues and journals that depend to a relatively large extent on subscription income. We rank journals in terms of subscription revenues (defined as subscription price multiplied by circulation) and approximated advertising revenues (defined as advertising price for a one-page ad multiplied by publication frequency). We subtract both rankings to get a new ranking in terms of the relative importance of subscription and advertising revenues, and subsequently divide them equally into two groups.

According to the *Handboek* (1991 until 2000), there were on average 73.5 journals published per year between 1991 and 2000. Total circulation of these journals declined from a maximum of 1.16 million copies in 1992 to a minimum of 1.02 million copies in 2000. The number of providers declined likewise, from 53 (1991) to 40 (2000). Non-traditional providers had an aggregated share in total circulation that varies between 18% (1991), 14% (1996) and 20% (2000).

Focusing on different types of journals, we observe a decline in the number and aggregate circulation of journals published by content producers. This results from market exit by agricultural extension organisations (which reduced their number from 8–10 to 5). The number and aggregate circulation of journals that are primarily offered on attention markets, on the other hand, increased, even though the number of providers of those journals declined as well (from 13 to 7). The explanation is that the remaining publishers offer more journals (on average, 3.9 instead of 1.7). The numbers of attention-seekers and publishers that operate primarily on information markets, as well as the average number of journals provided by these players, remain more or less the same.

Product and pricing strategies, and resulting circulation numbers, vary between the different types of journals (see Table 4.1). Journals offered by publishers on information and attention markets have the highest average circulation. Attention market journals in particular have the highest frequency (and hence highest annual circulation), and also highest advertising prices. Information market journals in contrast have highest average subscription prices. Prices of non-traditional providers' journals are lowest, as expected. Advertising prices of attention-seekers' journals, finally, are low but increasing, which suggests that these journals start to play a larger role on the attention market.

Livestock Farming Journals

To assess what diversity is offered by agricultural trade journals, we analyse the content of all but the smallest journals that target six trade- and region-specific groups of livestock farmers—keeping in mind that these farmers generally read a general national agricultural trade journal, a regional one that is associated with a particular farmers associations, and one or more trade-specific journals (J. Proost, personal communication, March 2001). We include all agricultural trade journals that are mentioned in the *Handboek* or the Dutch libraries' National Central Catalogue, for the odd years in between 1991 and 2000, that are likely

Table 4.1. Agricultural Trade Journals: Number, Average Circulation and Price Per Type

	number of titles		av. circ. (*1000)		average frequency		av. subscr. price (fl)		av. price 1-page ad (fl)	
Year	1991	2000	1991	2000	1991	2000	1991	2000	1991	2000
Attention seeker	13	13	12	13	10	13	16	8	893	2483
Attention market	22	27	13	18	37	35	64	70	1941	3161
Infor. Market	23	28	20	12	16	18	68	108	1878	2194
Content producer	8	5	13	6	14	16	23	21	2304	1551
Unclass-ified	6	1	10	2	26	6	84	56	n.a.	n.a.

to reach a significant section of the selected farmer groups (defined as 10% of dairy, meat cattle or pig farmers; 15% of livestock farmers; 20% of farmers in Gelderland or Noord-Brabant; or 33% of all Dutch farmers). This selection includes between 10 (1991) and 24 (1999) titles, with a total circulation that ranges between 463,000 (1993) and 642,000 (1999) copies. Non-traditional providers account for 13% (until 1995) to almost 30% (in 1997 and 1999) of total circulation.

The strong increase in the number and circulation of these journals from 1991 to 1999 follows from increases in the number and circulation of information market and content producers' journals, and from an increase in the number (but not circulation) of attention market journals. The growing number of information market journals in turn results first of all from the introduction of new titles by existing publishers, and only secondly from entry by new publishers. The increase in the number of content producers and attention market journals, in contrast, results first of all from new entry by new players and only secondly from the introduction of new titles by existing players. Again, the number of attention seekers and the number of journals per attention seeker remain stable.

Prices and product strategies vary once more per type of journal (see Table 4.2). The frequency with which attention market journals are published is highest, making that these journals reach the highest annual circulation.

Publication frequency is lowest for journals provided by non-traditional players. Both subscription and advertising prices are highest for information market journals, followed by attention market journals. Journals provided by non-traditional players in this market segment are free for readers and have low advertising prices.

Table 4.2. Livestock Farming Journals: Number and Average Circulation, Frequency, Prices and Diversity Per Type

	number of titles		av. circ (*1000)		average frequency		av. subs. price (fl)		av. price 1-page ad (fl)		average diversity	
Year	*'91*	*'99*	*'91*	*''99*	*'91*	*'99*	*'91*	*'99*	*'91*	*'99*	*'91*	*'99*
Attention seeker	1	1	40	40	4	4	0	0	n.a.	3113	0.22	0.49
Attention market	1	8	120	14	52	27	97	56	6544	3142	0.78	0.57
Info. Market	7	12	43	33	26	22	57	97	3179	4070	0.47	0.4
Content producer	1	3	22	42	4	4	0	0	2304	2406	0.31	0.32

What interests us most in this particular selection of journals, however, is that the highest degree of diversity is provided by attention market journals, followed subsequently by information market journals, journals from attention seekers and journals from content producers. These conclusions are based upon content analysis of the first one or two issues for May of the selected journals (depending on publication frequency). Articles in these issues are classified into 19 categories. Diversity (D) is defined $- \Sigma (p_i *\ ^{19}\log(p_i))$ where p_i is the relative number of pages in a journal per information category i.

Attention market journals are in particular more diverse because they pay more attention to short-term and long-term agricultural market developments (including prices for agricultural products), and to environmental policies and financial management. They also pay more attention to issues of agricultural tradesmen- and entrepreneurship from an environmental or ecological perspective. Information market journals, in contrast, pay more attention than other types of journals to international trade and competition issues, whereas journals from attention seekers and content producers pay more attention to employment-related issues. Different types of journals, therefore, have their own particular orientations.

THE AGRICULTURAL ONLINE INFORMATION MARKET

Modern farming practices have become increasingly information and ICT-intensive. We observe, for example, that farmers increasingly use PCs and other information equipment to monitor their farms. We also observe a growing number of (experimental) electronic information exchange systems and projects. Finally, we observe that farmers are, in increasing numbers, connected to the Internet (reaching 40% in 2001; Wary Dutch farmers ..., 2000).

Web Sites of Providers of Print Titles

A relatively large number of providers of agricultural trade journals respond to these developments by creating their own web presence. Of the 40 publishers and 74 agricultural trade titles mentioned for 2000 by the *Handboek* (2000), 29 publishers and 60 titles are reported to have a corresponding web site. These are the larger publishers and the larger titles (with an average aggregate circulation per publisher that is almost three times higher than for publishers without a web site; and an average circulation per title that is about half as high as for titles without a web site). Two-thirds of these web sites can be described as (extended) "web presence" sites. They merely give the publisher and/or its journal a presence on the web. They provide information about the publisher, its journal(s) and its other products (which makes a limited web presence site); or they provide (in 15 out of 26 cases) some additional news and/or background information (which makes an extended web presence site). In contrast, only two sites (out of 34) are full-fledged information sites that offer similar information as a trade journal for free; and six other sites offer full-fledged information to registered members or registered subscribers to their print journals.

The two free informative sites are provided by (semi-) governmental organisations that play the role of original content producers in the professional information value chain; namely the Ministry of Agriculture and the Agricultural Economics Institute. The information sites requiring registration by members or subscribers are provided by the largest commercial publisher, Elsevier Business Information, by collaborating with regional farmers' associations (that have their own web site but outsource publication of their regional print journals to a dedicated agricultural publisher), and by the major flower auction company. Traditional publishers that operate on attention markets are the major providers of "limited web presence" sites. Publishers that operate on information markets provide both limited and extended web presence sites. Attention seekers, finally, provide mostly extended web presence sites.

Web Only Publications

Web sites provided by traditional and non-traditional providers of print agricultural titles make up only a small portion of all Dutch web sites that inform about farmers, their suppliers, their advisors, their business customers and other relevant organisations. Startpagina.nl, one of the major Dutch directories of WWW sites, lists, for example, a total of 3,219 different links to "professional agricultural information" web resources that can be found on 2,005 different Dutch web sites (as of 23 November 2001). We included all links that are mentioned on 11 index pages that are listed as "agricultural business" pages on <http://categorie.pagina.nl/>, and on additional index pages to which these first pages refer, excluding links in subcategories that obviously are not relevant. Of course, an unknown percentage of these links and web sites will on closer inspection not be really relevant to farmers; and another unknown percentage will offer only very little information. Nevertheless, the number of available agricultural web sites dwarfs the number of web sites that is provided by commercial and non-traditional publishers of print journals.

According to their classification by Startpagina.nl, most of these 2,005 agricultural web sites provide information that concerns relatively general clusters of farming activities (general and livestock farming, and horticulture) rather than specific farming activities (e.g., dairy farming). Most of these sites also present information on farmers, on farm products, or on products and companies that farmers need (equipment, buildings, wholesale, and advisory organisations), rather providing specific (and valuable) price or weather information, or cultivation advice. Sites on which these more detailed types of information can be found, tend to be the largest sites. Comparing the 52 largest sites (defined as those sites that are listed on at least 5 or more relevant index pages of Startpagina.nl) with all other sites, we find that these major sites offer more information about specific farming activities (such as cultivation of fruits, and sheep keeping), as well as more specific types of information (e.g., on environmental issues, research, and weather). It therefore comes as no surprise that these major sites offer more diverse information than all other sites (see Table 4.3).

The traditional and non-traditional publishers of print journals that we discussed above are responsible for about 1% of all web sites mentioned by Startpagina.nl, and provide 6 of the 52 largest web sites. When we compare these web sites with web sites that do not have a print counterpart, we find that publishers' sites offer more information concerning some specific farming activities (e.g., cultivation of sugar beets, and ecological farming) but also less information concerning other specific activities (like cultivation of fruits, and glass horticulture). We also find that publishers' web sites provide less information on equipment, buildings, and farming products; and more information on wholesale trade, financial issues, research, weather, animal health and pest protection. These are arguably the more "informative" categories than other types of information that are less frequently offered by publishers. Nevertheless, in the end, publishers' web sites together provide less diversity than either the web sites of non-publishers, or the major web sites.

Table 4.3. Diversity Provided by Web Sites

in terms of ...	farming activities	types of information	overall
Major sites	0.81	0.91	0.72
Non-publishers	0.81	0.87	0.70
Smaller sites	0.80	0.86	0.69
Publishers	0.71	0.81	0.58

CONCLUSIONS

This chapter investigated how digitisation affects the professional information market in the Netherlands. Interviews with publishers and literature review suggested, firstly, that digitisation stimulates market segmentation by making it economically feasible to produce smaller printruns and circulations. Secondly, digitisation stimulates market entry of non-traditional information providers by reducing information reproduction and distribution costs. And thirdly, digitisation threatens to cause disintermediation of the professional information value chain. According to professional information publishers, the best response to these opportunities and threats is to reinforce product differentiation strategies. On theoretical grounds, we predicted that publishers that operate primarily on information markets differentiate by customising products for small groups of professionals; whereas publishers that operate primarily on attention markets differentiate by offering very diverse information products to relatively large groups of professionals.

Agricultural Trade Journal Market

Analysis of the agricultural trade information market in The Netherlands in the period 1991-2000 confirms these observations and expectations, with one major exception. The number of non-traditional information providers on the agricultural information market does not increase (as expected) but rather declines. However, we believe that this result directly reflects the privatisation, in that period, of agricultural extension organisations, which subsequently exited the market. This result, therefore, does not contradict the overall argument.

More in line with expectations, we observe on the agricultural trade journal market a decline in average circulation and a strong increase in subscription prices of journals that depend to a relatively large degree on subscription income. In the market segment for livestock farming journals, we moreover observe that these journals offer relatively little—and declining—diversity. These findings support the prediction that publishers that operate primarily on information markets adopt customisation strategies. Secondly, we observe that average circulation and advertising rates increase for journals that depend to a relatively large extent on advertising income. We also observe that these journals offer highest diversity on the livestock market. These findings support the expectation that publishers that operate primarily on attention markets and differentiate by offering diverse products with a wide appeal. A striking result, thirdly, is that diversity and advertising prices of journals produced by attention seekers increase, too. This suggests that these journals start to look more like journals that are offered by publishers that operate on attention markets. Journals produced by content producers, finally, show declining advertising rates and low subscription prices, and offer little diversity. These journals, therefore, remain dedicated information channels for content producers only, and do not become more similar to information market journals.

These findings suggest that competition between attention seekers and publishers on journal attention markets is increasing. This results in more diversity and lower prices on attention markets. Publishers that operate primarily on information markets, on the other hand, have been able to fend off competition by content producers (and have increased the number of their publications)—a result to which the privatisation of agricultural extension organisations probably has contributed. These changes result in lower diversity and higher prices on information markets. Both trends together contribute to an overall improvement of market performance. Professionals have a wider choice between low-priced diverse and high-priced specialised information sources. As long as attention market journals cover the same areas with acceptable quality as information market journals do, professionals therefore can choose their own particular combination of low-priced general and high-priced targeted information.

Agricultural Online Information Market

On the Internet, relations are different. Publishers of attention market journals only have a limited web presence. Attention seekers play a more important role, at least quantitatively. Available information suggests that many of the agricultural web sites listed by Startpagina.nl are provided by attention seekers; and therefore that attention seekers contribute significantly to diversity of Internet information. On the other hand, our research also shows that attention-seeker web sites are mainly extended web presence sites. We therefore do not expect that the large number of attention-seeker sites contribute significantly to the quality of available Internet information; although more research on these web sites is required.

Most valuable information on the web is offered by a few selected information market publishers and a few content producers. Both types of players offer full-fledged information sites. Content producers do this "for free", whereas publishers offer full information only to registered subscribers to their journals. It is not yet clear whether publishers refrain from charging money directly for their web content because of a general reluctance of users to pay for web content, because of competition with "free" web sites provided by content producers, attention-seekers and attention market publishers, or for other reasons. Again, more research is necessary. It is our educated guess, however, that when publishers want to make money on Internet information markets, they need to cut content producers out of the Internet markets, as they did on the trade journal market.

Future performance depends on whether publishers will succeed in this respect. Currently, Internet information supply is very diverse, but only few sites offer high-quality information. Overall quality of information will increase, when providers of attention market journals increase their Internet information offer—which will only happen when they can earn more advertising revenues. Both quality and prices of Internet information will increase, when information market publishers succeed in cutting content producers out of Internet markets and charge information prices. But only when both developments take place, will the Internet market reach similar levels of quality and accessibility as the trade journal market.

REFERENCES

ABN AMRO (1998). *Electronic publishing*. London: ABN AMRO Media Sector Research UK.

Bakker, P., & Scholten, O. (1997). *Communicatiekaart van Nederland*. Houten/Diegem: Bohn Stafleu Van Loghum.

Gordon-Murnane, L. (1999). Government search tools. *Searcher. The magazine for database professionals*, 7 (8), pp. 66-76.

Handboek van de Nederlandse Pers en Publiciteit. (1991–2000). [Electronic editions; Nijgh Media Disc]. Schiedam: Nijgh Periodieken.

Hayes, M. (1998). The ripple effect. *Folio. The magazine for magazine management*, 27 (13), 15 September 1998, pp. 18-21.

Leeuwis, C. (2000). Learning to be sustainable. Does the Dutch agrarian knowledge market fail? *The Journal of Agricultural Education and Extension*, 7 (2), pp. 79-92.

Lennon, D. (1999). The future of "free" information in the age of the Internet. *Aslib Proceedings*, 51 (9), pp. 285-289.

Liebman, B. (1998). A quick tour around value-added IPO web sites. *Database. The magazine of database reference and review*, 21 (5), October/November 1998, pp. 35-38, 40.

Media Group (2000). *Competitiveness of the European Union publishing industries*. Brussels: European Commission.

Meulenberg, M. T. G. (1995). Evolutie van marketing en marketing-informatie in landbouw en agribusiness. *Agro Informatica*, 8 (2), pp. 10-15.

Multiscope (2000). Visiscan top 10 archief. Top 10 - Financieel (oktober 2000) [WWW document]. Multiscope. URL http://www.multiscope.nl/visiscanar chief2.phtml?titel2=Top_10_-_Financieel.&periode2=Oktober_2000.

Neyssen, P.-E. (1995). Internet: een risico of een kans voor uitgevers? *Boekblad*, 162 (29/30), pp. 10-11.

Porter, M. (1985). *Competitive advantage*. (Reprinted 1998 ed.). New York: The Free Press.

Raeder, A. (1997). Financial and investment sources on the Web. *Searcher. The magazine for database professionals*, 5 (4), pp. 44-50.

Reed Elsevier (s.a.). *Jaaroverzicht & verkorte jaarrekening 1999*. Reed Elsevier.

SDU bestrijdt... (1997). SDU bestrijdt Wolters liefst samen met Elsevier. *Het Financieele Dagblad*, 13 February. [Electronic archive].

SIDN (2001). Aantal geregistreerde domeinnamen over de afgelopen jaren. Stichting Internet Domeinregistratie Nederland. [WWW document]. URL http://www.nic.nl/statistieken.html#2.

Shapiro, C., & Varian, H. R. (1999). *Information rules*. Boston, MA: Harvard Business School Press.

Stichting Speurwerk (1999). Aantal boektitels uitgebracht in 1994-1997. URL http://www.speurwerk.nl/bc/97asw.htm.

Van Ankeren, J., Bakker, P., Crombags, B., & Hendriks, P. (1996). Vakinformatie in Nederland (Research report). Amsterdam: Universiteit van Amsterdam/NVJ.

Van der Wurff, R., Bakker, P., Van Cuilenburg, J., & Hellenberg, J. (1999). De huidige en toekomstige markt voor vak en wetenschap (Research report). Amsterdam: The Amsterdam School of Communications Research ASCoR.

Van der Wurff, R. (2001). Het nieuwe uitgeven: Content- en aandachts-markten in de nieuwe economie. *Tijdschrift voor Communicatiewetenschap*, 29 (1), pp. 2-22.

Vergouwen, M. (Ed.) (1992). *Kennis maken: Informatiestromen in agrarisch Nederland*. Ede: Informatie en Kennis Centrum Veehouderij.

VNU (s.a.). *Jaarverslag 1999*. Haarlem: VNU.

58   van der Wurff — Competition, Innovation and Performance

Wary Dutch farmers lured to internet. *Het Financieele Dagblad*, 7 April 2001, p. 20.

Wolters Kluwer (s.a.). *Jaarverslag 1999*. Amsterdam: Wolters Kluwer.

Chapter 5
Competition Between New and Old Media in Economic and Financial News Markets

Angel Arrese and Mercedes Medina
University of Navarra

The new media and the new media companies have monopolised a good part of the academic and professional discussion for the last decade. The emergence of the Internet and firms dealing in information business on the network have spelt both threats and opportunities of all kinds for the strategies of old media and traditional businesses in practically all markets. Nevertheless, the concept of a "new medium" has not been associated exclusively to the appearance and development of the "digital business" of E-conomics in all the markets (European Communication Council, 2000).

Online media and online information services have not been the only new media to join the increasingly relevant new market of specialised economic and financial news in the last decade. For that sector, the incorporation of radio and television in the daily supply of content was, at the time, as important as the subsequent advent of the Internet. During almost a century, the print media had dominated that type of information. Neither radio nor television managed to develop competitive products. A few specialised businesses, unequivocally focused on the peculiar nature of their products, had managed to consolidate their leadership around prestigious journalistic brand names.

The new competitive situation resulting from the incorporation of new media into this sector poses fundamental challenges for the survival of those journalistic brand names as well as for the future of their publishing companies. They have had to change from monomedia to multimedia strategies in an environment of increasing interrelations with new businesses whose profiles are growing in the sector.

This study attempts to analyse the change in the competitive environment of the economic and financial news sector. Firstly, a general outline of the historical construction process of the sector will serve as a basis for justifying the consideration of media such as radio or television as "new media" in this market. A description of how new media (audiovisual and electronic) made their way into the economic and financial news market follows. Thirdly, the way that the media and traditional businesses reacted to this new competition is explained generically. Lastly, some conclusions are drawn about common interrelationship patterns among new and old media from both the information and managerial points of view.

ECONOMIC AND FINANCIAL NEWS MARKETS IN PERSPECTIVE

The history of the economic press and of journalism specialised in economics during the 20th century is a great information and managerial success story. Businesses such as Dow Jones, the Financial Times Group, Bloomberg, Nikkei or Reuters,[1] to mention the most significant, have managed to become international paradigms in the development and circulation of this type of content. Likewise, all developed countries have a healthy specialised information media sector competing for the growing attention that the rest of the media, new and not so new, pay to the economic world.

Nevertheless, a long road led to this situation. For many years, topics related to the "dismal science" played second fiddle in the journalistic agendas of the large media. Only a few publications for those in the know managed to shine in the media universe (Arrese, 2001a).

Very similar to what happened during the last quarter of the 20th century, the development of financial capitalism directed much attention to trade and finance in the last third of the 19th century (Parsons, 1989). In few years, the direct predecessors of some of today's most important economic newspapers were born. *Il Sole* was founded in Italy in 1865; in 1876, *Chugai Bukka Shimpo*—precedent to *Nihon Keizai Shimbung*—started up in Japan. The following decade witnessed the birth of the *Financial News* (1884) and the *Financial Times* (1888) in London, and the *Wall Street Journal* (1889) in New York. These newspapers joined the ranks of a whole set of economic and opinion journals that, with *The Economist* (1843) as the principal exponent, had been circulating since the middle of the 19th century. Likewise, from then on, the recently born news agencies, with Reuters in the lead, were to pay special attention to financial content.

---

[1] Although Reuters is obviously one of the businesses and brand names with a long history and important weight in the sector, it is only of marginal interest to this study because it is a business based primarily on the news agency model, in spite of increasingly promoting end-user products in recent years.

Periodicals continued to proliferate during the first decades of the 20th century, particularly with the appearance of the business magazines. The birth of *Forbes* (1917), *Business Week* (1929) and *Fortune* (1930)—"The Big Three," as they have been known in the United States—symbolised the managerial euphoria of the 1920s. They also marked the end of a period that concluded with the crash of the New York exchange. These were also the years when the first media groups specialised in economics and finance came into being, managing several publications in that market. Dow Jones, under the editorship of Clarence Barron, and the Financial Times Group, run by Brendan Bracken, were undoubtedly the two most representative (Arrese, 2001b: 122–127).

The 1929 financial crisis and the decade of the Great Depression punctuated a new paragraph in the history of that century's economic journalism. The financial newspapers, in general, were unable to interpret the magnitude of the economic disaster properly. This laid bare the poor professional qualifications of financial journalism, afflicted by serious deontological problems almost from its birth. Moreover, the decade of the 1930s was to leave financial and business news in the background to spotlight the importance of "the economy," which emerged as the real news sphere (Emmison, 1983). These were golden years for analysis magazines such as *The Economist* and *Fortune*, and years of transformation for financial dailies such as the *Financial News* and the *Wall Street Journal*. The latter started reorganising as true business newspapers, having broken their excessive dependence on Wall Street and the City news.

The end of the Second World War imposed reconstruction of the sector in the main western economies during the 1950s and 1960s. In the least affected market, the United States, the *Wall Street Journal* opted to become the country's first national daily. It also climbed to top position in circulation in competition with large quality newspapers such as the *New York Times* or the *Washington Post*. The *Financial Times*, already a single newspaper after the merger of the old *Financial Times* and *Financial News* in 1945, followed a similar strategy, albeit without such extraordinary results. The arrival of newcomers such as *Handelsblatt* (1946) in Germany and the Italian *24 Ore* (born in 1946 and merging with *Il Sole* in 1965), and the remodelling of some already veteran papers—the French *Les Echos* (established as a weekly in 1908) and the *Nihon Keizai Shimbun*, which integrated four newspapers starting in 1945—established the bases for creating solid specialised news groups during the booming 1960s. This was all supported by the lack of interest for economic and financial news of the general news media, including radio and television, at a time when the western countries were on their honeymoon with the "Keynesian consensus" (Arrese, 2001a).

The development of the sector accelerated in the 1970s after the collapse of the Bretton Woods exchange system and the 1973 oil crisis. As Krugman (1994) points out, "in 1973 the magic went away" (p. 3). The coexistence of high inflation and heavy unemployment hit the average citizen hard, and the economy became a priority public interest issue. Then came a new oil crisis and a vigorous neoliberal wave symbolised by "Thatcherism" and "Reaganomics," which was to conclude with the fall of the wall of Berlin and a good number of economic challenges as a result of growing globalisation and economic and financial integration on a planet where the economy of knowledge co-exists with the economy of poverty. All together, the relevance of economic and financial issues grew exponentially in the last quarter of the 20th century.

As it could not have been otherwise, most mass media have been echoing that new leading role of the economy, business and finance. Since the 1970s, the financial press has had to cope with new competition that had hardly existed before. Quality—and even popular—dailies, generalist television channels and radio stations have all tried to satisfy the citizens' growing information needs. In addition, there has been a veritable publishing "boom" in the print sector itself since the mid-1980s. Italy, Spain, France, and even the United States have new economic newspapers that continue to challenge the already consolidated mastheads, albeit with varying success.

Meanwhile, the large Anglo-Saxon publications, partly due to the commercial exhaustion of their national markets and partly to establish the new rules of the game for the sector, started a race to become brand names of truly world-wide influence—or at least international. Dow Jones with the *Wall Street Journal*, Pearson through the *Financial Times*—and other national newspapers, including *Expansión* and *Les Echos*, and Nikkei with its economic information system around the *Nihon Keizai Shimbun*, had become the "three big ones" of the daily economic news. In turn, brand names such *as The Economist, Business Week, Forbes* or *Fortune*, sought similar status in the magazine world.

This development of traditional print products and of economic and financial content in all types of generalist media had to coexist, in the 1990s, with a new range of competitors: the specialised broadcasting and electronic media.

THE GROWTH OF NEW MEDIA BUSINESS AROUND ECONOMIC AND FINANCIAL NEWS

Although a breeze of crisis is starting to blow currently, there is no doubt that the 1990s can be defined as a "prodigious decade" from the economic point of view. A similar definition can also be applied from a technological point of view, primarily within the scope of information technologies, to the expansion of the digital revolution and the Internet. In some sense, the last decade was also the decade of the free market, of "popular capitalism"—materialised in the extraordinary growth of the "citizen investor"—and of globalisation—primarily corporate and financial. All of this explains our entry into the new millennium at a time of renewed preeminence of economic, business and financial information, stimulated by the challenges of the "new economy" and favoured by the information frenzy generated by the information technologies (Arrese, 2001a; Parker, 1999; Saporito, 1999).

The conjunction of all these trends in the media world, in turn transformed from the business and technological point of view, was to be responsible for the new stardom of economic and financial news in the broadcasting and electronic media. That new leading role has materialised, among other manifestations, in the emergence of economics- and finance-theme channels on television and radio, and in the swift incorporation of the Internet as an indispensable supplier of that type of content.

Economic and Financial TV and Radio Channels

The emergence of the first channels specialised in economic and financial news can be set in the 1980s. The first important channel of this type in the United States was Financial News Network (FNN), founded in 1981, with an initial program schedule of five hours for a handful of UHF stations. In 1988, partly as a reaction to the success of FNN, the Consumer News and Business Channel (CNBC) was launched. The channel started broadcasting in 1989. With more varied and less finance-world-focused program planning than its competitor, CNBC was controlled by NBC (50%)—responsible for program planning--and Cablevision Systems Corp (50%)—in charge of distribution. Its impact on the market was immediate and six months after launch, it already had 13 million subscribers. In view of the effect that the appearance of this channel could have on CNN operations, increasingly interested in attracting business- and finance-oriented audiences, Ted Turner tried to get control of FNN, but the operation fell through. Finally, the competition between the two specialised channels was resolved in 1991. CNBC acquired and then integrated FNN. Since then, CNBC has continued consolidating as an economic information channel, increasing its international projection, especially since the mid-1990s.

While this was going on in the United States, a short-lived specialised television channel project was put into operation in Europe to serve businessmen on the Old Continent. To a degree, the European Business Channel was a kind of response to the impact of the launching of CNN International in 1985, as well as to the success of its economic content. Similar was the 1991 initiative of the Asian channel, Business News Network, also as an answer to the impact of CNN's attraction for transnational business audiences.

In any case, without underestimating these and other pioneer experiences, the importance of the phenomenon of television channels specialised in economics and business was not to be noticed until later in the 1990s, in terms of the national as well as the international markets.

After Financial News Network was absorbed in 1991, CNBC remained as the principal economic cable channel in the United States. The network maintained that position until the mid-1990s. The first serious competition arrived at the hand of Bloomberg, who launched the Bloomberg Information Television channel in 1994. But the real challenge for CNBC was to come in 1995, when CNN launched its own specialised channel, CNNfn. Of course, these three television channels also extended their competition to the Internet, where each made good use of the privileged situation of their brand names.

Especially beginning in 1997, with the stock market boom and the Internet business fever, the three channels thrived and became very popular with investors. One day in October of that year, the Dow Jones industrial average plummeted 554 points. The CNBC audience surpassed a million viewers, a landmark figure for this type of television content. By the end of the decade, CNBC had become an indisputable television phenomenon (Serwer, 1999). Its potential full-time coverage area reached 70 million households in the United States—as opposed to CNNfn's 12 million and Bloomberg TV's 10 million. It was constantly on in innumerable businesses and public places, and each week around 7 million persons would tune in at some point in time.

The North American experience had no match in Europe or Asia, but it did have a decisive influence on the launching of similar projects in those territories. Moreover, the main United States channels leapt their borders very soon to become international channels. The development of transmission technologies, particularly via satellite, was a key facilitating factor.

During the first half of the 1990s, several pan-European channels sprang up to capture the attention of businessmen. Some were generalist channels that joined CNN International's pioneer transnational activity. Others followed the economic channel model of their North American counterparts.

Euronews and BBC World were among the first. With respect to economic channels, the first that was completely specialised, European Business News, was launched in January 1995. This Dow Jones project was similar to that of its business channel in Asia. From London before the year was over, Bloomberg announced the start-up of European Bloomberg Television. CNBC Europe started broadcasting the following spring. In this case, NBC already had experience in economic program planning in Europe. It had oriented its first project in that market, NBC Super Channel, towards that type of content. In a few short months, pan-European television specialised in economics had practically staked out its battlefield.

During the following years, these projects continued to develop with increasing penetration into European homes, especially in those of the higher income brackets. The merger of European Business News and CNBC Europe made 1997 a key year. With the Dow Jones' publishing impulse, the new European CNBC was to end up being Bloomberg Television's only direct competitor. By then, Bloomberg had already intensified his efforts to break into the main national markets. With a strategy different from that of its competitor, Bloomberg Television designed, from London, the launching of national channels through associations with local media, alternating programs in English with their own programs and content. The French channel started up in 1996 and the Italian at the beginning of 1997 followed by the Spanish and German channels. By the end of the decade, CNBC Europe also initiated some program localisation projects, specifically, for the Scandinavian countries and for Turkey. This practice was already very consolidated in the international channel par excellence, CNN.

In most European countries, the economic content offering of these international channels through cable or via satellite began to be rounded out with content supplied by national specialised channels during the 1990s. Most followed the "all news" scheduling format, which allowed complementing the economic news with another type of information.

Germany was the European country with the greatest tradition of televised economic information. This explains why it was the first to have a highly successful channel of this type, n-tv. It started broadcasting in 1993 and the network gradually gained viewers. From a daily net audience of around 2 million a year after launching, it grew to almost 4.2 million in 1999. Some of its economic programs, such as "Telebörse," attracted up to almost a million people to the small screen at times of special activity in the securities market. Furthermore, the channel chose excellent publishing partners, including CNN International and the Handelsblatt group. It turned a profit for the first time in 1998. At the end of the decade, with a potential coverage area of 30 million homes (90% of the German market), the channel was the undisputed leader of the sector. It had little reason to fear competition, which actually came upon the scene in 2000 with the creation of N24. This channel, launched by the ProSieben group, had Bloomberg information support.

There were no such clear successes in other countries, although there was a channel specialised in these topics practically everywhere by the year 2000, or at least news channels devoting special attention to economic information. They were all part of the increasingly rich supply of digital theme channels distributed via satellite and cable. French viewers found quite specialised information on La Chaine Info (LCI). TF1 founded this all-news channel in 1994 with very important economic and financial program planning. Something similar happened in Italy with the program planning of Rainews 24, which was created with an eye to broadcasting content of special interest for the ruling classes. In addition, Raisat, a digital theme channel company of the Italian public television, signed an agreement with the Il Sole 24 Ore group in 1999 to develop a strictly economic channel. Likewise, the leading group of the Spanish economic press, Recoletos, had promoted the channel, Expansión TV, in 1998. This was the first project of that type on the market. Lastly, the Money Channel was launched in the United Kingdom in February 2000. This finance channel was to be distributed through Sky Digital. ETV Europe appeared in the Netherlands in 1998.

The radio medium underwent a process similar to that of television. At the beginning of the decade and for the first time in history, the implantation of radio stations focusing primarily on economic and financial content became widespread. One of the first important initiatives was the creation of Bloomberg Radio with the purchase of the New York station, WNEW-AM, in 1993. From then on, through program syndication, Bloomberg was to spread its programs to a great many stations, in the United States as well as in the rest in the world.

In Europe, French Radio Classique, one of the stations pioneering this type of program planning, normally combined news, economic content and music since 1982. But it was in the 1990s when this type of channel became widespread. With the French model in mind, Radio Intereconomía was born in Spain in 1994. At the end of the decade, this station initiated its expansion to the international Spanish-speaking market, from Buenos Aires to Miami. Other initiatives of interest were, for example, German Frankfurter Business Radio and Italian Radio 24, promoted by Il Sole 24 Ore, British Radio London, Dutch Business Nieuws Radio and French Bfm. Precisely in 1999, certifying the extension of this radio model and to facilitate collaboration among some of these stations, the European Economic Radios Association was founded.

The strategies of the specialised television channels and radio stations, as well as of the print media, contemplated developing their content and transmission modes through the Internet. After all, the Internet broke the traditional barriers among media from the point of view of the development and dissemination of content, so that all competed on the network with similar weapons for attracting and holding readers, viewers and listeners. Text, image and sound, all integrated, became a basic raw material for any information service whether it was promoted by one type of traditional medium or another.

Economic and Financial Web Sites

Financial information had flooded the network since the mid-1990s (Barber & Odean, 2001). The causes of that phenomenon were varied, but some evident ones are mentioned here. On one hand, the consumer of that type of content had a particularly attractive web user profile: high income and capital, the habit of using electronic information services at work and otherwise, day-to-day use of the computer, an intensive consumer of economic information, etc. On the other hand, financial and business news was particularly apt to be consumed in real time, as the markets change, as well as to be valued, and in many cases paid for, depending on its level of analysis, quantity, complexity, depth, etc. In addition, if any sphere of current events had played an important role in the phenomenon of globalisation, that was the financial market sphere. This made it even more sensible to consider the Internet, as a universal communication infrastructure, for sharing information about those topics. Finally yet importantly, the various financial service industries also saw the possibility of developing their relationship and transaction systems with their subscribers through the Internet, which included satisfying their information needs. If, besides all this, one considers the special conditions of the economic bonanza of the time, encouraging the interest of a lot of citizens in financial issues, it is easy to understand the proliferation of economic, business and financial news services on the Internet.

Some web sites of conventional economic media such as wsj.com, ft.com, cnbc.com, bloomberg.com and economist.com were among the 20 most visited web sites dealing with economic and financial issues during November 2000, according to the ranking developed by 100hot.com. What is interesting, however, is that these brand names springing from specialised media, old and new, only constituted one fourth of those most visited sites. The rest, with their corresponding position in the ranking, were: quote.com (1), yahoo.com (3), bigcharts.com (5), quicken.com (7), nasdaq.com (8), marketwatch.com (11), hoovers.com (12), fool.com (13), barchart.com (14), datek.com (15), wellsfargo.com (16), etrade.com (17), x.com (18), fidelity.com (19), thestreet.com (20). Although this list refers primarily to the U.S. market and can vary in time, it nonetheless serves to reflect what happened in other markets, too. In fact, the most interesting thing was not seeing what specific web sites dominated the sector, but rather considering their nature. At least four categories of new competitors could be distinguished: search engines/portals; new online financial media; online financial services; financial institutions' websites.

Search Engines/Portals. The search engines, evolved into the large Internet portals, held the first privileged positions when it came to distributing economic and financial information. Yahoo Finance and Quote, the latter brand name belonging to Lycos, are examples of this category in the ranking. Of these two portals—each quite different, however—undoubtedly Yahoo! Finance perfectly exemplified the capacity of those large electronic portals to become information media. Moreover, Yahoo was a truly international brand name, occupying the top positions among portals and Internet service suppliers in most countries. The same happened with the Microsoft portal, msn.com, and its financial area, "MoneyCentral", and with the America Online services, at least in the countries where it was present.

In the different European markets, global brand names such as Yahoo and Lycos were joined, in most cases surpassed, by portals developed by national Internet providers, in many cases promoted by the main operators in the telecommunications sector. T-Online in Germany, Freeserve in Great Britain, Wanadoo in France and Terra in Spain and other Spanish-speaking countries, to mention some outstanding cases, had their own business and finance information services.

New Online Financial Media. A second group of web sites competing with those of the more conventional specialised media was made up of economic and financial information services created expressly for the net, although, in some cases, they originated from firms that already offered similar services off this platform, marketing database information. Still, according to the Hot100 list, for example, two web sites were of the latter type: barchart.com and hoovers.com. They primarily provided business and finance documentation and analyses.

The fool.com site was much more interesting as an information phenomenon. It developed into a special community of investors that exchanged information, opinions and analyses about all types of financial assets, particularly stock market securities. Other sites pertaining to this group included TheStreet.com and CBS MarketWatch.com.

Almost every European country had a good number of informative web sites of a similar nature to those mentioned in this second group, composed of economic and financial information services created expressly for the Internet. In Great Britain since 1999, for example, ukinvest.com had been the model for the creation of similar services in many other countries, all promoted by GlobalNetFinancial.com Inc. Two of the more important German web sites were boerse.de and wallstreet-online.de. Italy also had interesting initiatives, including Wallstreetitalia.com and Italia-iNvest.com. The latter, like the Spanish espanainvest.com, followed the ukinvest.com model.

Although the examples mentioned so far were essentially information services, in some cases they also, directly or indirectly, acted as actual financial intermediaries. It was easy to combine the supply of information useful for investment decision making with the availability of tools for making those investments through the web site itself. The third type of portals used this function primarily to get into the audience-capture game.

Online Financial Services. Web sites such as quicken.com, datek.com, wellsfargo.com, etrade.com, x.com and fidelity.com were only a few of the many promoted by financial brand names, products and services, old and new, with the main goal of fostering the use of the Internet for making transactions on behalf of their subscribers. By strengthening their information elements as part of their services, they ended up becoming windows for distributing their own as well as third-party content. In the North American case, in addition to those mentioned, the Hot100 ranking also distinguished sites such as: americanexpress.com, schwab.com, bankrate.com, prudential.com, chase.com, etc. Banks, e-brokers and other finance companies were equally active on the Network in Germany (comdirect.de, deutschebank24.de, conconsors.de), Great Britain (barclays.co.uk, first-direct.com), France (socgen.com, bnp.fr), Spain (lacaixa.es, ebankinter.com), etc. Obviously, they could not compete with other established media from the point of view of content development, but in basic information –data about financial markets, interest rates, exchange rates, etc.- they were able to offer useful services for their subscribers.

Financial Institutions' Web Sites. One last type of site with high news content is made up of the portals of other organisms, such as the stock exchanges, that made information that had traditionally arrived through the media available to the general public. To mention only a few, sites such as nasdaq.com and nyse.com in the United States, londonstockexchange.co.uk in Great Britain and infobolsa.es in Spain took on a new information dimension, thanks to the Internet.

One of the fundamental characteristics of the news services described so far, particularly those of the second type, was their capacity to generate income by subscription. This was something that, as Compaine and Gomery (2000) point out, only generally happened with another type of content: sex (p. 451). In fact, most of the web sites mentioned were built around free areas and pay areas. This made the economic model of those businesses particularly attractive, since it could generate income by subscription and for advertising (Mahadevan, 2000; Picard 2000).

The development of this entire information infrastructure through the Internet focused particularly on financial information targeting the investor. Although that was only one of the many realms that the economic press addressed, it certainly was the fundamental one during the 1990s. This is why the competition of all these services with the traditional newspapers and journals and with their Internet editions became increasingly relevant. They not only captured their readers' and advertisers' time and money; they also recruited a good number of professionals from among them.

THE STRATEGY OF THE OLD MEDIA: DEVELOP MULTIMEDIA BRAND NAMES AND ALLIANCES

The proliferation of these new media during the 1990s forced most large economic dailies to stop identifying with a single journalistic product—the traditional newspaper—to become "journalistic brand names" that integrate new content and media around that basic product. To a large extent, the same also happened in the case of the best-known magazines, both national and international. Although this process had already commenced in the preceding decades, brand name extension became easier in the last decade of the century. This strategy was to become obligatory with the development of the Internet (Arrese, 1998).

From a managerial point of view, businesses such as Dow Jones and the Financial Times Group (Pearson) with international scopes, or Groupe Les Echos, Handelsblatt and Recoletos in their respective national markets, were forced to intensify the creation of various types of networks and alliances to benefit as much as possible from the new conditions of the environment.

Brand Development

From the perspective of brand name development, the Wall Street Journal and the *Financial Times* are the paradigms. In fact, both dailies were the only two newspapers in Interbrand's yearly ranking of the 100 overall most powerful brand names.

Both dailies considerably intensified their internationalisation strategy starting in 1992. By the end of the decade, their "global battle" was newsworthy for magazines and newspapers all over the world (Labi, 2000: Renaud, 2000; Tomlison, 2000). If, in the past, both newspapers had become strong in some markets and paid less attention to others, now direct competition spreads to all the geographical areas of the planet. *The Wall Street Journal* flings itself into the conquest of the European market, while the Financial Times disembarks in the United States with an aggressive publishing and marketing proposal. In some places, like in the German market, the struggle leads the London newspaper to launch a German edition, *Financial Times Deutschland*, while the Wall Street daily reinforces its alliance with that market's leader, *Handelsblatt*. They even find scopes for the two newspapers to collaborate, as in the case of the joint launching of a new economic daily, V*edomosti*, in Moscow. Competing in most markets and collaborating in a few—applying a "coopetition" strategy, increasingly common in this and other Business sectors—, both the Wall Street Journal and the *Financial Times* were brand names with a truly global information proposal in the 1990s.

In addition to the press, where each newspaper was also the flagship of a fleet of printed products, the commercial news services, television and Internet had become suitable channels for distributing content guaranteed by those brand names. On the Internet, the *Wall Street Journal* and the *Financial Times*, with radically different business models, had managed to successfully implant the brand names wsj.com and ft.com (Steinbock, 2000). Furthermore, both profited from synergies of a different type with other brand names well positioned on the Internet, as in the case of the *Financial Times* with CBS-MarketWatch. As to the audiovisual media, their commitment had been much less determined, perhaps forecasting that the boom of audiovisual economic and financial news was to be short-term. Nevertheless, there also existed ways to foster the brand name through those media, as in the case of the *Wall Street Journal* providing certain specialised content for radio and television networks (CNBC).

The spreading of brand names through the most consolidated media was a common phenomenon in most markets. *Handelsblatt, Il Sole 24 Ore, Les Echos* and *Expansión*—the latter two under the control of the British group Pearson—not only dominated their respective markets of daily economic information, but also extended their prestige to audiovisual and electronic products. The capacity of the electronic portals of those newspapers to capture users and compete, as a result, with other periodical brand names and new information services normally exceeded that corresponding to their printed circulation (Dans, 2000). Unlike what took place in the Anglo-Saxon markets, in these countries, the involvement of the main journalistic brand names in the development of specialised television channels was much more determined, especially in Spain and Italy.

Their publishing companies developed the mentioned brand names, in response to the growing competition from the new media, parallel to the implementation of geographic expansion and corporate diversification strategies.

Multimedia Alliances and Networks

The corporate development required of businesses such as Dow Jones and the Financial Times Group—and other national groups specialised in this type of information—by the new competitive environment of the 1990s can be called paradoxical. On one hand, the situation described has forced these groups to adopt multimedia strategies, particularly developing their range of non-print products. In many cases, this has necessitated playing the growth game of the large media groups. At the same time, however, they have had to do so while maintaining their historical focus on economic and financial news, a market niche with clear growth limitations when considered nationally. In general, the result of this paradoxical situation has been the patent internationalisation of the sector—both of businesses and of products—with the proliferation of networks, associations and alliances while the main actors maintain the niche approach appropriate for specialists.

Again, the Dow Jones and the Financial Times Group cases can serve as the model. Although on a different scale, national groups such as Handelsblatt (with its growth in the German-speaking market) and Recoletos (through its expansion in the Spanish-speaking markets) followed similar strategies.

As to Dow Jones Co., in addition to the intense promotion of the *Wall Street Journal* and of other journalistic brand names such as SmartMoney and Barron's, the backbone of its growth has been the reinvention of its electronic news services, heirs of one of the company's foundational businesses, the news agency, Dow Jones News Service. In those two fundamental lines of business—print and electronics—the group maintains various strategic alliances with other specialists, including *Nikkei* (for Japan and southwest Asia), *Handelsblatt* (Europe) and Reuters (for everybody using the Factiva service). In the audiovisual arena, Dow Jones is a partner with NBC for developing CNBC in the markets outside of the United States.

Although the multimedia, international and specialised approach of the Financial Times Group is largely similar to Dow Jones', their business situations and business strategies have differed notably. With respect to the business situation, while Dow Jones is an autonomic specialised group, the Financial Times Group is part of Pearson, a conglomerate with clearly differentiated business units: education, publishing, media. As to the business strategy, while the U.S. group has traditionally opted for alliances with other companies with an eye to promoting its own brand names, the British group has generally opted for purchasing businesses and products. Throughout the 1990s, it acquired the first French economic news group—*Les Echos*—and the first Spanish-speaking economic information group—Recoletos. Furthermore, it controls 50% of the capital of The Economist Group, 50% of the first New Zealand economic news group, and 34% of MarketWatch.com.

In spite of the differences between Dow Jones and the Financial Times Group, and between these and other national companies, the extension of traditional brand names and their transformation into multimedia brand names as well as the internationalisation strategies and reinforcement of the specialization have been common patterns in the response of the "old" companies and media to competition in view of the challenges posed by the new environment of economic and financial news in the decade of the 1990s.

CONCLUSIONS

Everything points to the economic and technological boom of the last decade being replaced by a new period of adjustment characterised by the revision of expectations of all kinds. The economic and financial news sphere, too, can expect that adjustment, which will undoubtedly help clarify the future of new and old media. The definitive incorporation of the audiovisual and electronic media into the sector, which took place in the 1990s, is no longer a process that can be expected to reverse itself. Especially in the case of the electronic media, no one doubts that they will play an increasingly important role in satisfying the information needs of businessmen, executives, investors, and citizens in general.

Moreover, as this study has attempted to show, after almost a century in a privileged and comfortable situation, the main economic newspapers have tried to adapt and play a leading role in the renovation of the sector. Most of them have become content brand names with business models that are particularly attractive on the Internet and have a great capacity to apply brand name expansion strategies. In this regard, we can assert that they have been in the vanguard of the transformation of the press. Moreover, the special nature of economic news and of its audience has endowed the sector with an international growth potential that few journalistic markets have achieved.

Lastly, by establishing alliances and creating networks, the main businesses of the sector have managed to become multimedia companies. Most of them have sought an international projection, while maintaining and even reinforcing their image of specialisation. All of this has allowed the same companies that dominated the various national and international markets three decades ago to currently occupy key positions in the sector, even though, obviously, new competitors have appeared on the scene.

Perhaps with the doubt about what might happen with economic and financial information in the audiovisual media, the potential of traditional journalistic brand names such as the *Wall Street Journal*, *Financial Times*, *The Economist*, *Nikkei or Il Sole 24 Ore* does not appear substantially threatened by the new media. Among other reasons, for quite some time, those publications founded more than century ago—like their publishing companies, are new media—and new businesses—as new as the rest.

REFERENCES

Arrese, A. (1998). Marca y relaciones de autoridad en el mercado. *Comunicación y Sociedad*, 9, 1, 91-124.

Arrese, A. (2001a). *Economic and financial press. From the beginings to the first oil crisis.* Pamplona: Colección Media Markets Monographs, Eunsa.

Arrese, A.(2001b). Viejos y nuevos medios de información económica. In J. Benavides & E. Fernández (Eds.). *Valores y medios de comunicación. De la innovación mediática a la creación cultural.* (pp. 61-94). Madrid: Ediciones Universidad Complutense.

Barber, B. M. & T. Odean (2001). The Internet and the investor. *Journal of Economic Perspectives*, 15, 1, 41-54.

Compaigne, B. M. & D. Gomery (2000). *Who owns the media? Competition and concentration in the mass media industry.* 3ª Ed. New Jersey: Lawrence Erlbaum.

Dans, E. (2000). Internet newspapers. Are some more equal than others?. *The International Journal of Media Management*, 2, 1, 4-13

Emmison, M. (1983). The Economy: its emergence in media discourse. In Davis, H. & P. Walton (Eds.). *Language, image and media.* Oxford: Blackwell.

European Communication Council (2000). *E-conomics. strategies for the digital marketplace.* Berlin: Springer.

Krugman, P. (1994). *Peddling prosperity. Economic sense and nonsense in the age of diminished expectations.* New York: W.W. Norton & Company.

Labi, A. (2000). Revamped and ready to rumble. *Time*, February 21, 61.

Mahadevan, B. (2000). Business models for Internet-based e-commerce: An anatomy. *California Management Review*, 42, 4, 55-69.

Parker, R. (1999). The revolution in America's financial industry: How well is the press covering the story? *Money, Markets and the News Monograph* 3. The

Joan Shorenstein Center on the Press, Politics and Public Policy, John F. Kennedy School of Government, Harvard University.

Parsons, W. (1989). *The power of the financial press. Journalism and economic Opinion in Britain and America.* Aldershot: Edward Elgar.

Picard, R. G. (2000). Changing business models of online content services – Their implications for multimedia and other content providers. *The Internationational Journal of Media Management*, 2, 1, 60-68.

Renaud, D. (2000) Presse: les seigneurs des marchés. *L'Express*, March 10, 69-72.

Saporito, B. (1999). The business century. How the economy became hot news in the last 100 years. *Columbia Journalism Review*, March/April, 48-51.

Serwer, A. (1999). I want my CNBC. *Fortune,* May 24, 139-141.

Steinbock, D. (2000). Building dynamic capabilities. The Wall Street Journal interactive edition: A successful online subscription model (1993-2000). *The International Journal of Media Management*, 2, III/IV, 178-194.

Tomlinson, R. (2000). The war to report on our financial times. *Fortune*, November 27.

Chapter 6
Reinventing Newspapers:
Readers and Markets of Free Dailies

Piet Bakker
University of Amsterdam

On June 21, 1999, two newspapers were launched in the Netherlands. This was news because the last new title had entered the market 20 years before and lasted had only a week. The Dutch newspaper market is a market of mergers and concentration. In 1995 three firms controlled 73% of the circulation. In 2000 this figure rose to 90%; the number of newspaper publishers and the total circulation dropped in this period. Both new papers were distributed free to users of the public transport system and were available from Monday through Friday. Now, after two years, the joined circulation of these free newspapers is 700,000 in a market where "regular" newspapers sell 4.4 million copies each day, which means that the free papers have 14% of the total weekday circulation.

Free papers are not new. From the beginning of the industrial revolution, so called "free sheets" have been produced. But most of them were (and still are) published on a weekly basis and serve mainly as an advertising platform for local businesses and carry some news and service for local communities. The new free newspaper is a different kind of animal. It is produced on a daily basis and is aimed at the general public in metropolitan areas. They are true competitors for existing newspapers, with a comparatively cheap distribution system and an editorial staff of only 15 to 25 journalists. These new papers penetrated an almost closed newspaper market. In the period 1996–2000 in the United States and Europe the number of newspapers dropped slightly, while circulation is also falling (*World Press Trends*, 2001; *Editor & Publisher International Yearbook*, 2001).

Newspapers were hardly prepared for these new competitors. Publishers mainly invested in online editions. The amount of dailies with online editions doubled or tripled in most countries in the last four years (*World Press Trends*, 2001), although it has been very hard to make a profit with these online publications. The rise of free dailies has occurred in the same period.

The successful introduction of these free dailies suggests that there is a growing market for printed newspapers. Not only for new firms, but also for traditional publishers. It could be the innovation the industry needed: a new product for a new audience.

THE RISE OF THE NEW FREE DAILIES

The Netherlands was not the first country where these phenomena took place. One of the papers published in the Netherlands, *Metro,* was originally founded in Stockholm, Sweden in 1995; editions in other countries soon followed. In 2001 publisher *M*etro International S.A. (formerly Modern Times Group) claimed that it had a readership of 8.5 million and publishes 21 editions in 15 countries. The 16th country will be Hong Kong in 2002. Metro International is not the only publisher of free daily newspapers (their version is usually called *Metro*, *Metropol*, *Metro Directo* or *Metro Directe*). The Norwegian firm Schibsted publishes its version of the free daily (*20 Minutes*) in Switzerland (Bern, Basle, Zurich) and Spain (Madrid, Barcelona) and until recently in Germany (Cologne). Other free daily newspapers are or were published by firms like Springer (Germany), Associated Newspapers (UK), Mediaprint (Austria), and De Telegraaf (The Netherlands). In 2001 there were free dailies in the Czech Republic, Hungary, the Netherlands, the UK, Germany, Belgium, Finland, Switzerland, Italy, Poland, Greece, Denmark, Austria, Spain, the United States, Canada, Chile, Argentina, and Singapore. In some cases (Cologne, Toronto, Zurich) it led to a genuine newspaper war (Fitzgerald, 2001; Wyss, 2000).

So far, more than 40 free papers have been introduced the last six years in more than 20 countries on three continents (see Table 6.1). In some cities or countries (Stockholm, Cologne, The Netherlands, Zurich, Basle, Bern, Toronto, Newcastle, Singapore) more than one free paper was published. Some papers were terminated or merged with their competitors (Cologne, Toronto, Newcastle, Singapore, the Netherlands). Now, about 30 free dailies exist and there are more to come. Almost every paper seems to have a circulation between 100,000 and 400,000. The total estimated circulation is around 8 million. The market is far from stable. *Metro*—as was noted above—wants a Hong Kong edition in 2002, Rupert Murdoch (*The Times*) is planning a second London free paper. Other free papers are planned in Brazil, Australia, Berlin, and Paris.

Table 6. 1. Introduction of Free Newspapers, 1995–2001

Europe	
	Sweden (Stockholm, 1995; Göteborg, 1998; Malmö 1999)
	Czech Republic (Prague, 1997)
	Hungary (Budapest, 1998)
	The Netherlands (1999)
	Finland (Helsinki, 1999)
	UK (London, 1999; Glasgow, Birmingham, Leeds, Manchester, Newcastle, 2000)
	Belgium (2000)
	Switzerland (Zurich, Basle, Bern 2000)
	Italy (Rome 2000, Milan, 2000; Turin, Naples 2001)
	Germany (Cologne, 2000)
	Poland (Warsaw, 2000)
	Greece (Athens, 2001)
	Spain (Barcelona, Madrid 2001)
	Denmark (Copenhagen, 2001)
	Austria (Vienna, 2001)
Americas	
	Chile (Santiago, 2000)
	USA (Philadelphia, 2000, Boston, 2001)
	Canada (Toronto, 2000; Montreal, 2001)
	Argentina (Buenos Aires, 2000)
Asia	
	Singapore (2000)

Sources: www.clubMetro.com, www.telegraaf.nl, www.gmgplc.co.uk, www.associatednewspapers.co.uk, www.editorandpublisher.com, www.adageglobal.com, www.schibsted.no, www.zurichexpress.ch, www.20min.ch

FRAMEWORKS FOR ANALYSIS

So far relatively little research has been done on the subject of free dailies. There is some research on the Swedish situation (Wadbring & Weibull, 2000). In other countries free newspapers were introduced much later—from 1998 on—which explains the lack of research. In the Netherlands some doctoral theses exist (Schaap, 2001; Van der Veer, 2001) and there is also a recent study on the Swiss situation (Bachman, Brander, & Lenz, 2001). Furthermore, there are research reports from the industry itself (mainly from free papers to prove their value to potential advertisers) and news items and commentaries on recent developments, especially during a "newspaper war".

The main questions from all these sources can be divided into two categories: economic questions concerning readership, business models for new and existing firms, competition, circulation, entry barriers, advertising and marketing; and legal questions on unfair competition, cartels, the right to carry the "*Metro*" title, unfair treatment by authorities and public transport systems. This chapter is devoted to economic issues.

ECONOMIC ISSUES

The most important question concerns the development of the newspaper market as a whole. How do readers react to free dailies? Is the market growing or do readers change from a "regular" newspaper to a free one? Important is the claim from free dailies that they attract a new and much younger public than "regular" newspapers. We should bear in mind that in a lot of markets (UK, the Netherlands, Sweden, Switzerland, Germany, the U.S.) readership is falling (see also Hendriks, 1998). Also, attracting a young audience is indeed a serious problem for newspapers.

We will use a substitution/cumulation model to map changes in readership and shifts in the newspaper market. When a new competitor enters the market four things can happen:

- Users will not change their behaviour.
- Users can trade in the old for the new (substitution) because readers find it "substantially similar in format and content" (Picard, 1989, p. 30).
- They can use both products at the same time (cumulation).
- The product can attract new users.

These options are presented graphically in Figure 6.1.

Figure 6.1. Cumulation and Substitution—Short-Term Effects

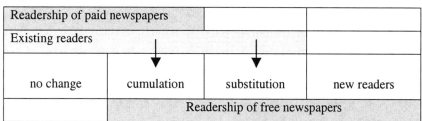

Readership of paid newspapers			
Existing readers			
no change	cumulation	substitution	new readers
	Readership of free newspapers		

The implication of this model is that a new competitor can take away some of the existing readers. How small this amount may be, there is no doubt that some readers will move to the new paper. There is also little doubt that the new medium will attract new users. A quantitative model is presented later but it is clear that when the amount of readers who trade the paid newspaper for the free one is substantial, this will harm existing firms.

This is only the short-term effect. In the long run two other movements are possible and these are illustrated in Figure 6.2:

- Readers who read free and paid papers can change to paid or free newspapers only. Research on newspaper reading and gratifications received could shed some light on the possible future behaviour of this group.
- On the other hand new readers could move over to a paid newspaper in the future. This hypothesis needs to be explored. Roger Parkinson, the President of the World Association of Newspapers (WAN) stated there is evidence that not only are these media attractive to young readers, but they may also be attracting young people to the paper product itself" (Quotes from the conference, 2001).

Figure 6.2. Cumulation and Substitution—Possible Long-Term Effects

Readership of paid newspapers			
Existing readers			
no change	cumulation	substitution	new readers
	Readership of free newspapers		

When constructing a quantified model some problems arise. Reliable data are hard to come by, particularly when new firms are not welcomed by existing ones. This, for instance, is evident in sources like *World Press Trends* (2001) and the *Editor & Publisher International Yearbook* (2001) where in some cases free newspapers are mentioned but their circulation is not included in the statistics. Regular publishers ignore these figures because, in most cases, they don't see free newspapers as a genuine product. Because organisations of established publishers are the main source for the statistics mentioned above, comparable data are hard to come by. In almost every case data from the publishers of the free newspapers themselves have to be used.

The second problem has to do with the definition of what we see as the "relevant market". In the Netherlands publishers of regular newspapers have argued that the influence of free newspapers on total sales of newspapers was negligible. But is the total market the relevant market? A more reliable method would be comparison with morning papers (when the free competitor is a morning paper), or even better with the single issue sales of morning papers on weekdays in the metropolitan areas where the new competitors are published. Alternative models should be used when free papers are published in the afternoon or six days a week. For the Netherlands, data about the four national daily morning papers is used. Figures indicate that subscription has hardly suffered, but also that single copy sales have dropped more than 10% in the period of competition from free dailies (Table 6.2). Wadbring and Weibull (2000) indicate that in the Stockholm market subscription was also affected.

Table 6.2: National Morning Newspaper and Free Newspaper Circulation (* 1000) in the Netherlands, 1997—2001

	subscription	Index 1997 = 100	single copy	Weekday (5/6 of single copy)	Index 1997 = 100	Circulation free papers
1997	1,321	100	306	255	100	
1998	1,325	100	305	254	100	
1999	1.328	101	285	238	93	515
2000	1,327	100	275	229	90	594
2001	1,305	99	263	219	86	695

Sources: *Oplagespecificaties Dagbladen 1996–2001*; *Persmediamonitor 2001*.

A quantified model can be useful for answering question about readership and circulation, the effects on the total market and shifts within that market. Although single copy sales have dropped by more than 10%, the absolute figures

(40,000 copies) compared to the total circulation of the free papers (695,000) indicate very clearly that substitution is—at least in the short term—not that important. Cumulation (reading paid and free papers) but mostly "new readers" seem to be more important. It should be noted, however, that there is some substitution and long-term effects are not yet known. The claim that "Readership of free newspapers may...be considered independent of, and therefore not a competitor, to paid-for newspapers" is not exactly true (Free paper readers ..., 2000).

A more detailed research is needed to reveal the nature of the new readership. Where do these new readers come from? Are they indeed younger than the audience of the paid newspapers?

READERS OF FREE DAILIES

To answer questions about readership we are compelled to use statistics from the new papers themselves and from some academic research. In 2001 Bachman, Brander and Lenz concluded after interviewing more than 800 readers in Zurich (where three free newspapers exist) that younger readers (under 30) were far more inclined to read free newspapers than older readers. Research from *20 Minuten* shows almost the same pattern; in 2001 29% of the age group "Kids" (10–13 years) consider themselves regular readers of *20 Minuten* (D&S Institut für Markt und Kommunikationsforshung, 2001). Another survey shows that the three free Zurich newspapers reached 36% (*ZürichExpress*), 40% (*20 Minuten*) and 22% (*Metropol*) of the age group of 14 to 34 (Mach Basic, 2001).

Dutch research shows that 55% to 57% of the readers of free newspapers are 35 or younger; for paid newspapers this percentage is 34 (Bereik- en lezersonderzoek *Spits & Metro*, 2000; see also Van der Veer, 2001; Schaap, 2001). *Metro* claims that 41% of their daily readers are under 30 (Sjöwall, 2001).

BUSINESS MODELS

Free dailies always compete with paid newspapers, and sometimes with other free papers. We can distinguish between different kinds of publishers and different objectives:

- First are the non-local or foreign firms entering a new market. This is the *Metro* and *20 Minutes* model of Metro International and Schibsted. This is the invasion model. Publishers are entering the market for profits. The Swedish example proved that this was indeed possible, it took *Metro* only one year to make profits in Stockholm (Wadbring & Weibull, 2000).

On the other hand, a lot of free dailies are published by local firms who also publish local or national dailies in the same market where the free dailies are published. Three different models can be distinguished:

- The defence model, when the second paper is only published because of the launching of another free paper. This was visible in the Netherlands where the publisher of the biggest morning paper *De Telegraaf* introduced a free paper the same day as the Dutch *Metro*. In Cologne two local firms (Springer and DuMont Schauberg) launched free papers when Schibsted published *20 Minuten*. After one year *20 Minuten* gave up whereupon the other two publications ceased publication. In Stockholm and Göteborg an existing newspaper published a weekly free paper (Wadbring & Weibull, 2000).
- The prevention model, where publishers launch a free paper to prevent another firm from entering the market; in the UK and Austria this has been the case. In Norway two free papers were released twice a week to prevent new competitors from entering the market (Wadbring & Weibull, 2000).
- The expansion model, when local publishers launch a free paper, not to prevent another publisher from making profits but for profit themselves. It may be difficult to distinguish between expansion and defence.

Only in the invasion and expansion models firms are entering a market with a new product for profit; in the other two cases publishers are willing to lose money. Often their paid papers cross-subsidise the free dailies. This means that markets where free papers are published are often imperfect (see also Ludwig, 2000), and competition is by definition "not fair". Price dumping, cross subsidising, and operating publications at a loss are not "fair" practices, and are therefore possibly harmful for customers. Furthermore it may hinder innovation.

CONCLUSION

Free newspapers are here to stay; in the last few years more than 40 new titles have been launched and more than 30 have survived. It has been proved that it is possible to make a profit and even to publish more than one newspaper in a metropolitan area. Because free dailies have also proven to be attractive to a younger audience, the future looks relatively bright. Problems may arise because of "unfair" behaviour of competitors. The readers of the free dailies are likely to be "new readers" indeed; (young) people who did not read a newspaper before, although some substitution is visible in local weekday single copy sales (The Netherlands) and in subscription (Sweden). Other markets and possible long-term effects should be studied in the future.

REFERENCES

Bachman, A., Brander, C. & Lenz, S. (2001). *Gratiszeitungen im Raum Zürich; Eine Befragung der Leserinnen und Leser.* Zurich: Universität Zurich, IPMZ.

Bereik- en lezersonderzoek Spits & Metro. (2000, January). Retrieved April 17, 2000, from http://spitsnet.nl

D&S Institut für Markt und Kommunikationsforshung. (2001). *Kids - Teens - News.* Eine Studie im Auftrag von: 20 Minuten. Zurich. Retrieved December 10, 2001, from http://www.20min.ch/intern/mediadaten/

Editor & Publisher International Yearbook. (2001). New York: Editor & Publisher.

Fitzgerald, M. (2001, December 5th). Toronto's Newspaper War Fissles. *Editor and Publisher.* Retrieved December 10, 2001, from http://www.editorandpublisher.com

Free paper readers are big media consumers. (July 1, 2000). World Association of Newspapers Research Centre. Retrieved December 1, 2001, from http://www.wan-press.org/rp/research/news.html

Hendriks, P. (1998). *Newspapers: A Lost Cause? Strategic Management of Newspaper Firms in the United States and The Netherlands.* Amsterdam: University of Amsterdam.

Ludwig, J. (2000). The Essential Economic Problem of the Media: Working Between Market Failure and Cross-Financing [Electronic version]. *The Journal of Media Economics* 13(3), 187-200.

Mach Basic. (2001). *Zurich Express Mehr Zurich*. Retrieved December 13, 2001, from http://www.zueriexpress.ch/pictures/new/zemachbr.pdf

Oplagespecificaties Dagbladen. (1996-2001). Amsterdam: Cebuco.

Persmediamonitor 2001. Retrieved December 13, 2001, from MediaMonitor Database http://www.mediamonitor.nl/

Picard, R. G. (1989). *Media Economics; Concepts and issues*. Newbury Park: Sage Publications.

Quotes from the conference (2001, November). World Association of Newspapers Newsletter nr. 19. Retrieved December 12, 2001, from http://www.wan-press.org/downloads/newsletter19/eng19.pdf

Schaap, A. (2001). *Metro & Spits*, Twee nieuwkomers op de dagbladmarkt. (doctoral thesis, University of Amsterdam)

Sjöwall, J. (2001, May). *The Metro Concept*. Retrieved December 12, 2001, from http://www.club*Metro*.com

Van der Veer, C. (2001). De substitutiefunctie van gratis dagbladen. (doctoral thesis, University of Amsterdam)

Wadbring, I. & Weibull, L. (2000). *Metro on the Swedish Newspaper Market*. Mediatique, nr. 20. Retrieved December 13, 2001, from http://www.comu.ucl. ac.be/ORM/Mediatique/*Metro*.htm

World Press Trends. (2001). Paris: World Association of Newspapers.

Wyss, T. (2000, June). *Vom Tram in den Hörsaal*: Welche Gratiszeitung schaft den Weg? Retrieved December 13, 2001, from http://www.meltingpot. unizh.ch/magazin/

Chapter 7
Media Business Online:
Features and Strategies of Runet

Marina Pavlikova
Moscow State University

At the end of the 20th century, in the period of economic instability and—at the same time—the beginning of economic revival and growth of purchasing power of population in industrial centres, there was a peak of activity in developing professional media resources on the Russian segment of the Internet (Runet). It was expected that online media could be a real source for making a profit. The idea of creating and promoting media projects oriented on the Internet capacities was rather attractive for commercial investors and media "oligarchs"—leaders in the offline media market.

The chapter analyses what the Internet has brought to the Russian media market. Its purpose is to measure media content and diversity on the Runet and define what actually affected success in the sphere.

WHO "PLAYS" ON RUNET? MAIN ACTORS

If the Internet is regarded as a part of natural human progress and as a technology, around which an information market forms, instead of considering it a new centre of the universe and virtual reality, it's worth understanding how to make profit of online issuing, analysing some tendencies of the social adaptation to the innovation and defining the best way for promoting information product on the Net.

At the third annual conference IFRA/Wan it was noticed that the Internet mainly consists of three "Cs": Content, Commerce and Communities (Bol'she, chem pechatnoe slovo, IFRA/WAN, 1999), and of three "Ps": Portals, Partners, and Possibilities. Since the Internet in Russia has recently transformed from entertainment for groups of enthusiasts into the sphere, which is suitable for mass media, acting as business enterprises, it is still rather difficult to apply those particular game rules that the use of the progressive technology dictates. Nowadays there are some successful projects based on principles of economic welfare, which in turn are achieved if there are suitable conditions for competition, development, employment, consumerism, and innovation. A vertical (or sometimes so-called sticky) portal Ireland.com (*The Irish Times*), a regional portal BerlinOnline (*Berliner Zeitung*), a portal entirely devoted to sailing, Sail Online (*Le Telegramme*), New Jersey Online, targeted at virtual communities (Advance Publications), New York Times online with experience of capitalising on banner advertising (*New York Times*), alliance of Canadian newspapers *Globe and Mail*, *Toronto Star*, which created a site of classifieds—their joint venture, etc.; all of these are good examples of mass media adaptation to the rules of new communication market. In other words, media firms and newspapers survive if they use three "Cs" and "Ps" combined in different variations.

What strategies do Russian media owners and media managers follow to play the game? At first sight it seems so easy to turn to western models for experience. But it's rather often said that Russia has own way. There is certainly a grain of truth in that. What is happening on the Runet? Can we argue that network media and online newspapers are not able to compete with traditional media if the latter intend to be seriously presented on the Net? Let's briefly look at the main trends of the Runet developing.

The Russian Media Sector on the Net

At present the situation of the Runet media sector can be defined as a problematic, in spite of the fact that the attitude of Russian business and population on the whole to the Internet possibilities becomes more comprehensive and more serious.

The Internet media developing in Russia can be conditionally divided into four periods.

The First Period: 1990 to 1998 In 1990 the domain .su was officially registered and there appeared the first Russian Internet resources (Informacionnoe obshestvo, 2000). At the beginning a lot of resources were designed by the Russian Diaspora abroad, in most cases in the United States and Israel. This period is characterised by the absence of dominant players and low investments in the Runet media sector. There were many authors' sites that could be classified in the amateur league and providers' portals, which played an important role in content providing and representing different media projects. At that time the Internet in Russia was a marginal sphere, accessible to a rather negligible quantity of users. However, there was forming a circle of playmakers, which would direct development of the media sector on the Runet in the future. The fact is that top-management of the leading media projects "came" to the Internet namely in this period.

The Second Period: 1998 to 2000   We could observe the first peak of activity in creating professional media resources from the end of 1998 to the spring of 2000. This was the second period. Almost all resources, which today represent the media of the Runet (Gazeta.ru, SMI.ru, Utro.ru, Vesti.ru, Lenta.ru and some others), appeared (or took the leading positions) during this period. Besides, two main strategies (some experts call them primitive [Davidov, 2000]) of constructing online media: newswires and analogues of the offline editions were successfully adopted in the scheme of net media promoting. The success of newswires mirrored on the realisation of media projects in so-called "investments boom " (see below), but as it was revealed the projects couldn't become a lottery ticket. As for the activity in the online media sector in this period, it wasn't accidental. It was directly connected with the State Duma elections (December 1999) and Presidential elections (March 2000). During 1999–2000 new players came to the Net. They pursued their own interests both in mass media and politics and began investing in the network media. Thus, media and political groups became the dominant players on the Runet.

Constructing and promoting media resources on the Net cost much less than the same preparations in the offline sector. Since the elections were approaching and agiotage for political information among the Internet users was growing, network media, surpassing the traditional ones in efficiency, were in great demand. Hence, the number of visits considerably increased. The situation before elections required a lot of information channels that one could attend to. Therefore, online media were often mentioned in different newspapers, TV and radio programs. That raised their significance. The situation was favourable for realising online media projects; a visible success of some of them really changed the status of the Internet among plenty of Russian information consumers and was one of the stimuli for investments as well. As for the estimates of perspectives and place of the Internet media in the communication sphere in that period, Russian experts emphasised that the success was particularly situational. Use of online resources during and before elections was not caused by their extremely qualitative content. The information resources were popular because of technical inability of newspapers and traditional electronic media to satisfy the growing requirements for news. The achievement of the Internet media in that period was not considerable enough to break some other election projects, which didn't rely on the Internet.

Planning of large-scale projects was directly connected with optimistic forecasts of the stable and rather fast growth of Internet users. The ground for such forecasts was a presumption that the majority of users regarded the Internet first of all as an information source. However, because very cautious experts analysed it, media on the Runet was not the best sphere for investments. Even such an indicator as 50,000 visitors per day, the achievement of interactive political channel Polit.ru in 1999 could not justify those millions, which were planned for investment in the sector. However, the Runet was exposed to an investment boom in 2000.

The Third Period: 2000   At the beginning of 2000 Russian experts began using the term *investment boom* in reference to the Internet. Russian business circles, in cooperation with western investment companies (first of all with American venture enterprises), made a start: they were buying the most popular Runet resources and developing some new ones. In spite of the fact that the investors were actively operating in the spheres connected with the Internet services and electronic commerce as well, changes took place in the media sector too. But it's worth mentioning that journalists created a great fuss about investing and often mistook the wish for the reality. Actually there were few companies that really invested in online media projects.

New players, unlike the second period actors, did not have any special interests in politics and were profit-oriented on the whole. They aimed to follow some Western or American strategies, implementing into life large-scale information projects (or projects just including some information components, for example, newswires) called "portals". Despite the cases of bankruptcy of among "dot-com" firms, Russian companies nevertheless still exist and the big portals of the Runet are still afloat. However, services of the Russian portals are not so diverse as those of Yahoo!, Excite or Lycos, for instance. Table 7.1 shows the spread and use of traditional western services in some Russian portals.

What was very important during this period is that leaders (read: media oligarchs), who were very active in the offline media market, showed a real interest in the Internet. Here it's necessary to mention Vladimir Gusinsky, whose holding "Media-Most" created a special structure elaborating online media projects called "MeMoNet"[1] and Boris Beresovsky, who controlled resources, which were united in the frame of the "Postfactum" portal. The fact is that after the media giants had come to the Net (for instance, portal "NTV.ru" created on

---

[1] Gusinsky's flight to Spain and the collapse of his company *Mediamost* resulted in the death of MeMoNet. This event was the most noticeable one on the Runet during the year 2001 (E-business 2001).

the base of the Russian Independent television company NTV, etc.), quality requirements to the online media resources were raised to higher levels. Today research emphasises the fact that the players made a number of mistakes, which seriously influenced further development of the Runet media. First, instead of creating new content product they imitated electronic versions of traditional newspapers. Secondly, they yearned to establish the same relations in "online" as in "offline" sphere, not taking into consideration features and demands of a new (different) market.

The Fourth Period: 2001 forward Complication and specificity of the situation was that there was a lack of media firms that could demonstrate a good business plan to investors, which would confirm further perspectives of the project. Since schemes of financing the Internet projects in Russia are the same as financing of venture business all over the world, nobody can pay millions of dollars for a text with pictures; they want a real business model. Russian media actors need partners to survive and prosper.

Partnership is a special term. It rather often consists only in exchange of the banners, so-called buttons, links, mentions. Thus, the Internet edition (not version) of the national newspaper *Izvestia* places banners of the television company NTV.ru, online newspaper Utro.ru, the search buttons of the portal Rambler on its own page, and in return for the service places its own banner on these sites. The concept of the World Wide Web means availability of links and references to some other web-resources. So, it's obvious that such exchange exists. It can hardly be regarded as serious partnership, but on the other hand it would be rather difficult to promote its own brand without such exchange and attract visitors. During the September 2001 tragedy (it's not a secret that network media are primarily interested in scandals and tragedies) in the United States a lot of Russian information portals used entertainment sites or sites of amateur league to place their own banners and actively exchanged references with each other (Gazeta.ru, Lenta.ru, Mail.ru, NTV.ru, Utro.ru, RBK.ru [Kak rabotali rossiiskie Inernet SMI, November 2001]).

More professional players cooperate into groups and follow united marketing strategy. They can use different strategies: some of them expect advertising profit, others deal with electronic commerce, and others hope for complex projects. It can rather often be observed that information agencies consolidate with Internet companies, PR-companies and industrial firms. The best example of it is RBK—RosBusinessConsulting—leading Internet holding in Russia (formed in 1992). Its information structure (http://www.rbk.ru/) is based on the activity of information agency RosBuisnessConsulting and its resources. Today among projects created by RBK are news servers (www.rbk.ru/, www.informer.ru/), Internet editions www.utro.ru/,

Table 7.1. Services Provided by the Major Portals, 2001

Categories	Services	Big Portals			
		Port.ru	Golden Telecom	Yandex	Rambler
Connection	E-mail	+	+	+	+
	Rating	+	+	+	+
	Search		+	+	+
	Free hostings	+		+	
	Catalog	+	+	+	
				+	
Information	TV program	+	+	+	+
	Information distribution	+	+	+	
	Weather	+	+		+
	Advertisements	+	+		
	Dictionaries		+		+
	Bills	+			+
	Job	+			+
	Finance, quotations				+
	Yellow pages	+			+
	Maps				
Commun-ication	Chats	+	+		+
	Cards	+	+	+	
	Forums	+	+		
	People search	+	+		
	Acquaintances	+	+		
	Instant Messenger		+		+
				+	
	Communities				
Personal	Addresses	+			
	Calendar	+			
	Bookmarks			+	+
	Photos			+	+
Commerce	Web malls	+	+	+	+
	Auctions	+			
Options	My...		+	+	+
	Toolbar	+		+	+

www.sport.rbk.ru/), entertainment and chats (www.krovatka.ru/), mail service (www.hotbox.ru), and banner network (www.lbn.ru). Frequency of visits confirmed by open and independent statistics, show that RBK controls more than 1/3 of the Internet advertising market. Recently RBK signed a contract with AltaVista and now search on the Net is under way of taking into consideration morphological features of Russian.

Different TV companies as partners of the Runet online media play the market rather successfully as well.

Looking at Table 7.1, we notice also that the Russian portals offer some services, which are not typical for western patterns. First of all there are ratings of online resources, including media. We find the reasons for such specific phenomenon in the history of the Runet developing. Rambler's Top 100, the first serious rating, appeared when nobody intended to invest big money in the Internet. Rambler took the place of a catalogue and became the most popular site on the Runet. However, at present Russian portals have mainly technological services to offer: search, hosting and mailbox. Media projects are more often not included into a portal structure. But in spite of such a pessimistic situation, media on the Runet are nevertheless involved in different ratings and measuring.

RATINGS OF MASS MEDIA ON THE RUNET: MENTIONABLE AND INFLUENTIAL

In all time of existence of information for mass consumption online there was a lot of talk about the frequency of visits as a criteria of success of sites. Today we see that frequency still remains an important factor, but now we would not define it as the synonym of economic efficiency and successfulness of an information project. What does the frequency show? It shows that a banner campaign was good and an electronic newspaper, for example, has gained odd visitors. Why does it need odd visitors? An advertiser, who is interested in "undifferentiated" consumers, is just driven by curiosity when placing his products on the Net: he will use the Internet capacity as an experiment, nothing more, the experts conclude. Audiences are still too small to compensate advertising expenses, and the situation will hardly change in the nearest future, they say (Davidov, Reitings vliyatel'nosti SMI Runeta, 2001). These producers and advertisers, whose aim is to reach target audiences, are not interested in odd visitors at all. However, there are mass media on the Runet that encourage odd visits, because, first of all, they want to be first in ratings. More often, online newspapers and online versions compete with each other for the leading positions in the ratings. "A rating shows how we are working during the day, how we are managing with news and etc. For example, today we have left famous "Komsomol'skaya pravda" behind, and I know we have won owing to the sensational report about TV6 project "Za steklom" made by our journalists. Thanks to the ratings I can understand how popular we are, in comparison with other sites,"web-editor of "Izvestia.ru" Natalia Loseva says. "Ratings let me watch our competitors and define the direction we go."

Runet Ratings

- Rambler top 100 (counter.rambler.ru/top100/)
- List 100 (counter.list.ru/)
- 1000 Stars (www.stars.ru/stat?r1.htm)

On the other hand, professionals agree that number of readers and pages they look through doesn't directly correlate to successfulness of the Internet edition and, accordingly, to price of advertisement placed on the site. Success can not be assessed either by ratings hits or by banner clicks. The main criteria of successfulness of media outlet online should be its ability to attract concrete readers with definite and clear interests. Such readers are the most suitable audience for target advertising. But a lot of web publishers in Russia lack knowledge about audience segmentation and in most cases don't understand that frequency of visits is a secondary parameter, and the editor's policy should not entirely depend on it. Number of visits can not be regarded as a site's circulation; presence of archives and at the same time updated information makes impossible the definition of "issue."

Today it's not a secret that network media in Russia in most cases exist thanks to investments. As an instrument of political and economic influence and power, network media are not so attractive for investors as, say, traditional ones. Authority of print publication is still higher than that of Internet ones. The matter is that the Internet media, producing exclusive content, are few. Though the Net brands of some mass media on the Runet are well known and rather independent from offline, their future is rather vague: neither notorious efficiency nor famous brands will lead to prosperity, if the project is not supported by exclusive content.

There is a hypothesis that leadership of Internet media is defined by so-called influential power. As a rule, the hypothesis follows discussions about specificity of the Internet audience in Russia, which is supposed to consist of people, who make decisions, in other words, businessmen, top-managers, etc. However, any detailed sociological research shows that such conclusions lack serious grounds. Nevertheless, ratings that measure the influential power of mass media on the Runet already exist. The project (SMI.ru), designed by Fund of Effective Policy (FEP) in Russia, indicates frequency of mentions and references to media outlet, counts how many times it is quoted in central and regional newspapers, in radio and TV programs. According to databases, which include all publications of central newspapers and almost all serious regional periodicals, and monitoring of radio and TV, they count mentions of the Internet media in traditional information sources during a week. As a result they publish two tables on SMI.ru. The first one is a ranked in decreasing order of number of mentions list of the Runet media. The second one, targeted to professionals (editors, web-editors, media managers), gives information concerning the given media: how many times, when and in what sources it was quoted. The sources are divided into central information agencies, regional information agencies, central press, regional press, central TV and radio, regional TV and radio, and foreign Russian-language sources.

The measurements involve certain definitions and assumptions. Referral to the given media in news stories demonstrates the fact that mass media have a status of a newsmaker and a real player in public and political sphere. Mentions and quotations in central press and central electronic media confirm a great reputation of the given media in the information field. Mass media are able to reach target audiences in small towns, which are remote from capitals, and generate so-called secondary media activity in regions. People reaction to an article or a program is more significant than counter statistics; audience response is better evidence of influence than position in ratings.

One can notice there is some dependence: the more reference to the given media (in our case media existing on the Net) gives more reasons to refer to its influential power in some circles, and, accordingly, on the contrary; more power supposes more mentions and references.

Of course, it's difficult to avoid critical remarks addressed to such measuring: there would be a lot of citations in traditional media caused by primitive desire to fill empty space in periodicals; impossibility to reveal all cases of direct and indirect citing and so on. Nevertheless, Runet's experts emphasise that counting mentions is almost the only veritable way to define more precisely what "influential power" means in the framework of the Internet.

Thus, the first table is a peculiar rating, which shows the power; the second table is a peculiar basis for analysing its own activity on the Net. The person responsible for media planning in newspaper (electronic version, the Internet edition, etc.) can judge newspaper work by the information: whether publications have reached target audiences or not.

There are not many users turning to online press in Russia (see Table 7.2). The Internet audience mostly looks through newswires, which in their turn exist as an information addition of portals. The political and economic nature of news really attracts visitors. All actors specialising in producing operative and readable news are leaders of news, business, and political segment on the Runet.

Table 7.2. Information Consumption on the Runet, 2000

	Number of Internet users (in percentage of max. Audience)
Political and Economic News	**27.7**
Music, video	26.8
New software	26.2
Computer games	25.7
Entertainment and leisure	25
Techniques	15.1
Goods and services	15.0
Erotic	11.6
Sport	11.5
Online Press	**11.1**
E-commerce	10.1
Job search	9.9
Weather broadcast	8.8
Art	8.3
Travel and Tourism	7.1
Science	6.9
Medicine	4.7
Other	32.2

Source: Komkon-Vector. Gotovnost' Rossii k informacionnomu obshestvu, 2001
*Notice: a respondent could choose several variants of answer, so the sum on the column cannot be 100%.

Though TV channels, transmitting fresh news several times per day, have maximum audience, there are situations when people need more operative information (in case of extreme situations, for example). And first of all they look for the information mainly on sites, which are updated in the process of news delivering. Electronic versions of newspapers or sites of print media, working in daily or weekly mode, are not able to satisfy short-term information needs, as newswires do it. News pages, which are familiar to audiences or immediately remembered by users if necessary—in other words, sites with the most promoted brands—are the most popular sources for getting information. To illustrate, let's turn to the American tragedy of 11 September 2001. The events have caused explosive growth of Runet news resources on politics, finance and business. In particular, traffic of "Rambler media", measured in hits and hosts, has increased by several times as seen in Figure 7.3 (Rumetrica, 23 October 2001). Number of users measured in visits has increased as well. At the same time sites not connected with above-mentioned themes lacked attention; their traffic was declining and as a result it has decreased by 10–20%.

Practically all newswires increased foreign news traffic—Gazeta.ru, Lenta.ru 55% (sometimes – 80%), RBK 25%.

Table 7.3. Growth of Rambler's Traffic, September 2001 (x/times)

Site	Growth of attendance	Growth of audience
Rambler Media	2.80	2.14
Rambler–Finance	2.16	2.40
Rambler–Sport	0.74	0.9
Rambler (average)	1.25	1.11

Source: Rambler

The active segment of Internet users also changed during that period. Specialists in financing, insuring, sphere of credits became much more mobile and more involved in electronic communication via the Net.

As to online newspapers and electronic versions of traditional media on the Runet, they could not compete with newswires in news providing and news delivering. But they still have a niche: exclusive content. Internet media, producing diverse and qualitative content, are scarce. Nowadays developing exclusive content is rather problematic, because of so-called secondary use of information by Internet media; especially it concerns those media elements which are included into a portal structure as information components, combining newswires and texts with hyperlinks.

CONTENT PRODUCING:
A VARIANT OF "SECOND HAND"?

From 1 January 1999 to 26 June 2000, 176 web sites have been officially registered as mass media on the Runet. There began a big confusion: what access to information should be, free or paid? It became clear by the year 2000 that the orientation towards paid access for mass audience was wrong (see Table 7.4). Free content has won. The only niche where paid content could prosper was placing specialised information for professionals and corporate users.

Today, paid services and paid content growth is hampered because of the rather small quantity of Internet users in Russia (according to Spylog research statistics, 16.9 million people surf the Net in Russia; the figure is 12.5 million according to Rambler), rather low paying capacity of the population and lack of distanced payment. Subscription, payment for data, and more seldom, payment for work-time—all these ways are often used to realise paid services. However, sometimes difficulties with online services do not depend on the absence of suitable infrastructure or the purchasing power of the population. Table 7.5 shows that the Internet in regions with rich natural resources and, hence, relative welfare of population, was mostly driven by the enthusiasm of users than by commercial initiative and interests. Diffusion of the Internet in Moscow and St. Petersburg was higher than anywhere in regions: 8.5% of population make 36% of weekly audience; in East Siberia and the Far East the spread of the Internet is approaching the average index; in the Ural and West Siberia it is below the average level.

Table 7.4. Content Service Providers in 1998: Turnover ($ thousands per year)

Information Services	Turnover
Free access to information resources	6,000
Paid access to information resources	5,000
Advertisement producing and placing	500

Source: Gotovnost' Rossii k informacionnomu obshestvu, 2001

Table 7.5. Use of the Internet in Russia (summer, 2000)

	Moscow, St. Petersburg	European Part of Russia	The Urals and West Siberia	East Siberia and Far East
The core (%)	36.7	41.5	8.6	13.2
Weekly audience (%)	36.1	38.6	12.2	13.1
Maximum audience (%)	26.7	40.3	18.4	14.6
All population(%)	8.5	56.0	21.9	13.6

The core – more than 3 hrs per week
Weekly – minimum one time per week
Maximum – all users
Source: Monitoring.ru

Since the majority of population groups in Russia do not yet realise the role of the Internet in satisfying their information demands or their information needs, it's rather difficult to develop a serious content market on the Runet. Today's offline and online editions are supposed to be content providers. But traditional newspapers and magazines come to the Net, following, firstly, their readers, secondly, their advertisers. Both of these factors are directly connected with growth of the Internet audience in Russia. Though sociological research forecasts vary, they let us think optimistically about the future of traditional media on the Internet. It was recently believed that electronic versions of traditional newspapers had some immanent advantages, the use of which would help them to supersede especially Internet editions in the market. But nothing of the kind happened. Electronic versions in ideal patterns were unprofitable or at least could not yield a fair return and, hence, offline media giants didn't find any serious commercial interest in actively promoting their product in the Internet. In spite of the facts that free information online is accessible practically to a global audience (Chyi, 1998) and, as it was already noticed, paid services often remain unclaimed, there is only one way that print newspapers can follow to have some profit from the Runet: paid subscription, paid access to archives (for instance, "Kommersant", "Vedomosti", "Expert"). Subscription profits were enough to partially or entirely compensate the expenses of Web representation, not more. Despite relatively low subscription prices (for example, to subscribe for electronic version of a specialised financial magazine "Expert" in 2001 one paid $36 a year), subscribers are still few, and the turnover of the business remains rather small. According to Vladimir Konovalov, owner of auction www. molotok.ru it's better to have such portals as Yahoo or eBay, which are more like a mix of e-commerce and information.

Actually Russia follows American trends in the Internet: 1) developing: promotion of popular sites, 2) the appearance of portals transition to retail trade (business-to-consumer), and 3) forming an intercorporate sector (business-to-business). Professionals agree that e-commerce in Russia develops more rapidly than in the West. But as to target policy in content market, it has started being used on the Runet in the framework of big portals, which in their turn are often built by offline publishing business and its funds. Since it should be based both on formed consumer requirements and on necessity to make the attitude toward information like that toward a precious resource, the role of mass media on the Internet must be essential. However, in most cases information filling of portals can be characterised as second hand. Today, the media sector of the Runet experiences the so-called *secondariness crisis*. The problem is as follows. Except for information agencies, which exist on the Net, and some electronic versions of print media, mass media on the Runet have no exclusive information resources. Portals' builders intend to offer maximum services in the framework of one site or system of interconnected sites, which belong to one company (for example, Port.ru). Since most users in Russia, as everywhere in the world, regard the Internet as a source of news, the builders place different newswires in a portal's structure. But information choice is rather poor, because newswires of different Internet media very often have the same information source (or information sources: Interfaks, ITAR-TASS, RIA "Novosti"). "Correspondents visit the same press-conferences, talk to the same makers, write the same stories," Nezavisimaya gazeta writes. It leads to levelling the newswires. Sometimes the situation becomes absurd. For example, the media section of the portal "Yandex", working as "an organiser of news", delivered the same news with different headlines borrowed from different online editions to different newswires.

Thus, it's all the same for a user no matter what news page he will turn to. Hard competition inside the news sector doesn't influence users' choice anyhow. For many Net publishers, the media business isn't the main focus of activity. We can say that all vices of Russian Internet media descend from their poverty, or more precisely, from their stinginess. Quality is not a factor of the victory. Orientation towards number of visits entails the situation when quality is sacrificed for its cost. There are online editions on the Runet, whose managers prefer not to spend money either on their own correspondents able to handle raw information or even on professional journalists able to write comprehensible stories, using e-mail and telephone. Initial texts, which are reproduced into leaderettes usual for readers, are intermediate products delivered from information agencies or already published in print newspaper materials. "Professionalism isn't required for such 'journalism of palimpseston', it is enough to have skill in writing essays and dictations"(see Bessudonov & Dugaev, 2001).

But things are not so simple as it may seem. Potential of a newswire and any other information project is great enough. Its influence on print media is one of the main attractive features often used by different structures simply for informing, wide discussions, propaganda and promoting ideas. Thus, central and regional newspapers often turn to information resources on the Net, because they are forced to reduce their expenses on information agencies' subscription and correspondents' network in regions and abroad. New agencies, which in their turn cut staff maintenance costs, also stimulate the use of the Internet.

Online information edition can be an important influential resource connected with activity of leading groups of financial and industrial structures. Analysts themselves become involved in the community of a politically or economically oriented site: on the one hand they take part in its development, on the other hand they use information (analyses, opinions) placed on the site for their professional reports.

Such resources can be sold or used by order. For example, by state order (Strana.ru) or by order of a political party (Vesti.ru). However, none of those projects which specialise on political and economic news is able to make up for PR and advertising expenses. Some scheme suggested and already realised by Fund of Effective Policy, according to which mass media on the Runet should be created not as business but as an influential resource, works best of all.

REFERENCES

Bol'she, chem pechatnoe slovo-99. Materials of the 3rd IFRA/WAN Conference, Amsterdam, October 1999. // *Gasetnie Technologii/ Newspaper Techniques.* P. 4.

Informacionnoe obshestvo, 2000. N4.

Davidov I. Mass-media Runeta. Osnovnie tendencii rasvitiya i analiz tekushei situacii. // *Russkii Jurnal.* http://russ.ru/politics/20000928_davydov.html. 28.09.2000

E-business 2001: vse kto mog umeret', umerli. http://www.rambler.ru/ db/news/msg.html?mid=2167686&s=5. 28.12.2001

Kak rabotali rossiiskie Internet SMI v dni tragedii v Soedinennix Shtatax. // Planeta Internet (the Internet Planet), &8470;51, November 2001. http://www.rbc.ru/press?112001?smi1109.shtml

Davidov I. Reiting vliyatel'nosti SMI Runeta – obosnovanie novogo proekta.// SMI.ru, 18.09.2001. http://www.smi.ru/2001/

Rumetrica: Zametki nablyadatelya. http://www.rambler.ru/db/rumetrica/article, 23.10.2001.

Spylog Research. Global statistics. http://gs.spylog.ru/short_news.phtml? offset=20

Gotovnost' Rossii k informacionnomu obshestvu: Osenka vozmozhnostei i potrebnostei shirokomasshtabnogo ispol'sovaniya informacionno-kommunikacionnix texnologii. Moskva, 2001.

Chyi H.I. The medium is Global; the Market is Not: The Umbrella-Opgrading Model of Online Newspaper Markets. Robert G. Picard, ed. *Evolving media markets: effects of economic and policy changes.* Turku: Turku School of Economics and Business Administration 1998.

Expert, #16 (227), April 24, 2000.

Makarov R. Kak poluchit' pribil ' ot setevogo SMI. //Nezavisimaya gazeta, #26 (2336), February 14, 2001. http://ng.ru/ideas/2001-02-14/8_profit.html.

Bessudnov A., Dugaev D. Ot Nosika k Gutenbergu.// Internet. Ru. 24.01.2001. http://internet.ru/article/preview_articles/2001/01/24/4883.html.

Chapter 8
The Top Six
Communication Industry Firms:
Structure, Performance and Strategy

Alan B. Albarran and Terry Moellinger
University of North Texas

Unparalleled mergers and acquisitions during the 1980s and 1990s led to the formation of an oligopoly of global media conglomerates (Albarran, *Management of...*, 2002; Demers, 1999, Maney, 1995). These companies, also called *megamedia* (Alger, 1998), or *transnational media corporations* (Gershon, 1997), are multi-divisional companies, operating in numerous media markets such as broadcasting, publishing, motion pictures and sound recordings. Their goals are rather simple—dominate the markets in which they are engaged by attracting as much market share and revenues as possible, as well as engage in economies of scale and scope to improve efficiencies and lower the cost of operations.

But who are these conglomerates? This chapter analyses the top six media companies in terms of structure, performance and strategy in order to gain a better understanding of their activities and roles in the global communications marketplace. The six companies reviewed in this chapter include AOL Time Warner (later referenced as AOL TW), Bertelsmann AG, News Corporation, Viacom, Vivendi Universal and the Walt Disney Company. These companies were chosen because their divisional structure consists of at least two or more media-related divisions and media activities account for at least half of the company's asset base. As such, the world's largest company in terms of revenues, General Electric, is omitted from this analysis because the company's media holdings are limited to a single division that consists of NBC and its branded cable networks (CNBC, MSNBC). Likewise, Sony was also rejected because its media holdings are limited with most of the company's revenues obtained through its consumer electronics division and the sale of video players and games.

Of the six companies analysed in this chapter, three are American companies (AOL TW, Disney, Viacom). Bertelsmann is based in Germany, Vivendi in France and Canada, and News Corporation in Australia. But every company is in fact a global company, presenting their respective brands and entertainment/information products to consumers around the globe.

STRUCTURE OF THE TOP SIX FIRMS

This section presents an overview of the internal structure and organisation of the top six media conglomerates. Table 8.1 presents basic description on each company in regards to revenue, market capitalisation, number of employees, and the number of officers and corporate directors.

Table 8.1. Descriptive Data on Top Six Media Companies

Company	Revenue (in $ billions)	Market Value (billion)	Employees	Number of Officers	Number of Directors
AOL Time Warner	$36.2	$166	88,500	14	16
Walt Disney Co.	$25.4	$53.2	120,000	10	16
Vivendi Universal	$24.3	$59.4	253,000	11	19
Viacom	$20.0	$80.6	57,840	8	18
Bertelsmann AG	$18.0	$70	82,162	11	8
News Corporation	$13.8	$15.6	33,800	14	16

Source: Ur..ess otherwise noted, all information retrieved from Compact Disclosure CD-ROM, October 12, 2001, and reflects 2000 information. Revenue figures (except for Bertelsmann AG) taken from: *Broadcasting & Cable*n "Top 25...," (2001). All information regarding Bertelsmann AG was taken from *Bertelsmann: Facts and figures* (2001). Bertelsmann's market capitalisation is drawn from a press release. The market value for News Corporation was found in *News Corporation—Investor relations* (2001).

In several areas the companies are remarkably similar to one another. The mean revenue in 2000 was $22.9 billion, the average number of corporate officers is 11.3 and the average number of corporate directors is 15.5. In terms of market capitalisation, AOL TW outdistances the other companies by $85 billion. In terms of employees, Vivendi Universal is the largest employer, News Corporation the smallest.

Each of these enterprises is a holding company for other media concerns and each is organised accordingly. The structure of every media company is in constant flux as a result of change and strategic initiatives. To better understand each company's purpose, we next review each company's mission statement.

Mission Statements of the Conglomerates

The company mission statement typically identifies the organisation's purpose and values (Albarran, *Management of...*, 2002). The actual mission statements vary in length from several paragraphs to a single paragraph. The authors have distilled the material down to present the key aspects of the mission statement. This material is presented in Figure 8.1.

As might be expected, the mission statements espouse similar goals and objectives. For example, all but one company (News Corporation) mention the word "entertainment" in their statements. Disney emphasises "family entertainment" while other companies use the terms "consumers," "customers" and "people". Vivendi, Viacom and News Corp. emphasise their role as creators and distributors of content. Financial goals are inferred or explicitly stated by AOL TW, Disney and News Corp.

In addition to the mission statements, much insight can be gained by looking at each company in terms of its current structure and historical development. Each company is reviewed in the following sections.

AOL TW Compact Disclosure lists AOL TW's primary business activities as "information retrieval services; cable and other pay TV services; photographic equipment and supplies" (AOL Time Warner, 2001). However, there is much more to this company than this list of business ventures implies. The company is further described by the Disclosure database as a company that:

> Develops and operates branded interactive services including: a worldwide Internet online service and an Internet portal; creates and distributes branded information and entertainment throughout the world; and owns and operates cable networks consisting principally of interests in film entertainment, television production and television broadcasting (AOL Time Warner, 2001).

Figure 8.1: Excerpts from Corporate Mission Statements

Our mission at AOL Time Warner is to become the world's most respected and valued company by connecting, informing and entertaining people everywhere in innovative ways that will enrich their lives.

The Walt Disney Company's key objective is to be the world's premier family entertainment company through the ongoing development of its powerful brand and character franchises. The company's primary financial goals are to maximise earnings and cash flow from existing businesses and to allocate capital profitably toward growth initiatives that will drive long-term shareholder value.

Vivendi Universal will be the world's preferred creator and provider of entertainment, education and personalised services to consumers anywhere, at any time, and across all distribution platforms and devices.

Bertelsmann is the most international media corporation, striving to be the world's leader in the markets in which they operates. Bertelsmann provide customers with information, education and entertainment through every possible outlet and in every conceivable format.

Viacom is a leading global media company, with preeminent positions in broadcast and cable television, radio, outdoor advertising, and online. With programming that appeals to audiences in every demographic category across virtually all media, the company is a leader in the creation, promotion, and distribution of entertainment, news, sports, and music.

The News Corporation Limited is one of the world's largest media companies [involved in] the production and distribution of motion pictures and television programming; television, satellite and cable broadcasting; the publication of newspapers, magazines and books; the production and distribution of promotional and advertising products and services; the development of digital broadcasting; the development of conditional access and subscriber management systems; and the creation and distribution of popular on-line programming. News Corporation's success worldwide is attributed to teamwork, communication, creativity and determination. These skills, combined with the breadth of our assets, enables us to create customised media and marketing solutions that impact consumers one by one.

Sources adapted from corporate websites as follows: AOL Time Warner—About us (2001); Walt Disney and Company—About us (2001); Discover Vivendi Universal (2001); Bertelsmann profile (2001); About Viacom (2001); and News Corporation—Investor relations (2001).

The term "branded," used twice to describe the nature of AOL TW's business, is important. Each of the media conglomerates has experienced a history of acquiring additional properties that are known brands. Each of these companies uses these brands to differentiate itself from the other media companies.

AOL TW is divided into seven segments comprising one or two principle companies with other acquisitions folded in. Each segment has its own Chairman and Chief Executive Officer, each of whom reports to AOL TW's Board of Directors, its Chairman, and its CEO. These segments are: Interactive services and properties (America Online), networks (Turner Broadcasting and Home Box Office), publishing (Time Inc. and Time Warner Trade Publishing), music (Warner Music Group), filmed entertainment (Warner Bros. and New Line Cinema), cable systems (Time Warner Cable), and their Interactive Video Division, comprising AOL Time Warner Interactive Video.

Key events in the organisational development of AOL Time Warner are presented in the timeline presented in Table 8.2.

The Walt Disney Company The Walt Disney Company was organised in 1923. Disney achieved notoriety with the debut of the animated character "Mickey Mouse" in 1928. Disney became known as an animated film company and cartoon creator. Later, the company developed theme park operations and moved into merchandising of the Disney family of characters and retail through the Disney stores around the world.

The company is currently organised in a similar fashion to AOL TW, with certain key companies—all brand names—dominating each division. Although each media company assigns their executive officers different responsibilities, the functions of the Walt Disney Company offer a clear picture of the priorities of every media concern.

The 1950s saw the company develop early examples of synergy. Disney used two television programs, "The Mickey Mouse Club," and "Walt Disney Presents," to promote Disneyland, the first truly national theme park. This type of relationship is still important to the company and is reflected in its choice of executive officer positions, as there is a Vice President for Corporate Synergy.

The desire to find alternative revenue streams is also reflected in the position of Executive Vice President of Merchandise and Creative Services for Disney Store and Disney Direct Marketing. There is also a Senior Executive Vice President and Chief Strategic Officer, indicating the company's commitment to further acquisitions, mergers and alliances.

Table 2. AOL Time Warner Timeline

1918	Henry Luce and Briton Hadden conceive the idea for Time magazine. (Time Inc. is incorporated in 1922.) The Warner brothers open their first west coast studio on a 10-acre lot on Sunset Boulevard.
1968	Time Inc. acquires Boston publishing house Little, Brown and Company.
1969	Warner-Seven Arts acquired by Kinney National Co. and becomes Warner Communications Inc.
1972	Home Box Office transmits first programming to subscribers in Wilkes-Barre, PA.
1976	Turner Communications Group purchases MLB's Atlanta Braves. Turner Broadcasting's WTCG (later renamed WTBS) in Atlanta is beamed via satellite to cable homes nationwide, becoming cable's first superstation.
1978	Time Inc. acquires cable operator American Television & Communications
1980	CNN, the world's first 24-hour, all-news network, premieres with 1.7 million subscribers.
1989	America Online is launched. Time Warner Inc. is created as the world's largest media company due to merger of Time Inc. and Warner Communications Inc.
1993	AOL becomes the first online service to release a Windows version of its software; Steve Case is named CEO of America Online.
1994	AOL links members to the Internet for the first time. Turner Broadcasting System and New Line Cinema merge. Turner Classic Movies launches. Warner/Chappell Music acquires CPP/Belwin, becoming the world's largest music publisher.
	1995 The WB Network debuts.
1996	Time Warner Inc. and Turner Broadcasting System, Inc., merge, creating the world's leading entertainment, information and media company.
1997	AOL reaches 10 million subscribers.
1998	AOL acquires CompuServe and ICQ.
1999	Netscape is acquired by AOL.
2001	America Online and Time Warner complete merger announced in 2000 to become AOL Time Warner.

Source: *AOL Time Warner timeline*, 2001.

The company's concern for its image—a family and community friendly corporation—is reflected by the positions of Senior Vice President for Corporate Public Service and Vice President for Communications. A timeline for the Walt Disney Company is presented in Table 8.3.

Table 8.3. Walt Disney Co. Timeline

1923	Walt Disney and Co. begins as Disney brothers sign a contract to produce the "Alice Comedy" series for $1500 each.
1928	"Steamboat Willie", the first animated film with synchronised sound, introduces Mickey Mouse to the American public.
1937	Disney enters the merchandise arena with the licensing to Ingersol of the Mickey Mouse watch and the creation of the first Mickey Mouse magazine.
1937	"Snow White and the Seven Dwarfs", the first feature-length animated movie debuts.
1939	The Academy of Motion Picture Arts and Sciences awards "Snow White and the Seven Dwarfs" a special Oscar.
1940	Fantasia, the first film to introduce stereophonic sound, is produced.
1946	"Song of the South" is the first production to combine live action and animation.
1954	Disney announces the plans for Disneyland; the park opens in 1955.
1957	Disney enters the live-action market with the release of "Johnny Tremain" in theatres and Zorro on television.
1971	Walt Disney World and Resort opens in Florida.
1982	Epcot Center in Florida celebrates its grand opening. Tron, the first film to make extensive use of computer imagery, is released.
1983	The Disney Channel is launched as a premium service.
1991	"Beauty and the Beast" becomes the first animated film to be nominated for an Oscar for Best Picture.
1992	Euro Disneyland opens.
1993	Disney acquires Miramax Films.
1995	Disney and Capital Cities/ABC agree to merge.
2001	Disney acquires the Fox Family Worldwide assets for $3.0 billion in cash plus debt. Renames channel ABC Family.

Sources: Ellis (1995); Polsson (2001); Smith & Clark (1999); *Walt Disney and Company corporate acquisitions* (2001).

Vivendi Universal Vivendi Universal is the newest global media entity, created in December 2000 as a result of a merger between Vivendi, the Seagram Company Ltd., and Canal +. However, its base company is older than any other media company except Bertelsmann. The merger combined Vivendi's assets with Seagram's film, television and music holdings (including Universal Studios) and Canal +'s programming and distribution capacity (*Merchants of Cool*, 2001).

Vivendi Universal has operations in water, waste management, energy, transport services and nonferrous wiring (Vivendi Universal, 2001). These interests provide an industrial economic base that separates it from other media giants and relieves them from downturns in the economy as advertising revenue declines. In fact, Vivendi Universal only receives 48% of their total revenue from media ventures (Leonard, 2001).

The company's formula for success, according to Guyon (2001) is to "first, separate your old-fashioned, reliable, cash-generating utility business from your glamorous but risky media business. Then take most of your debt—in Vivendi's case, $16.9 billion—and stick it in the utility business." This strategic division of assets has encouraged further acquisitions by removing the necessity to raise extra cash to retire existing debt. Vivendi's timeline is presented in Table 8.4.

Table 8.4. Vivendi Universal Timeline

1853	Creation of Compagnie Générale des Eaux (CGE) in France.
1924	Seagram, which deals in spirits and wines, is created.
1980-1986	CGE expands, diversifies and starts international operations in water, waste management, energy, and transport services and also expands in telecom and Media.
1983	CGE participates in the creation of Canal+, the first Pay-TV channel in France.
1996	Creation of Cegetel to provide telecommunications services—it becomes the second largest operator on the French market.
1997	Acquisition of NetHold, a Dutch set-top box manufacturer; a major step in Canal+ Pay TV successful internationalisation. Launch of the digital TV offer in Spain and Italy.
1998	Company changes its name to Vivendi.
2000	Vivendi launches Vizzavi (a multi-access portal) in France in June.
2000	Vivendi completes acquisition of Seagram; becomes Vivendi Universal.
2001	Vivendi invests $1.5 billion in EchoStar; acquires USA networks for $10.3 billion.

Source: *Discover Vivendi Universal group: The group history*, (2001); *Vivendi seals deal*, (2001).

Viacom   Viacom's strategy is built around brand names that appeal to audiences in every demographic category across all media.   The company is heavily identified with its CEO and majority owner, Sumner Redstone.   In terms of divisional structure, the company divides its segments into seven areas.   The Broadcast and Cable Television Group consists of the CBS Television Network and the United Paramount Network (UPN); Comedy Central; Showtime Networks Inc.—Showtime, The Movie Channel, FLIX, and the Sundance Channel—and the Viacom Television Stations Group.   Also included in this division are the MTV Networks, which comprise MTV, Nickelodeon, VH1, TNN, MTV2, Nick at Nite, TV Land, CMT, and The Digital Suite.

The network has also extended its brand identity by sponsoring films, books, and other online and consumer products.   This division also includes BET (Black Entertainment Television), The Jazz Channel, BET International, BET Books, BET Pictures, and BET.com.   Paramount Television has six production units: Paramount Network Television, Viacom Productions, Spelling Television, Big Ticket Television, Paramount Domestic Television, and Paramount International Television.   CBS Enterprises consists of King World Productions Inc., the domestic syndication branch, CBS Broadcast International and King World International Productions.   Viacom Plus—the company's sales and marketing arm—is also in this division. The Radio and Outdoor Division contains Infinity Broadcasting and Viacom Outdoor.

The Motion Pictures and Theatrical Exhibition Division includes Paramount Pictures, Paramount Home Entertainment, Famous Players—Canada's oldest theatrical exhibitor—United International Pictures (UIP), United Cinemas International (UCI), Viacom Consumer Products (entertainment licensing), and Famous Music Publishing. Blockbuster—the world's largest renter of videos, DVDs, and video games—comprises Viacom's Video Division. The company also has an Internet Division, a Publishing Division and a Paramount Theme Parks Division.   Significant developments in the history of Viacom are presented in Table 8.5.

Bertelsmann A.G.   Bertelsmann is the only privately held media conglomerate; with 71% of its shares held by the Bertelsmann Foundation, 21% by the Mohn family (descendants of the founder), and 7% by the ZEIT Foundation. Thomas Middelhoff is the company CEO.   The members of the board, except for the Chairman/CEO, are responsible for one of the company's corporate divisions. Two divisions are not represented on the board, the RTL Group and BertelsmannSpringer. The RTL Group is in the process of moving towards limited public ownership.

Table 8.5. Viacom Timeline

1967	Sumner Redstone named President of National Amusements, Inc.
1975	Simon and Schuster purchased by Gulf + Western (later becomes Paramount).
1976	Showtime debuts as a premium service and competitor to HBO.
1979	Viacom debuts Nickelodeon, and The Movie Channel, a second pay channel.
1981	Viacom launches MTV.
1986	Sumner Redstone named Chairman of National Amusements, Inc.
1987	National Amusements acquires controlling interest; Redstone named Chairman.
1993	Along with Chris-Craft Industries, Viacom launches UPN.
1994	Viacom acquires Paramount Communications, Blockbuster and Simon and Schuster in separate transactions.
1999	Viacom acquires CBS in largest media transaction to date.
2000	BHC Communications sells its half-interest in UPN to Viacom for $5 billion.
2001	Viacom folds Infinity Broadcasting into company; acquires BET.

Source: *About Viacom*, 2001.

Eight of Bertelsmann's ten divisions are under an over-arching strategic business unit. The Content unit includes most companies (entities with book, music, magazine, newspaper, television, radio and professional information interests). The Arvato division, with its thirty subsidiaries, forms the Media Service unit. The Direct-to-Customer Businesses unit encompasses Bertelsmann's DirectGroup (Bertelsmann, "Facts and Figures," 2001). Table 8.6 lists key events in the company's history.

News Corporation Like Viacom, News Corporation is best known through its Chairman and CEO, Rupert Murdoch. In the early 1950s, Murdoch inherited a regional Australian newspaper and in the span of fifty years has been transformed into one of the world's most recognised media moguls. Like other media giants, News Corporation consists of many brand name companies, e.g., Twentieth Century Fox, The Times, the New York Post, and the Los Angeles Dodgers. The company operates several divisions: book publishing, cable and satellite television, filmed entertainment, magazines and inserts, newspapers, television, and other assets.

Table 8.6. Bertelsmann Timeline

1834	Carl Bertelsmann founds C. Bertelsmann Verlag, a book printing company.
1921	The fourth generation of ownership led by Heinrich Mohn (1885-1955) succeeds in achieving a broad readership for the company.
1962	Bertelsmann establishes a Spanish book club, Circulo de Lectores, in Barcelona.
1969	Bertelsmann acquires interests in magazine industry through Gruner + Jahr.
1980	Bertelsmann acquires Bantam Books.
1986	Bertelsmann acquires RCA records.
1997	Bertelsmann merges the Ufa Film- und Fernseh-GmbH with Compagnie Luxembourgeoise de Télédiffusion (CLT), to form the largest television enterprise in Europe. Bertelsmann also established the first book club in China.
1998	Bertelsmann acquires Random House; merges it with Bantam Doubleday Dell.
1999	Bertelsmann launches BOL – the most international media shop in the world, with operations in Germany, the Netherlands, France, Great Britain, Spain, Switzerland and a huge selection of books and music.
2000	Bertelsmann arranges for a merger between CLT-UFA and the British company Pearson TV, forming the RTL Group—the first complete corporate division of Bertelsmann to go public.
2001	Establishes alliance with Napster music service; with other partners launches MusicNet online music service.

Source: *Bertelsmann history*, 2001.

Rupert Murdoch and his family dominate the organisation of the company. Murdoch and two of his sons serve on the board of directors of the corporation. Compact Disclosures reports of the 2,037,326,936 outstanding shares, as of June 30, 2000, the corporation's officers and board members own 2,084,37 (over 10%) (News Corporation, 2001).

In addition to 10% of the voting stock held by News Corporation's officers and board members, the Cruden Trust—an entity controlled by the Murdoch family—controls 40% of the company's outstanding stock (Shawcross, 1997: 381). A timeline of News Corporation's Development is listed in Table 8.7.

Table 8.7. News Corporation timeline

1952	Rupert Murdoch inherits *The Adelaide News.*
1960	Acquires the Syndey *Mirror.*
1968	Acquires *News of the World* (United Kingdom) and *The Sun* (U.K., 1969).
1969	Acquires *The Sun* (United Kingdom)
1976	Acquires *The New York Post.*
1980	Acquires Collins Press and later Harper and Row and combines them into the HarperCollins General Book Group.
1984	Acquires Twentieth Century Fox. Forms the Fox Broadcasting Company following an agreement to purchase the Metromedia TV station group.
1986	Fox Broadcasting Network begins operation.
1988	Acquires TV Guide.
1990s	Numerous acquisitions including British Sky Broadcasting (1990), Star Television (Asia, 1993); launches Fox News Channel (1996), Fox Kids Network, Fox Sports (1996), The Health Network, FX Network, National Geographic's cable channel (owns 50%), the Golf Channel, and the TV Guide channel (owns 44%).
2001	Acquires Chris-Craft television stations to become leading TV broadcaster in U.S.

Source: *Merchants of Cool*, (2001); Shawcross, (1997).

PERFORMANCE OF THE TOP SIX FIRMS

Having examined organisational structure and development, we now turn attention to the issue of performance. Performance can be studied in many ways. For example, performance can be tied to industrial organisation analysis, by focusing on the variables of production and allocative efficiencies, as well as progress and equity (Albarran, *Media Economics*, 2002). For our purposes, performance is best reflected in financial data on the six firms to indicate their ability to increase profits, and in all cases but Bertelsmann, shareholder value.

Table 8.8 presents basic financial information for each firm except Bertelsmann, with data on total assets, total debt, and debt-to-equity and total assets-to-equity ratios.

Table 8.8. Financial Information on Publicly Traded Companies.

Company	Total Assets (in billions)	Total Debt (in billions)	Debt to Equity	Total Assets to Equity
AOL Time Warner	$ 10.827	$ 1.411	0.21	1.60
Disney Company	45.027	6.959	0.39	1.87
Vivendi Universal	150.738	.150	0.00	2.60
Viacom	82.646	12.473	0.26	1.72
News Corporation	38.315	6.959	0.47	1.99

Source: *Compact Disclosures CD-ROM* (2001).

Vivendi's large asset base is attributed to the company's industrial sectors. Viacom has the largest debt load of the public firms. All five companies have very low debt-to-equity ratios, indicating good financial management. Total assets-to-equity ratio is also very similar, with all companies having an asset base at least 1.5 times as large as their equity.

Performance ratios such as profit margins, return on equity, and return on assets provide other indications of economic performance, as well as estimates on earnings per share. Table 8.9 lists these data for the five publicly traded firms.

Table 8.9. Company Performance Ratios (2000) and Earnings Per Share (2000-2001).

Company	PM (%)	ROE (%)	ROA (%)	EPS-01 ($)	EPS-02 ($)
AOL TW	15.0	17.0	10.6	1.20	1.35
Disney	3.6	3.8	2.0	.59	.80
Vivendi	5.4	4.1	1.5	N/A	.03
Viacom	-1.8	-.26	-.4	0	.14
News Corp.	6.0	4.5	2.0	.64	.80

Source: All financial information adapted from *Wall Street Research Net* for year 2000.

As the table illustrates, AOL TW has the strongest performance ratios and EPS estimates, followed by News Corp. Viacom's high debt load led to negative performances for all 2000 performance ratios. While these data help analyse the company, the poor American and global economy in 2000 and 2001 are reflected in the subdued performance data and EPS estimates for all companies except for AOL TW.

STRATEGY OF THE TOP SIX FIRMS

This section considers the primary strategies used by these six media firms in executing their business plans. We can only assess strategies at the macro level, because within each company their respective divisions and brands within these divisions all operate with individual strategic business models and objectives.

There are two broad strategic objectives that each of these companies is engaged in: content and distribution. In terms of content, every firm has either developed or acquired significant content brands well known to consumers. The "richest" companies in terms of content include Viacom, Disney, AOL TW and News Corporation. Vivendi Universal's most visible content is in their motion picture (Universal Studios) and music divisions, while Bertelsmann is best known through its publishing and music divisions.

In terms of distribution, all six companies are engaged in distribution, but utilising different forms. For example, AOL TW and Viacom distribute content via broadcasting, cable, the Internet and print. Disney concentrates on broadcasting, cable and the Internet. News Corporation is the leading distributor of content via satellite, but also offers distribution via broadcasting, cable and publishing. Vivendi's and Bertelsmann's distribution efforts are primarily on the European continent, yet both companies are targeting the United States through their successful Internet operations. Vivendi's December 2001 acquisition of USA networks provides a much needed distribution platform in the United States that the company will build upon. Vivendi also acquired a $1.5 billion stake in EchoStar, increasing its U.S. distribution options (Vivendi seals deal, 2001).

The joint emphasis on content and distribution lead to another common strategy among media firms known as *repurposing*. First coined by Negroponte (1995), the term has come to mean content produced in one arena that is reused or repackaged for other arenas. Albarran and Dimmick (1996) refer to repurposing in economic terms as "economies of multiformity." During the 2001–2002 television season, examples of repurposing was found among the broadcast and cable networks owned by AOL TW, Disney, and News Corp.

The program *Charmed* is first broadcast on AOL TW's WB television network, then repurposed on cable networks TBS and TNT. Two programs airing on the Fox network, *24* and *Nathan's Choice*, are repurposed on FX. Disney regularly repurposes *Good Morning America* and other portions of their prime-time lineup on the cable network ABC Family.

Strategic alliances and partnerships is a fourth generic strategy used by these firms. Strategic alliances and partnerships offer several benefits to companies, including the sharing of risks and rewards, providing access to new markets and increasing shareholder and company value (Albarran, *Management of...*, 2002). With the beginning of the 21st century, most strategic alliances between these companies and other firms were devoted to developing and marketing programming and other forms of media content; expanding into non-domestic markets, and developing e-commerce and Internet strategies.

Producing and distributing television and film content became the first logical areas where strategic partnerships were widely used among media companies to lower costs, but partnerships have expanded to other areas. In the recording industry, the impact of the Napster controversy led to two different consortiums offering online music distribution. MusicNet's principal partners include AOL TW, Bertelsmann, EMI and RealNetworks, while Pressplay's initial partners consist of Vivendi Universal, Sony, Yahoo and Microsoft.

Finally, diversification is a fifth strategy used by these companies. Diversification refers to the different segments or divisions that the company draws revenues (and losses) from. In reviewing the histories of all six of these firms, one can easily see that these companies became more diversified over the years through a series of mergers and acquisitions. Likewise, in some cases the companies divested of assets that were considered non-essential to the core mission of each firm.

At the end of 2001, each of the six firms reviewed in this study were diversified to the extent that they had multiple divisions with media-related activities. But several firms hold assets that are non-media related. For example, Disney, AOL TW and Viacom holdings include theme parks, retail stores and merchandising opportunities. Disney and News Corporation both own professional sports franchises. Vivendi Universal has about half of its assets in the areas of water and waste utilities, telecommunications, and manufacturing.

SUMMARY AND CONCLUSIONS

This study provides a review and analysis of the world's largest media firms by focusing on their organisational structure and development, financial performance and business strategy. Three of the top six companies are based in the U.S., two are based in Europe, and one in Australia. In regards to structure, each company operates multiple divisions, and each company has a similar number of corporate officers and directors. Revenues, market capitalisation and number of employees vary among the six firms. All firms are publicly traded companies with the exception of Bertelsmann, which is privately held.

A review of performance data found variation among the six firms in terms of selected financial ratios. Vivendi Universal has the largest asset base and also the lowest debt. Viacom currently carries the largest debt load of the firms, and the debt has negatively impacted the company's performance in terms of profitability estimates and earnings per share projections. Of the six firms analysed, AOL TW had the strongest profitability margins and the largest EPS estimates for 2001–2002.

Regarding strategy, each of the six firms represents a conglomerate structure, with many divisions having their own leadership and support staff. As such, they have multiple strategic plans in place reflective of the needs of the various divisions.

Five macro-level strategies were observed by examining all six firms. Each firm is heavily engaged in creating and developing media content, in many cases across a number of different platforms and mediums. Every company is involved in producing for motion pictures and television; a number of companies are involved in publishing. All of the companies are also engaged in a distribution strategy, or delivering content to consumers either via over-the-air broadcasting or some type of subscriptions.

Repurposing of content is a third generic strategy used by these firms. Repurposing allows content to be repackaged or reused over different media markets and products. A fourth strategy is in the area of strategic partnerships and alliances, designed to share rewards and risks and develop new products and services across markets. Finally, diversification at the corporate level is another observed strategy, enabling these companies to draw revenues from multiple business segments composed of both media- and non-media related assets.

These billion-dollar media companies, whether identified as megamedia corporations or transnational media companies, dominate the global media landscape at the start of the 21st century. In reviewing their corporate history and development, it is unlikely these companies are finished in terms of future acquisitions. AOL TW and Bertelsmann both tried to acquire EMI records but were thwarted by regulators. AOL TW is one of several suitors after the cable television assets of AT&T. In reality, the question is how big might these companies eventually become? And how much of the various media markets (e.g., publishing, motion pictures, television, etc.) might these firms one day control?

Clearly, these giants have put considerable pressure on "smaller" firms to also grow in size and stature in order to compete with these established leaders. General Electric, through its NBC division is one such company. In the fall of 2001, NBC acquired the assets of Telemundo, the second largest Spanish-language broadcaster in the United States. NBC is also frequently rumoured to be trying to buy the movie studios owned by Sony, as NBC is the only broadcast network not affiliated with a major studio. AT&T has decided to sell its cable television assets, rather than attempt to grow larger. Telefonica acquired Terra Lycos in order to strengthen its Internet divisions and also gain a stronger position in the growing Latin American market.

In conclusion, there is little doubt that a global media oligopoly is now in operation, dominating many segments of the media marketplace. For regulators and members of society, the challenge is not to try and figure out how to "breakup" these companies—but rather how to learn how to live and function in a world where the media industries are dominated by a handful of companies. Only time will tell if the number of players in this global oligopoly grows in size, or actually shrinks in the years ahead.

REFERENCES

About Viacom. (2001). Retrieved from the World Wide Web, November 23, 2001: www. viacom.com/announce.tin?

Albarran, A. B. (2002). *Management of electronic media*, 2nd. Ed. Belmont, CA: Wadsworth Publishing Company.

Albarran, A. B. (2002). *Media economics: Understanding markets, industries and concepts*, 2nd. Ed. Ames, IA: Iowa State Press.

Albarran, A. B. & Dimmick, J. (1996). Economies of multiformity and concentration in the communication industries. *Journal of Media Economics* 9, 41-49.

Alger, D. (1998). *Megamedia*. Lanham, MD: Rowman & Littlefield Publishers, Inc.

America Online. (2001). Retrieved from the World Wide Web, November 28, 2001: www. aoltimewarner.com/about/companies/americaonline.

AOL Time Warner. (2001). Retrieved from Compact Disclosure CD-ROM, October 12, 2001.

AOL Time Warner—About us. (2001.) Retrieved from the World Wide Web, November 28, 2001: www. aoltimewarner.com/about/.

AOL Time Warner timeline. (2001). Retrieved from the World Wide Web, November 13, 2001: www.aoltimewarner.com/about/timeline.

Bertelsmann: Facts and figures. (2001). Retrieved from the World Wide Web, November 14, 2001: www. bertelsmann.com/bag/facts/facts-content.ctm.

Bertelsmann history. (2001). Retrieved from the World Wide Web, November 14, 2001: www. bertelsmann.com/bag/chronicle.

Bertelsmann news. (2001). Retrieved from the World Wide Web, November 24, 2001:   www.bertelsmann.com.news,faq/faq-section-content.cfm?section= 2&a=3481.

Bertelsmann profile. (2001). Retrieved from the World Wide Web, November 23, 2001: www.bertelsmann.com/bag/profile/profile.cfm.

Demers, D. P. (1999). *Global media: Menace or messiah?* Cresskill, NJ: Hampton Press.

Discover Vivendi Universal group: The group history. (2001). Retrieved from the World Wide Web, November 16, 2001: www.finance.vivendiuniversal.com/ discover/overview/drover01.htm.

Dolan, K. A., & Kroll, L. (2001). The world's richest people. Forbes. Retrieved from the World Wide Web, November 25, 2001: www. forbes.com/people/ 2001/06/21/billionairesindex.html.

Gershon, R. A. (1997). *The transnational media corporation.* Mahwah, NJ: LEA.

Guyon, J. (2001, September 3). Can Messier make cash flow like water? Turning a 147-year-old water company into a global media giant takes more than finesse. *Fortune.* Retrieved from the World Wide Web, November 19, 2001: www. fortune.com/indexw.ihtml?channel-artcol.ihtml&doc.

Leonard, D. (2001, September 3). Mr. Messier is ready for his close-up: A maverick Frenchman auditions for a part of an American media mogul. Weird casting? Maybe. But he's sure having fun. *Fortune*. Retrieved from the World Wide Web, November 19, 2001: www. fortune.com/indexw.ihtml?channel-artcol.ihtml&doc.

Maney, K. (1995). *Megamedia shakeout*. New York: John Wiley.

Merchants of cool. (2001). Retrieved from the World Wide Web, March 21, 2001: www. pbs.org/frontline/merchantsofcool/meidiagiants.

Negroponte, N. (1995). *Being digital*. New York: Alfred Knopf.

News Corporation. Retrieved from Compact Disclosure CD-ROM, October 12, 2001.

News Corporation—Investor relations. (2001). Retrieved from the World Wide Web, November 13, 2001: www. newscorp.com/incestor/index.html.

New Line Cinema. (2001). Retrieved from the World Wide Web, November 28, 2001: www. aoltimewarner.com/about/companies/newlinecinema.

Polsson, K. (2001). Chronology of Walt Disney. Retrieved from the World Wide Web, November 29, 2001: www. islandnet.com/~kpolsson/disnehis.

Shawcross, W. (1997). *Murdoch: The making of a media empire*. New York: Touchstone Books.

Top 25 media companies. (2001, August 27). *Broadcasting & Cable*, p. 17.

Viacom. Retrieved from Compact Disclosure CD-ROM, October 12, 2001.

Vivendi seals deal. Retrieved from the World Wide Web, December 17, 2001: www.msnbc.com/news/673698.asp.

Vivendi Universal. Retrieved from Compact Disclosure CD-ROM, October 12, 2001.

Wall Street Research Net. Corporate data retrieved from the World Wide Web, December 10, 2001: www.wsrn.com

Walt Disney and Company. Retrieved from Compact Disclosure CD-ROM, October 12, 2001.

Walt Disney and Company—About us. (2001). Retrieved from the World Wide Web, November 13, 2001: www.disney.go.com/corporate/press/w/dig/disney/releases.html

Walt Disney and Company corporate acquisitions. (2001.) Retrieved from the World Wide Web, November 13, 2001: www.disney.com.

Walt Disney Company—Officers and Directors. (2001). Retrieved from the World Wide Web, November, 30, 2001: yahoo.marketguide. com/ MGI/offrdir. asp? re=ratio &target=stock.../offrdir&Ticker=DI.

Warner Bros. (2001). Retrieved from the World Wide Web, November 28, 2001: www.aoltimewarner.com/about/companies/warnerbros.

Chapter 9
The Internationalisation of Norwegian Newspaper Companies

Jan E. S. Helgesen
Norwegian School of Management BI

After the deregulation and internationalisation of the financial markets throughout the 1980s and 1990s (Helgesen, 1999), a process of mergers and acquisitions has taken place in the media sector in many countries, and is currently spreading across national barriers. In Norway, such national developments have so far been kept at bay by legislation that put limits to horizontal integration nationally. This is a push factor for the major Norwegian media companies to expand outside their domestic market, as European legislation outside Britain generally is less restrictive. At the same time, the newspaper industry in Norway has benefited from a VAT exemption, furnishing the companies with economical power to expand. However, the question remains why the newspaper companies invest in foreign markets, albeit the return in this sector is below average.

Greenfield ventures are the most studied form of internationalisation. Knickerbocker (1973:5-6) describes what he calls oligopolistic reaction. He observed that U.S. manufacturing firms tended to cluster their investments. Knickerbocker interpreted this as defensive investment behaviour. If a firm invests in a new country, an opponent firm will consider making a similar move or building some kind of blocking strategy. Aharoni (1966) considered a parallel phenomenon, viz. the bandwagon effect, which has also been given the sociological explanation of being mimetic behaviour.

In the newspaper industry, oligopolistic reaction effects seem less likely in the case of acquisitions. Firms may compete in buying a targeted foreign company, but once one of them has bought it, there is no reason to try to fight that in any other way than in a regular competitive situation considering market shares. The sale to readers and advertisers of general newspapers is local, and so is competition on the production side, thus it hardly affects the competition situation elsewhere. There may even be fewer reasons to fight as the situation approaches a full competition situation as one moves from the national level to the global level. By definition, the global level will have at least the same amount of competitors as the national.

The quest for growth might explain a good deal of international expansion. It also seems easier to act in a bluntly profit seeking manner abroad in the general newspaper market, as there may be little goodwill at bay; the company is foreign, and considered as profit seeking anyway. With the public listing of owners, there is also the recognition of being in an international milieu. The management of the company consists of professionals seeking profit through expansion and efficiency, while traditional leaders with their own money at stake may choose a less risky path, like reinvesting according to a portfolio strategy.

Professional management tends to be educated at business schools, or at least adhere to the idea of profit through replication of an already successful concept. Furthermore, if foreign operations are considered business-as-usual, the large media companies will regard foreign competitors as regular competitors. The advantage of national owners may then simply be reduced to superior market knowledge.

In this chapter, we present theory grounded in bounded rationality to analyse the economical foundation of foreign operations. A literature review of different forms of entry modes relevant to the newspaper companies is presented. This is linked to the different forms of internationalisation: the internationalisation of the newspaper through duplication, syndication of content, and the transfer of a business model. The business model may be the organisational structure, a technology based product standard, or a concept or an editorial formula that may be rooted in this.

A SWOT ANALYSIS OF NEWSPAPERS

The starting point for this chapter is why newspaper companies go abroad at all. The obvious answer in economics would be to earn money. However, the newspaper business is generally not very profitable in Europe, due to declining readership and competition from other media in the advertising.

Thus, following an economic reasoning, it can be fruitful to look at some underlying features of newspapers. Table 9.1 gives an overview of the various strengths and weaknesses of newspapers as well as the opportunities and threats confronting that industry. It seems that newspapers have a strong position in the local markets, and they satisfy these markets' need for information on a broad scale (Picard, 1999). Considering the strength of newspapers, the ad sales division could probably be more valuable to a big newspaper company than a

Table 9.1. A SWOT Analysis of the Newspaper Industry

Strengths	*Weaknesses*
• Newspapers are normally well known brands with a good image and a high integrity in their field. • They present new, interesting content in right time, day by day, year by year. • They have an established sales division for ads and subscribers. • A given attention in people's daily life. • Contact and knowledge about advertisers in the publishing area. • Effective distribution organisation. • Efficient, easy-accessed, known and bug-free user platform. • A newspaper contains a lot of information, but is still easy to orient in, and the reader himself chooses how much each article shall be studied. • A firm grip on the adult population. • Good at selecting content and formulating the content for a given reader strata, and presenting the material in a readable fashion. Good at handling text.	• Expensive distribution and production compared to the new digital alternatives. • They are in a satisfied market without growth, except from some branches. • Economically vulnerable to changes in income (e.g., production support, subscribers, advertising etc.) • A weak grip on the young audience. • Other media, like television, radio and the Internet are faster, and give competition especially on the national market. Media bureaus often neglect local papers. • Other media and channels (CD-ROM and the Internet) are better pertaining search on earlier published material. • They are not professional in the advertising market; short life span is negative for advertisers. • The biggest threat may be the resistance to change among management and employees. • Cyclical earnings from ad sales
Opportunities	*Threats*
• Reorganisation and technological update of the product. • Newspapers may capitalise on their brand and image, and by this expand into related products and areas. • Distribution of content through new channels like the Internet, digital television, etc. • Help the local environment to the cyberspace by web hotels, ads on the Internet etc. • Custom make news for those pressed on time. Online offers. • Help companies create interactive ads.	• Diminishing household coverage. Losing readers to companies in other industries that are expanding, like computer and telecommunication. • Losing the less beneficiated as subscribers in the 2/3 society – those who like but cannot afford the product of the newspaper, digital or traditional. • Risk of losing people that are choosing away newspapers to escape information stress. • Costs of employees rising more than earnings. • Free newspapers and rising environmental problems.

single newspaper, because the company then may offer ad campaigns on a larger scale. However, this is dependent on the company moving into several newspapers in that country. This is also where large firms can alleviate one of the traditional weaknesses of newspapers: large firms are often more professional in the advertising market. They may also have an advantage in implementing changes due to greater financial resources. The same holds for branding. Large firms may capitalise more efficiently on brand and image, and thereby expand into related products and areas. The threats remain largely the same even if you are a part of a big company. Nevertheless, having a greater financial power helps resisting the short run competition from (other) free newspapers.

THREE NORWEGIAN CASES

In Norway, three actors stand for most of the outward internationalisation in the newspaper industry: Schibsted, Orkla Media, and A-pressen. These companies also control the majority of the Norwegian newspaper market. Schibsted has moved into Sweden and Estonia, and into Switzerland and Spain through the free newspaper joint venture 20 Minutes Holding AG. Orkla Media has moved into Poland, and further into Lithuania and Ukraine. In 1997, Orkla Media moved into Sweden, and in 2000, they bought *Berlingske Officin* in Denmark. A-pressen has moved towards Russia through printing mills, a 49% holding in the weekly newspaper *Petersburg Ekspress*, a 45% holding in the daily newspaper *Nizhegorodskij Rabochij,* and an option to purchase one quarter of *Pravda* due August 2002 (A-pressen, 2001).

The Competition Situation of Schibsted, Orkla Media, and A-pressen

The three companies enjoy markedly different positions with regard to financial muscle. All of Schibsted's foreign operations show negative profit, except *Aftonbladet* AB (Schibsted, 2001). However, it is the largest of the three, with the biggest Norwegian newspaper VG as the engine of the company.

Schibsted's main concern is to protect their advertising incomes, along with keeping up profitability in their core operations. Thus, they started a competing free sheet, *avis1,* when *Osloposten* tried to invade the advertising market of the Oslo area. The launch of the free newspaper *20 Minuten* in Switzerland, Germany, and Spain may also be a part of a defensive investment strategy to obstruct the free newspaper *Metro*'s worldwide spread, ultimately threatening Schibsted's interests, if not mimetic behaviour to get their share of the international free newspaper market.

Orkla Media, being a business unit in the large conglomerate Orkla, has few problems with additional funding. Their operations in Eastern Europe were approaching their 15% profit standard (Orkla Media, 2001) before the downturn of the advertising market. However, *Berlingske Officin* is showing a deficit.

Few of the newspapers held by Schibsted and Orkla Media are in direct competition with each other—the biggest threat for Schibsted is Orkla Media's direct marketing. They have chosen to stay away from cut-throat competition at the national level, but rather concentrate their forces on the international arena. They probably both had interests in getting control over the Danish company *Berlingske Officin*, where Orkla Media ended up buying the company.

A-pressen is the smallest and has the tightest financial position. It is competing with Schibsted in the city Bodø (*Nordlands Framtid* and *Nordlandsposten*, respectively) and earlier in Harstad too (Bladet Harstad and *Harstad Tidende*). In both cases, they chose to fight. In the first case, it has turned into a stalemate. In the second case, A-pressen closed down their newspaper in November 2000. In addition, A-pressen has *Nordlys*, which is a regional paper for the northern part of Norway. As a regional paper, it is in a fix between the local papers and the national papers.

It seems that A-pressen is following a different strategy when competing with Orkla Media. Orkla Media's business idea is to focus on leading local papers, and together with their economical power, a direct competition is almost futile. Instead, one might see attempts at market sharing and cooperation in distribution and printing.

The Internationalisation Process of Schibsted

Schibsted became the majority owner of the Swedish companies Aftonbladet AB in 1997 and Svenska Dagbladet Holding AB in 1998. In 1998 the company became a dominating actor in the Estonian media market, through its 92% (now: 93%) holding in AS Eesti Media. Eesti Media has 1,000 employees, publishing two national newspapers, nine magazines, is excessively involved in printing, and being a sole or part holder of five local newspapers. The involvement in Estonia was Schibsted's first outside Scandinavia in newspapers. The Estonian newspaper market is shared between Bonnier and Schibsted (Schibsted, 1999).

In 1999, Schibsted entered the free newspaper market through the Swiss company 20 Minutes Holding AG. Schibsted now possesses 41% of this company. It started up in Zurich and Cologne. In 2000, *20 Minuten* was also produced in Bern and Basel. The German project is terminated, but the company may start up a French version in Paris. Recently they entered Barcelona and Madrid in Spain.

Schibsted (1999) states that its entry into Estonia is founded on careful consideration of geography, culture, and the political situation. Estonia has a tradition for reading newspapers, the education level is high, and Schibsted expected that it would become a member of EU right after the turn of the millennium. Furthermore, Schibsted has been a shareholder in the Estonian Kanal 2 since 1995. Thus, they already have some country experience. With respect to Sweden, Schibsted's perceptions of that market indicate that the company may have thought it had the required market knowledge due to its proximity to Norway. In contrast, when entering Switzerland, they chose to form a joint venture with a Swiss based company. Then they moved into Germany, apparently without any local partner. In Paris, they are also without a local partner. However, they have hired the editor-in-chief of *Libération*, Frédéric Filloux. This should be a great help on the editorial side, but still there is the question of local knowledge on the financial side of the venture, pertaining to, *inter alia*, advertising, choice of target group, and estimation of readership potential. A local partner should also be of great help in avoiding political risk.

Table 9.2. Schibsted's Acquisitions in the Newspaper Market

Acquired company	Country	Year
Aftonbladet AB	Sweden	1997
Svenska Dagbladet Holding AB	Sweden	1998
Eesti Media	Estonia	1998
20 Minutes Holding AG*	Switzerland	1999
20 Minutes Holding AG**	Germany	2000
20 Minutes Holding AG*	Spain	2001

*Joint venture
** Terminated joint venture

The Internationalisation Process of Orkla Media

Orkla Media (OM) was established in 1987. In 1989 the engagements of the old Orkla Communications unit in the new media sector were terminated (InfoFilm + Video, Janco Visjon, CCV and Filmco). From then on, OM consisted of newspapers and the publishing company Ernst G. Mortensen.

Orkla Media's Expansion in Poland and Eastern Europe In 1990, OM launched the newspaper *Dziennik* in a joint venture with *Solidaritet* in Wroclaw, Poland. It was terminated half a year later. In 1991, OM acquired 33.3% of the shares in the Polish regional newspaper *Slowo Polskie*. In 1993, OM bought shares in four other regional papers, *Wieczor Wroclawa, Nowiny, Gazeta Wspolczesna*, and *Glos Pomorza*, and in 1994 shares in *Kurier Poranny* and *Gazeta Pomorska*, also regional papers. At that time, Dagspresse Øst-Europa (OMP) was established as a business unit with focus on Eastern Europe.

In 1995, OMP bought 62.7% of the shares in the regional paper *Dziennik Wschodni*, and in 1996 51% of the national paper *Rzeczpospolita* and 33.8% of the regional paper *Nowa Trybuna Opolska*. In 1998, the holding company Orkla Press (OP) was established, unifying all the East-European newspaper investments. It acquired 100% of the regional paper *Gazeta Lubuska*, and in 1999 two new printing mills were opened in Poznan and Warsaw for the printing of *Rzeczpospolita*. In 2000, OP bought 40% of the advertisement company Media Tak in Warsaw, and 100% of the regional paper *Glos Szczecinski* and 38.5% of the regional paper *Glos Koszalinski*.

In 1998, OP also bought 100% of Lithuania's largest regional newspaper *Kauno diena*, and 50% of *Vysokyj Zamok*, Ukraina's largest regional newspaper. OP also has a 10% holding in the Ukrainian Industrialnoje Zaporozje. In 2000 OM acquired 100% of *Berlingske Officin*, the largest newspaper company in Denmark (with 40% of the total paid circulation). It also holds a 49% holding in the Swedish *Norrländska Sosialdemokraten* through Orkla Dagspresse, since 1997.

As there are high entry barriers and few greenfield investments in the regular newspaper markets, the risk of dissemination of knowledge was small when Orkla Media entered Poland through a joint venture with locals. This is a way to learn about the foreign market and to avoid political risk as a foreigner. Later on, OM bought parts of many Polish newspapers. It is now a majority owner in many newspapers, suggesting that OM is following a strategy of becoming the majority or sole owner in its foreign ventures. Control appears to be a priority.

In Norway, Orkla Media's investment strategy is to buy number one local papers, and it is expected that they plan to follow the same strategy abroad. This suggests that valuable brands are likely to be emphasised in its strategy. Having top brands provides a good position when moving into related markets. A challenge is nevertheless to get media bureaus to use regional newspapers at the same level as the larger newspapers. Another challenge is the organisation structure; newspapers are very traditional and not very welcoming to changes. Nevertheless, it seems that Orkla Media has control over the printing mills and workers.

Table 9.3. Orkla Media's Foreign Positions in the Newspaper Market

Substantial foreign positions	Country	Year
Dziennik, joint venture*	Poland	1990
Slow Polskie, 33.3%	Poland	1991
Dziennik Wschodni, 62.7%	Poland	1995
Rzeczpospolita, 51%	Poland	1996
Norrländska Demokraten	Sweden	1997
Nowa Trybuna Opolska, 33.8%	Poland	1996
Kauno Diena, 100%	Lithuania	1998
Vysokyj Zamok, 50%	Ukraine	1998
Gazeta Lubuska, 100%	Poland	1998
Media Tak, 40%	Poland	2000
Glos Szczecinski, 100%	Poland	2000
Glos Koszalinski, 38.5%	Poland	2000
Berlingske Officin, 100%	Denmark	2000

*Terminated operation

The Internationalisation Process of A-pressen

The stronghold of A-pressen is its portfolio of local newspapers. Another significant part of the economical foundation is the 33% share holding of TV2 AS, the largest commercial TV company in Norway. In addition, the production support (a government subsidy scheme) for local newspapers with unfortunate market situation and poor performance, gives room for some "innovative slack", if not preventing closures in recessions. This economic safety net is now under greater threat. Arbeiderpartiet (The Norwegian Labour party) is out of government after its disastrous election result in September 2001. Its policy has always been to protect the press support scheme, which has mainly gone to former labour party papers. Høyre, the conservative party, is the largest of the three parties in the ruling coalition of Conservatives, Christian Democrats, and Liberals. It is opposed to press support, but the other parties of the coalition are fighting to keep it.

A-pressen has founded the company A-pressen Eastern Europe AS (AEE), operating in Russia. Sixty-five percent is owned by A-pressen and 35% by EBRD and its regional fund Nordic Russian Management Company Ltd. The business strategy is to seek local partners, who will provide base investments (e.g. office facilities), and provide their share of the investment before AEE and EBRD contributes the additional capital. A-pressen will furthermore contribute with their competence in the development of the projects (A-pressen, 1999)

In the light of its domestic position, it seems rather hazardous of A-pressen to move into Russia. This might be interpreted as a "follower's" move, to use the reasoning of game theory. A-pressen is not in the position of being "first mover", and with limited economical resources, it has to take what is left and within the economical possibilities. Otherwise, they could stay at home, but then there would be few opportunities for growth. It is commonly known that growth itself can be an explanation for internationalisation.

Table 9.4. A-pressen's Foreign Positions in the Newspaper Market

Foreign positions	Country	Year
OGF Ekaterinenburg, 29%*	Russia	1999
Petersburg Ekspress, 49%	Russia	1999
Nizhegorodskij Rabochij, 45%	Russia	1999
OGF Nizhnij Novgorod, 29%*	Russia	2000

*Printing mill: Greenfield joint venture

INTERNATIONALISATION OF NEWSPAPERS

Internationalisation can be seen as a part of the product life cycle, i.e. production of mature products (old technology) in less developed countries. This idea originates in Vernon's seminal work on internationalisation (Vernon, 1966). In principle one could print the newspaper abroad for cost reasons, and sell it at home. The generally insurmountable obstacle is rapid distribution of the printed newspaper to a price less than the saved amount on printing.

Internationalisation of the product could also entail selling it abroad. However, it is highly questionable whether this is a practical opportunity, except for niche newspapers in, for example, shipping, oil/gas, and economics/business more generally (examples are *The Economist* and to a certain degree, *The Financial Times*). The difference from general newspapers is typically the global isomorphic understanding of the content. A hypothetical example of a market offensive way to duplicate would be to start printing and selling the Norwegian *VG* in Stockholm, Sweden, which is easily done by the same type of satellite transmission used to print *VG* outside Oslo. As it turns out, such moves have never been attempted. General newspapers are locally bound products, and the need for Norwegian newspapers in Stockholm is covered by aircraft shipment.

When speaking of newspapers it is important to remember that the product is twofold: It is both a journalistic product serving the reader market and a distribution channel for advertising. Thus, borrowing an example from the magazine world, there are one U.S. and six English-language editorial editions of *Newsweek*, but as many as 105 advertising editions globally (Hafstrand, 1995). However, this is unlikely to happen in the general newspaper industry, due to the local features of the newspaper markets. In the following we suggest that for most newspapers the reader market will coincide more or less with the advertising market, thus making it cost efficient to have only one advertising edition per editorial edition.

In the newspaper industry, duplication would normally be in the form of syndicated material. However, this can be problematic due to language barriers, cultural barriers, and the need for local content. Used on a large scale, it also commands that the branding strategy of the two newspapers is alike.

International Syndication of Material within Newspaper Companies

As an example of the use of syndicated material, there is a broad exchange of editorial content between the between their offices of the Swiss editions of Schibsted's free newspaper *20 Minuten* in Zurich, Basel, and Bern. They are possibly moving towards one common newspaper with local adaptations, a technique known from regular national papers. However, there were no exchanges with the German Cologne edition. This may give a hint in to how heterogeneous the newspaper product is believed to be, as the language is identical.

We also went to Brussels to investigate the case of *Metro*. In Brussels, there are two editions of Metro, reflecting the bilinguality of the city. However, there is also a cultural difference. Inspection of the two editions revealed that very few articles were common. For example, the leading front-page article often differs. Belgium is a divided country, still one could imagine that people from Brussels were more homogenous across language barriers. On the other hand, most of the sizeable ads and some of the small ones are common, except they are in French and Flemish, respectively. Then one could wonder if their taste in news really differs more than their taste in goods.

We have found some examples of translated newspapers. *El Periódico* in Barcelona is published in Castillan ("Spanish") and Catalan. They claim this is a success, as circulation rose. It is still an open question whether the two editions will differ in the future. One reason for this could be that the Catalan version would gain popularity throughout Catalonia, and therefore support a broader or different audience. There is also *Atuagdliutit/Grønlandsposten* and *Sermitsiaq*, both published in Greenlandic and Danish.

Internationalisation of the Business Model

Generally, for newspapers to sell abroad, the product needs local adaptation. Thus, instead of exporting the newspaper the business model could be duplicated. The business model is the manufacturing model, and it shows physically as the editorial formula and layout of the newspaper, made possible by the technological production process and the organisational model. The best example of this is *Metro*, which has the same layout and composition all over the world.

Historically, the Nordic and the continental European newspapers have mainly been run on an ideological and independent basis. Thus, newspapers have not been market-driven. This position is reflected in their traditional organisation model, with a fundamental split into two parts: the editorial and the administrative departments. It is understood that editors should be free to express and pursue any opinion and viewpoints of their own, fully independent of marketing objectives, strategies and programs.

From a marketing orientation point of view, this poses a dilemma, because any independent editorial line is potentially incompatible with the opinions, needs, and preferences of readers and advertisers. Thus, an implementation of a professional business model may be the essential competitive advantage of a multinational enterprise.

A potential threat to such strategic recipes is that format can be imitated or adapted by other firms for a low cost. Nevertheless, because it usually takes more than simply imitating a format to succeed in the market place over time—intangible capabilities and knowledge as essential additional components—copy-cat tactics are seldom enough to succeed with a product. There may also be important features of economics of scale, both for governing the business model and in the business model itself, for example by selling advertising campaign space in several newspapers.

FOREIGN MARKET ENTRY

Among the vast array of alternatives for a firm to organise its foreign business activities, Hill, Hwang, and Kim (1990) consider non-equity contractual modes (licensing), equity-based co-operative ventures (joint ventures) and wholly owned subsidiaries. Each mode of entry has different implications for the degree of control that the firm can exercise over the foreign operation, the resources it must commit to the foreign operation, and the risk of dissemination of firm-specific knowledge.

Licensing gives a low degree of control, but also a low degree of resource commitment. The dissemination risk, however, is high. If a firm grants a license to a foreign enterprise to use firm-specific knowledge to manufacture its product, it runs significant risk of the licensee, or a employee of the licensee, disseminating that knowledge, or using it for purposes other than those originally intended. For example, RCA once licensed its colour TV technology to a number of Japanese companies. The Japanese companies quickly assimilated RCA's technology and then used it to enter the U.S. market. Now the Japanese have a bigger share of the U.S. market than the RCA brand.

In the newspaper market, there is no question that the licensee could be well off breaching the contract after a while, when it has gained knowledge (and control) over the production process. It is harder for employees of the licensee to use that knowledge in a competing way, because of great startup costs in the newspaper market. The licensee could also use the knowledge for other purposes than intended. For example, instead of upholding the license they could move on to producing another kind of newspaper, centre newspapers, or direct mail.

The licensing of a newspaper business model could be a possibility with free newspapers like *Metro* and *Natt&Dag*, when entering a foreign market having little country experience and knowledge. However, in the regular newspaper market the idea of paying a license fee on a business model for an already existing newspaper seems rather far-fetched, and is likely to be resisted by managers. Thus, it appears to be a viable option only in the rare case of greenfield ventures.

A similar argument holds for joint ventures, although it seems reasonable to propose that the risks of dissemination are not as great as in the licensing case. The difference is that in a joint venture the firm's ownership stake may give it greater control over its partner's utilisation of firm-specific knowledge (Hill et al., 1990), as well as control in other fields. The resource commitment will be greater than that of licensing, depending on the ownership split and resource sharing between the venture partners.

The risk of dissemination of knowledge is likely to be lowest in the case of a wholly owned subsidiary. One reason for this is that internal organisation fosters an "atmosphere" conducive to a congruence of goals and values between members of the organisation. There is nevertheless always the risk that an essential employee with access to firm-specific knowledge leaves the organisation and joins or forms another company. Thus, a residual risk of dissemination remains, even if it is lower than that of a joint venture, which again is lower than in the case of licensing.

Anderson and Gatignon (1986) offer a more extensive list of entry modes. The medium-control modes are the most discussed, as they are theoretically most intriguing. Various kinds of balanced interests (plurality shareholder, equal partnership and balanced contracts) are based on the notion of "credible commitment" or "hostage" (see Williamson, 1983).

The hostage situation can be exemplified by the Norwegian TV2's holding in TVNorge, another Norwegian commercial TV station. In this case, the other large owner, SBS, has majority control, and may block any attempt from TV2 to use their holding strategically. Firms forming a venture with a high likelihood of trouble (such as equal partnerships) will have difficulty locating suitable partners. To attract a partner, the entrant may need to put up something to lose, a sort of good-faith collateral, known as *credible commitment*. For example, in a slightly unbalanced venture the partner holding more than 50% of equity may concede favourable contract clauses (such as veto power). Such clauses can be so favourable that a firm may have more control with a 49% share than with a 51% share (Anderson & Gatignon, 1986). As an example from Norway, Nagell-Erichsen's enterprise Blommenholm Industrier controls Schibsted with its 26.11% A-share.

Commitments may also entail the most critical positions in the foreign entity: the exposed partner can demand to fill them with its own personnel, a method preferred by Japanese multinationals (Hayashi, 1978). This is most relevant in the cases where the firm of the localisation country is in minority.

In a 50-50 relationship, the hostage is a peculiar one—the venture itself. However, Friedman and Beguin (1971) point out that equality in equity capital can "lend a special feeling of partnership to the two partners" (p. 372), adding that "the risk of deadlock itself acts as a powerful incentive to the partners, encouraging them to find solutions to disagreements by discussion and compromise" (p. 377).

There is also some non-equity modes that yield moderate control. Among these, franchising is a commonly used form of licensing, in which the use of a business system is granted. Franchising offers medium control because agreements typically include incentives to adhere to the system's rules and allow for a high degree of monitoring of the franchisee's activities.

Anderson and Gatignon (1986) offer several propositions on which level of control to use, some suggesting low control if applied on the newspaper markets. They have made no ranking of the propositions in, say, an order of importance. Although the article proposes high control when dealing with newer technology, the point in question is control over the process and implementation, not so much as possible opportunism from the partner or employee. However, following the reasoning of Schumpeter (1942: 84), it appears that what Anderson and Gatignon really consider is competitive advantage on the margin and not competition that commands decisive cost or quality advantages, which in turn yield supra-normal profits. Such competition is typically based on new technology and new type of organisation.

On the technological side, the acquisition of newspapers is often followed by construction of new printing mills, at least in developed countries. Modern printing mills provide substantial advantages especially on printing pictures, and using colours. In turn, this gives room for new layout and modern photojournalism.

In contrast, newspapers have not developed much on the organisational side in decenniums. In Europe, there is a strong heritage from the political press. Traditionally, most newspapers were not focused on earnings. Thus, many newspapers probably have an unrealised economic potential. Another heritage is "the wall" between the editorial and marketing side of the newspaper. Although newspapers should benefit from thinking along the lines of brand management (Gaustad, 1999), such moves are much more consistent with the thinking of professional owners than with the values held by traditional newspaper owners.

In both the cases of new technology and new organisational model, the need for control should be high due to lack of knowledge about host countries and resistance from top-management and employees. The issues of new technology and new organisation models should be highly relevant when analysing international ventures. When crossing borders, the differences are likely to be, *a priori*, greater than within a country. In the newspaper industry, which has so far been almost exclusively local, national differences give reason to believe that the situation in some countries is sub-optimal.

CONCLUSIONS AND IMPLICATIONS

There have been few attempts to get synergies out of syndicated material internationally, except for the use of news agencies. This seems to indicate that there are substantial barriers on the use of syndicated material in newspapers due to product specificity. However, it could also imply that there is an unrealised potential.

The duplication of newspaper business models seems to be an emerging approach to the internationalisation of newspapers. This is an area where companies may gain synergies, and we may apply the normal economical understanding of international business, typically with research and development in the home country and mature production abroad. However, little economical outcome seems yet achieved in the Norwegian cases. It might be a problem of local adaptation, i.e., a lack of knowledge of the newspaper industry and the implementation and transferability of business models.

The advanced technology of modern print mills gives a new potential for journalism and especially photojournalism. However, the resistance to change is strong in the newspaper industry, thus implying a high control mode, viz running the operation as a wholly owned subsidiary. Nevertheless, when entering a new market there is a need for local experience, and this can be gained through a joint venture with a local partner. A local partner may also be useful to avoid political risk.

REFERENCES

Aharoni, Y. (1966). The foreign investment decision process. Division of Research, Graduate School of Business Administration, Harvard University. Boston.

A-pressen (1999). Årsrapport 1998. A-pressen ASA. Oslo.

A-pressen (2001). *Årsrapport 2000*. A-pressen ASA. Oslo

Anderson, E. and H. Gatignon (1986). Modes of foreign entry: A transaction cost analysis and propositions. *Journal of International Business Studies*, Fall.

Baumol, W. J. and R. D. Willig (1981). Fixed costs, sunk costs, entry barriers, and sustainability of monopoly, *Quarterly Journal of Economics*, 96, 405-431

Friedman, W. G. and J.-P. Beguin (1971*). Joint international business ventures in developing countries*, New York: Columbia University Press.

Gaustad, Terje (1999). Creating the newspaper of the 21st century.. Paper. Senter for Medieøkonomi. Sandvika.

Hafstrand, Helene (1995). Consumer magazines in transition. *The Journal of Media Economics*, 8(1), pp. 1-12.

Hayashi, K. (1978). Japanese management of multinational operations: Sources and means of joint venture control. *Management International Review*, 18 (4), p. 47-57.

138 Helgesen — Internationalisation of Norwegian Newspaper Firms

Helgesen, Jan E. S. (1999). Analyse av sektorfordelte tap i finansnæringen. Hovedoppgave i sosialøkonomi. Sosialøkonomisk institutt. Universitetet i Oslo.

Helgesen, Thorolf (2000). Dagspressens fremtid. Senter for Medieøkonomi. Sandvika.

Hill, C. W. L., P. Hwang and W. C. Kim (1990). An eclectic theory of the choice of international entry mode. *Strategic Management Journal*, Vol. 11, 117-128

Knickerbocker, F. T. (1973). *Oligopolistic reaction and multinational enterprise*. Harvard University

Orkla Media (2001) *Orkla media informerer*. Orkla Media AS. Oslo

Picard, Robert (1999). *Competitiveness of the European Union publishing industries*, European Commision. Brussels

Schibsted (1999). *Årsrapport 1998*. Schibsted ASA. Oslo

Schibsted (2001). *Årsrapport 2000*. Schibsted ASA. Oslo

Schumpeter, J.A. (1942). *Capitalism, socialism, and democracy*. New York, NY: Harper & Brothers

Van Kranenburg, Hans (1999). Entry, survival or exit of firms over industry life cycles. Proefschrift. Universiteit Maastricht.

Vernon, R. (1966). International investment and international trade in the product cycle. *Quarterly Journal of Economics*, Vol. 80, pp. 190-207

Williamson, O. E. (1983). Credible commitments: Using hostages to support exchange, *American Economic Review*, 73 (September), 519-540.

Chapter 10
Company Size, Operational Type, Ownership Structure and Business Strategy: An Analysis of Taiwanese Satellite Channel Companies

Li-Chuan (Evelyn) Mai
Ming Chuan University

Since the Taiwanese Government amended the CATV Law and introduced the Satellite Law in 1999 (*Taiwan Daily*, 1999), the satellite and cable television (CATV) industry has been successful in attracting both local and foreign entrepreneurs, and their presence has translated into more competition.

STAR TV entered the market in 1991, and "STAR TV Chinese" was the first foreign channel to be broadcast via a CATV system. Successively, TVBS, Discovery, HBO, CNBC, Disney, ESPN, NHK, Super TV, and so on entered this market. These companies compete with domestic satellite channels, and competition has been very intensive since the 1990s. Therefore, how to formulate the business strategies in order to survive the environment is very important for both domestic and global satellite companies.

This research reviews the development of the satellite industry and market structure in Taiwan, analyses the business strategies in companies of different sizes and ownership structures, and attempts to investigate the relationships among company sizes, ownership structures, operational types and business strategies. Porter's strategic model was applied to examine the business strategies of these satellite companies.

BACKGROUND

In Taiwan, the development of the satellite channel industry is closely linked to the CATV industry. The major development of the satellite television industry occurred after the Taiwanese government introduced the Cable Television (CATV) Law in 1993 and the Satellite Law in 1999. The satellite and CATV markets attracted many investors, including foreign operators, who led the market into intense competition.

But in the 1980s, before the Taiwanese government legitimised the CATV industry, some illegal CATV stations utilised satellite dishes to receive foreign satellite channels, including NHK 1 and 2, WOWOW, and China Central Television. Those satellite channels were re-transmitted without the consent of the copyright owners. Therefore, the Taiwanese government used the "Broadcast and Television Law" to confiscated these illegal CATV stations' facilities and prohibited the installation of satellite dishes without permissions. Not until 1988, did the Taiwanese government legalise "little ear" (small satellite dishes). In 1992, the government allowed the private ownership of "middle and big ears".

In the early 1990s, the distribution of domestic channels relied on physical transportation, such as aeroplanes, trains, and taxis, to deliver their videotapes. When the global satellite channels were launched in Taiwan, the operators of the domestic channels started transmitting via satellite in order to compete with foreign channels. All of domestic satellite signals were up-linked via satellite transmissions from outside Taiwan. The reason was that the Taiwanese government did not regulate the satellite businesses. On the other hand, Taiwan was not allocated a satellite quota (the sovereignty of Taiwan is not recognised by most countries, and its diplomatic and other resources are allocated to the People's Republic of China). Therefore, all up-links were done through foreign satellite channels from Singapore, Indonesia, Hong Kong, Indonesia, and India. In 1995, the Taiwanese government permitted channel operators to up-link their satellite signals from Taiwan, and this policy allowed the operators to save some costs.

In 1990, there were about 20 channels in Taiwan (*China Times Express*, 1990), and most of the programmes were transmitted to CATV systems through landlines. In 1995, there were 200 channels, including 70 transmitting via satellite (Tsaur, 1995). In 1996, the number of channels had reduced to 120, most of which were distributed via satellite transmission (Yang, Kwan, & Mai, 1996). As a result of the intense competition, the number of channels was further reduced to just over 100 by 1999, with satellite channel operators having consolidated into about 30 companies. According to the latest (1999) survey by the author, the number of satellite channel operators has stabilised at around 30 companies, but they now offer just over 80 channels. About half of the broadcasting rights were owned by the three largest firms in the satellite channel market; China Trust offers 13 channels, ReBar offers 14 channels and Filmate offers 18 channels.

FOREIGN SATELLITE CHANNELS IN TAIWAN

"STAR Chinese" was the first satellite channel launched in Taiwan (Feng, 1998:95), and it was watched by most people with CATV systems. "STAR TV", the main company, was founded in Hong Kong and owned by a Cantonese entrepreneur, Chia-Chen Lee. In 1995, Rupert Murdoch (News Corporation International) took over the company and aimed to penetrate the greater Chinese satellite TV market further. Therefore, STAR TV provided STAR Chinese to CATV systems for free, later providing "STAR Plus", "STAR Mandarin Movies", "STAR Western Movies", "STAR Sports", "STAR World" (Western drama) and "Channel V" (music channel), increasing the cost of subscription for each additional channel, a typical Murdoch strategy employed in developing BSkyB in Europe.

Other satellite channel operators were also interested in the Taiwanese market. In 1993, Hong Kong TVB co-operated with the Taiwanese-born Fu-San Chu to establish the TVBS TV stations, providing the "TVBS Satellite channel" (a drama channel). They then founded "TVBS-N" (a news channel), "TVBS-G" (a comedy and lifestyle channel), "ERA Sports" and "ERA Business". HBO, CNN, CNBC (a business channel) and CBS Hour (an American Comedy channel) were licensed to TVBS. The competition in the satellite channel market suddenly became intense.

Furthermore, in order to expand distribution efficiently, most global channels were licensed to domestic channel agencies or companies (Liu, 1997: 9). For example, NHK was licensed to the "Commercial Group". The Taiwanese broadcasting copyright for TNT, the cartoon channel, and Discovery belonged to China Trust, one of the largest CATV companies. ESPN and the Military Information Channel belonged to the Tan-Tun Company, while Disney belonged to the "Po-Hsin" company. These domestic agencies owned most distributing channels, were experienced in distributing videotapes or films, and had good connections with CATV stations. Only STAR TV, MTV, Singapore TV and Discovery established branches in Taiwan and promoted their channels to Taiwanese subscribers and produced local programmes, but distributions still relied on their domestic channel agents.

Even though the quality of the Taiwanese domestic channels improved, the global satellite channels achieved greater popularity in Taiwan, particularly HBO, MTV, Disney, and ESPN. Following market growth, global satellite channels continued to expand into the Taiwanese market, including Cinemax, Hallmark, TV5 (French channel), and BBC during 1993 to 1995. National Geographic channel had been broadcasting since 1998. However, some of these channels have been withdrawn from the market, such as CBS Hour, the Military channel, TV5, and BBC (Liu, 1996). Meeting the copyright fees for the popular channels meant raised subscription costs every year. Therefore, to formulate suitable business strategies are important for these satellite channel companies.

LITERATURE REVIEW

Strategic management is focused on how the resources and skills of a company should be used to achieve goals (Bennett, 1996: 3; Chandler, 1962; Child, 1972; Chisnall, 1995: 181; Lorange & Vancil, 1976; Thompson, 1993: 1), increase performance (Gunnigle & Moore, 1994), and accomplish long-term objectives (Dubrin & Ireland, 1993: 143; Faulkner & Johnson, 1992: 17), and to be able to estimate external risks and environment (Hunt & Lambe, 2000). Business strategy is concerned more with adaptive management processes, planning, and actions, as from deliberative, rational, conscious, and intentional actions and thinking (Bailey & Johnson, 1992; McGrath-Champ, 1999; McCarthy, Markides, & Mintzberg, 2000; Mintzberg, 1978; Mintzberg, 1994; Mintzberg & Frances, 2000), and excellence in the implementation of strategies in order for the company to perform well (Thompson, 1993: 1).

Business strategy has been frequently studied since the 1960s (Kay, 1993: 6). The most influential model of business strategy was presented by Porter (1980: 13-39), and was applied in a number of studies (Bauer & Colgan, 2001; Fitzsimmons & Fitzsimmons, 1994: 46; Gunnigle & Moore 1994; Hit, Ireland, & Hoskissan, 1997: 123-131; Silva, Lisboar & Yasin, 2000;) although his model was seriously criticised by some academics (Bowman, 1990: 53-54; 1992: 64-83; Chan-Olmsted & Jamison, 2000; Pruet & Howard, 1996).

Some scholars have continued to develop other strategic models, they are either with broader and vague definitions or with narrow perspectives that has made further application difficult. For instance, Greiner and Schein (1989: 46) adopted three categories to classify strategies, namely "using social networks", "playing it straight" and "going around the formal system." "Using social networks" includes establishing alliances and coalitions, dealing directly with key decision-makers, etc. "Playing it straight" involves using data to convince others, being persistent, and focusing on the needs of a target group. "Going around the formal system" is concerned with working around obstacles preventing progress, not necessarily using organisational rules. These three aspects of the model could not be distinguished clearly one from another, and two or three different strategies may be adopted at the same time. For example, the "playing it straight" of the strategy sometimes involves using social networks.

Furthermore, several other models have been proposed, including linear strategy, adaptive strategy, and interpretative strategy (Thompson, 1993: 20).

Linear strategy focuses on achieving goals. Adaptive strategy is concerned with the development of the relationship between the firm's capabilities and resources for exploring business opportunities. Interpretative strategy presumes that the firm and its environment are clearly correlated, and managers continually respond to changes in the industry to ensure the success of their business. These aspects of the three models are vague. Companies plan strategies mostly aimed at achieving business goals, but whether they are linear or non-linear it is difficult to judge. For example, Helms, Dibrell & Wright (1997) found that there is not a linear relationship between competitive strategies and business performance and demonstrated that the adoption of a low cost strategy and differentiation is not inconsistent with higher profitability.

Moreover, MacMillam (1998) applied the game theory to strategic development. Game theory focuses on the reaction of other players in a particular situation, i.e., a company must pay careful attention to its competitors. This model is narrowly focused, concentrating on competitors and ignoring the business environment, company capabilities, and other relevant factors.

Therefore, these models are not appropriate to this research. Many academics (Bauer & Colgan 2001; Bennett, 1996: 66; Bowman, 1990: 54, 1992: 65; Bowman and Johnson, 1992; Dobson & Starkey, 1993: 62-63; Dubrin & Ireland, 1993: 144; Fitzsimmons & Fitzsimmons, 1994: 46; Gunnigle & Moore 1994; Hit et al., 1997:123-131; Segal-Horn, 1992; Silva et al., 2000; Smith, Arnold & Bizzell, 1991:263) have subsequently applied Porter's model to develop and discuss strategic models. Until now, his model has been widely adopted by most scholars (Silva et al., 2000). As a result, Porter's generic strategic model is applied to this research.

Porter (1980: 13-41) argued that business level strategies should take into account the three generic strategies of cost leadership, differentiation, and focus. Overall cost leadership strategy focuses on producing a highly standardised product, with the aim of becoming the lowest cost producer in the industry, with the product being the cheapest in the market. Differentiation involves a firm producing clearly differentiated products for customers, that means they have a unique position in the market. Focus strategy targets a particular group of buyers or a geographical market.

Porter (1980: 42) emphasised that the three generic strategies can be altered, but no two strategies can be adopted at the same time. He regards being "stuck in the middle" of two strategies as an extremely poor strategic situation. Porter's argument is challenged by some researchers. They question the notion that the adoption of two strategies would lead to a company being "stuck in the middle" and the failure to develop a clear strategy.

For instance, Bowman (1990: 53-54; 1992: 64-83), and Pruet and Howard (1996) attempted to examine Porter's arguments. Bowman (1990: 53) states that a cost leadership strategy should consider the firm's skills and resources, structure and system, culture, style and values, because these factors determine whether the firm can adopt the strategy. He (1992: 64-83) believes that a firm may pursue the cost-leadership strategy and simultaneously differentiate its products. Bowman (1992:64-83) notes that Cronshaw, Davis and Kay (1990) also have ideas different from Porter. They agreed that a company frequently adopts different strategies in response to the market, particularly when the market competition is intense. Moreover, Pruet and Howard (1996) doubted the validity and utility of Porter's approach, which advocated a single generic strategy.

Similarly, Chan-Olmsted and Jamison (2000) argue that there are many strategic adoptions in media industries. In practice, Porter's three generic strategies cannot contain all the possible strategies available to communication businesses. They found, for example, more than three strategies generally adopted by telecommunication operators, such as focus, strategic alliances, cost leadership, best product differentiation, customer-solutions orientation, etc.

Although Porter's strategic model is used by many researchers and professionals, some of them argue that his model cannot be applied to all firms. Consequently, there is a need to examine Porter's model in the Taiwanese environment.

COMPANY SIZE, OPERATIONAL TYPE, OWNERSHIP STRUCTURE AND BUSINESS STRATEGY

Some studies have demonstrated that a company's ownership structure, operational type, and size have a strong relationship with business strategies (Bennett, 1996: 123; Hanly & Cheung, 1998; Mansfield, 1984; Owers, Carveth, & Alexander, 1993: 3-46; Ralph, 2000: 77; Tayeb, 1988: 42). Some researchers have studied the relationships between ownership structures or sizes and the company's performance (Aw & Batra, 1998; Han & Suk, 1998; Kawahara & Speece, 1994; Picard & Rimmer, 1999). A specific strategy can help a company to perform well. In fact, strategies and performance have a cause–effect relation. Thus, this research reviews the relevant literature.

Company Size

Company size is one of the factors affecting performance. The most widely accepted definition of company size is the number of its employees (Tayeb, 1988:14), as opposed to some scholars who define it according to its total revenues (e.g., Picard & Rimmer, 1999) or capital. Whatever the definition, company size is related to corporate strength and economies of scale. Sometimes, large companies become difficult to manage, because of their hierarchical structures and slow responses (Picard & Rimmer, 1999). Furthermore, a company with a hierarchical structure has different proceedings compared to a company with a flat structure in terms of strategic planning and decision-making (Mansfield, 1984: 138; Tayeb, 1988: 42–43). Finally, because of different organisational structures, the results of strategic choice and adoptions might be different. Large corporations usually have a complicated structure with built-in inefficiency; therefore, in the 1980s, there was a "wave"; many large companies restructured their organisations, reducing their size or changing the set of operations substantially in order to implement strategies efficiently (Owers et al., 1993: 3–46). In other words, company sizes are significantly related to strategies, as well as to a corporation's performance and operations.

Operational Type

Different operational types affect strategic formulations. For example, companies with multi-products may have competitive advantages in operations, including economies of scope, risk reduction, and complementary demand (Hanly & Cheung, 1998).

Ownership Structure

Top management teams (TMT) are involved in strategic formulations, as are shareholders (Bennett, 1996: 33). In fact, shareholders and founders exert powerful influences on a business, which means that one of the manager's most important tasks is to balance the various stakeholder groups' opinions (Lynch, 2000: 467). Consequently, the TMT considers the shareholders' interests, the resources and the capabilities of the company in formulating management decisions and allocating resources in order to accomplish business purposes or long-term objectives. Some studies have reported companies with different ownership structures have different strategies and performances (Kawahara & Speece, 1994; Han & Suk, 1998). For instance, Kawahara and Speece found that Japanese-owned firms founded in Hong Kong attempt to maintain their Japanese identities and give more weight to Japanese products.

As a consequence, these three factors—ownership structure, company size and operational type—all have influences on the strategic adoptions of a company in general. However, whether they affect the strategic formulations of the Taiwanese Satellite companies needs more research. Therefore, the hypotheses of this research are stated:

H1: Companies of different sizes have different business strategies.

H2: Companies with different operational types have different strategies.

H3: Companies with different ownership structures have different strategies.

RESEARCH METHODS

A survey is employed to collect the data of this research in order to examine the different strategies among those of companies with different operational types, company sizes and ownership structures. To ensure accurate results and analysis of the various types of business strategies, all the satellite channel companies were studied. Due to mergers and consolidation, there are now about 30 satellite channel companies.

Strategic choices and decisions are generally made by the most senior staff who are in charge of the strategic business unit (SBU) or top management team (TMT) that is normally responsible for the planning, organisation, leadership and control of the business (Das & Teng, 1999). These managers are assessed according to the overall financial performance of the business and their ability to establish strategic directions. These managers usually understand their strategies well; therefore, this research aims at the TMT of the Satellite channel companies in order to collect more specific information. Non-probability (purposive) sampling was adopted, and the members of the TMT of each company were sampled.

The composition of the TMT is different from one company to another. In the satellite channel companies, there are at least four departments involved in strategic decision-making, namely the programming department, the marketing department, the news department, and the planning department. According to company structures, the samples are within these companies giving a sample size of 3 to 4 for each company, and a total of 93 targets.

A questionnaire was designed for the survey. It was sent by mail or facsimile or administered face-to-face to company presidents (or chairmen), vice-presidents, general managers, managers of marketing departments, planning departments, marketing departments or news departments between January 1999 and June 1999. Seventy-five managers responded to the questionnaires, representing an individual response rate of 80.75% of the population. Twenty-nine of 30 companies were surveyed, representing a response rate of 96.67% of the population.

Operational Definitions

The operational definitions of the independent variables, operational type, company size and ownership structure are defined as follows:

The size of the company Large companies were categorised as having more than 120 employees, medium sized companies between 81 and 120 employees, smaller companies between 41 and 80, and smallest companies with fewer than 40 employees. The scales were used in this research as "1-40", "41-80", "81-120", and "above 121" staff.

The operational type of the company These were defined as single channel operation, multiple channel operation, or multiple system station operation (MS0).

The ownership structure of the company Indicated whether a firm was family-owned, multinational, diversified, singleton, or foreign. The definitions of these ownership structures are as follows:

- A family-owned company—the owners of the company are mostly from the same family.
- A domestic multinational group—a group involved in many different industries, playing an important role in Taiwanese economic development, and owned by Taiwanese entrepreneurs.
- Diversified ownership—a company with some linked businesses in the same or different industries, but its economic scale is smaller than multinational groups, and owners of the company are also diverse.
- A singleton type of ownership was defined as one in which the capital of the company is limited or without establishing any linked businesses or companies.
- Foreign ownership— the owners of the company are foreigners.

The questionnaire for the quantitative research included four parts: the style of the company, economic scale of the company, generic strategy of company and sample profile.

The measurement of Porter's (1980, 1985) generic strategy, "overall cost leadership", "differentiation", and "focus" derives Dess and Davis' (1984), and Bowman and Ambrosini's (1997) statements concerned with these three strategies. Managers were asked to state the extent to which they agreed with the statements, ranging from "strongly disagree" (1) to "strongly agree" (5). There are nine variables for examining the "overall cost leadership" strategy, seven for the "differentiation" strategy, and five for the "focus" strategy.

Factor analyses and reliable tests are used to examine the reliability and validity of the 21 variables of the strategic model. The results show that these variables can be classified into seven factors, which explain 69.624% of total variance (see Table 10.1), with a high validity.

Table 10.1: Explained Variance of 7 Factors of Porter's Strategic Model

Factor	Eigenvalue	Explained Variance	Cumulative Variance
Factor 1	2.973	14.158	14.158
Factor 2	2.318	11.036	25.194
Factor 3	2.300	10.953	36.147
Factor 4	2.154	10.256	46.403
Factor 5	1.863	8.871	55.274
Factor 6	1.519	7.232	62.506
Factor 7	1.495	7.118	69.624

The results of the factor analysis show that there are a minimum of seven different strategies adopted by these CATV companies (see Table 10.2). The results indicate that Porter's three generic strategies—overall cost leadership, differentiation, and focus—cannot contain all the strategies adopted. In other words, Porter's strategic model cannot fit these companies.

"Cronbach's alpha" examination was employed as a "reliability test" to confirm the internal consistency of each of the factors. Factor 6 did not achieve a reliability level of Alpha bigger than 0.5 ($\alpha = 0.2110$; see Table 10.3). It means the three variables of Factor 6 are not consistent and its validity can be challenged. Therefore, this factor is eliminated from subsequent discussions.

The six remaining factors are renamed according to the highest value or the characteristics of the set of the variables in each factor (see Table 10.2):

Factor 1 is explained by five variables: "focus on narrow targets" (explained value = .888), "narrow target, more competitive" (= .830), "focus on geographical markets" (= .662), "focus on particular buyers" (= .550), and "sale polices concern particular buyers" (= .530; see Table 10.2). This factor accounts for 13.85% of total variance with an Eigenvalue equal to 2.908 (see Table 10.1). The reliability test suggests that this factor has a high level of consistency ($\alpha = 0.8291$; see Table 10.3). Considering the highest value and characteristics of the set of variables, this factor is renamed "concentrated/focus strategy".

Table 10.2: Component Matrix of 7 Factors of Porter's Strategic Model

Variable /Factor	1	2	3	4	5	6	7
20 Focus on narrow targets	.888	-.157	-.112	-.193	.009	-.001	-.008
21 Narrow targets, more competitive	.830	.001	-.113	.001	-.005	.004	.103
17 Focus on geographical markets	.662	.339	.008	-.009	.001	-.005	-.006
19 Sale policies focus on particular buyers	.550	-.414	.483	.004	-.001	-.001	-.138
18 Channel focuses on particular buyers	.530	-.528	.378	-.007	-.001	-.009	-.209
16 Offer superior channels to compete with others	.008	.792	.009	-.003	-.008	-.009	.001
10 Emphasise distinctive channels in competition	-.007	.606	-.001	-.251	.319	.106	.154
11 Regularly develop new channels	-.163	.585	-.206	.002	-.179	.001	-.509
06 Monitor operations to keep costs under control	-.009	.103	.865	.009	.162	-.008	-.002
01 Emphasise on costs control	.148	-.003	.862	.008	.006	.003	.155
03 Make efforts to secure cost sources of supply	-.005	-.006	.416	.748	-.006	.136	-.115
04 Maintain maximum utilisation of resources	-.209	.003	.193	.721	.135	.004	-.256
13 Give new channels top priority	.002	.105	.136	-.720	-.007	.395	-.005
12 Offer unique channels enabling change	.002	.450	.151	-.546	.008	.239	-.002
08 To be the lowest cost producer	.172	.005	.009	.009	.722	.253	.006
05 Emphasise competitive price strategies	-.179	-.005	.179	.108	.720	-.179	-.159
09 Offer similar channels, compete on prices	.005	.006	-.001	-.110	.713	-.142	.258
02 Pressure to cut overheads	.206	.188	.009	.127	-.004	-.733	.101
15 Sales performance information is important	.145	.148	-.007	.005	-.001	.596	.461
07 Devote time and effort to improving efficiency	-.206	-.304	-.159	.117	.285	-.485	-.004
14 Our channel seldom changes	-.137	.006	.003	-.204	.108	-.002	.840

Table 10.3 (a): Reclassified Types of Business Strategies

Factors	Reliability Alpha	Reliability %
Factor 1 (Concentrated/focus strategy)	0.8219	82.19
20. Our programmes/channels focus on narrow targets/buyers/subscribers		
21. Because our programmes focus on narrow targets, we are more competitive, more effective or more efficient		
17. Our programmes/channels focus on a particular geographical market		
18. Our programme/channels focus on Particular buyers/subscribers		
19. Our company's sales policy always concerns particular buyers/subscribers		
Factor 2 (Distinctive Strategy)	0.5277	52.77
16. We aim to offer superior programmes/channels/services to those of our competitors		
10. We emphasise our distinctive programmes/channels/image in our marketing strategy		
11. We regularly develop new channels or significantly change the line of channels/service we offer		
Factor 3 (Cost-control strategy)	0.7761	77.61
1. We place considerable emphasis on the control of operating costs		
6. We carefully monitor operations to help keep costs under control		
Factor 4 (Cost/Resource maintenance strategy)	0.6606	66.06
3. We make extensive efforts to secure the cost sources of supply		
4. We try hard to maintain the maximum feasible utilisation of our capacity/resources		
13. We give the development of new programmes/channels/services top priority		
12. We try to offer unique programmes/channels/services enabling us to charge premium prices		
Factor 5 (Competitive-price strategy)	0.5968	59.68
8. We aim to be the lowest cost producer in our industry		
5. We emphasise competitive prices in our marketing strategy		
9. Because we offer very similar programmes/channels/services to our competitors;we try to maintain competitive prices		

N = 75

Table 10.3 (b): Reclassified Types of Business Strategies

Factors	Reliability Alpha	Reliability %
Factor 6 (eliminated)	0.2110	21.10
2. There is constant pressure here to cut the cost of overheads		
15. Information about sales performance is considered to be more important than cost control information		
7. As our customers are very price sensitive, we devote considerable time and effort into improving efficiency		
Factor 7 (Constant strategy)	0.9999	99.99
14. Our line of programmes/channels/services seldom change in a substantive manner		

N = 75

Factor 2 is explained by three variables: "offer superior channels to compete with others" (explained value = .792), "emphasise distinctive channel images of strategies" (= .606), and "regularly develop new channels" (= .585; see Table 10.2). This factor accounts for 11.12% of total variance with an Eigenvalue equal to 2.334 (see Table 10.1). The reliability test suggests that this factor possesses a high level of consistency (α = 0.5277; see Table 3). Considering the highest value and the characteristics of the set of variables, this factor is renamed "distinctive strategy".

Factor 3 is strongly influenced by two variables: "emphasise cost control" (explained value = .865) and "monitor operation to keep costs under control" (= .862; see Table 10.2). This factor accounts for 10.91% of total variance with an Eigenvalue equal to 2.290 (see Table 10.1). The reliability test suggests that this factor has a high level of consistency (α = 0.7761; see Table 10.3). This factor is renamed "cost-control strategy" in consideration of both the highest value and the characteristics of the set of variables.

Factor 4 is explained by four variables: "to secure cost sources of supply" (explained value = .748), "maintain maximum utilisation of resources" (= .721), "giving new programmes top priority" (= .720), and "offer unique channels enabling higher charges" (= .546; see Table 10.2). This factor accounts for 10.17% of total variance with an Eigenvalue equal to 2.136 (see Table 10.1). The reliability test suggests that this factor has a high level of consistency (α = 0.6606; see Table 10.3). Considering the highest value of the set of variables, this factor is renamed "cost/resource maintenance strategy".

Factor 5 is influenced by three variables: "to be the lowest cost producer" (explained value = .722), "emphasise competitive prices" (= .720), and "offer similar channels and maintain competitive prices" (= .713; see Table 10.2). This factor accounts for 8.79% of total variance with an Eigenvalue equal to 1.848 (see Table 1). The reliability test suggests that this factor has a high level of consistency (α=0.5968, see Table 3). After the highest value and characteristics of the set of variables, this factor is renamed "competitive-price strategy".

Factor 7 is explained by only one variable, i.e., "our line of programmes/ channels/ services seldom changes in a substantive manner" (explained value = .840; see Table 10.2). The factor accounts for 7.32% of total variance with an Eigenvalue equal to 1.538 (see Table 1). In consideration of both the value and the characteristics of the variable, this factor is renamed "constant strategy".

In summary, the result of the factor analysis shows that Porter's three types of generic business strategies—overall cost leadership, differentiation and focus—do not correspond with the business strategies of the Taiwanese CATV companies. The results show that there are at least seven strategies adopted by the CATV channel companies.

DATA ANALYSIS

Of the 29 satellite channel companies surveyed, five companies employ fewer than 40 (17.25%) staff, the lowest number of employees being 6. Twelve companies (41.38%) employ more than 121 staff. Twenty-three (79.30%) out of 29 are completely Taiwanese owned. Eight of 29 companies are with the singleton type of ownership structure, seven companies are with the foreign type, six are with the family type, six are with the diversified type, and only two of 29 companies are with the multinational type (see Table 10.4).

With respect to operational types, about 45% (13) provide one channel to their subscribers, nearly 50% (14) provide multiple channels, and about 6% (2) provide multiple channels and also operate stations. The capital of 19 (65.50%) of the companies is under NT$ 300 million (under US$ 8.57 million), but the capital of eight (27.50%) of the companies is higher than NT$ 501 million (US$ 14.31 million).

Table 10.4: Satellite Channel Companies

Variables	Frequencies (Co.)	Percentage (%)
Company Size		
1–40 staff	5	17.25
41–80 staff	8	27.58
81–120 staff	4	13.79
120+ staff	12	41.38
Company Owners		
All the shareholders are from Taiwan	23	79.40
Some shareholders are not from Taiwan	3	10.30
No shareholders are from Taiwan	3	10.30
Ownership Structure		
Family	6	20.70
Multinational	2	6.80
Diversified	6	20.70
Singleton	8	27.60
Foreign	7	24.20
Operational Type		
Single channel	13	44.82
Multiple channel	14	48.28
2 channel	6	
3 channel	2	
4 channel	1	
5 channel	2	
5+ channel	3	
Multiple Channel and Station	2	6.90
1 Station	0	
2 Stations	0	
3 Stations	0	

4 Stations	0	
5 Stations	0	
5+ Stations	2	
Programme Sources (Multiple)		
In-house productions	9	
Bought copyright of films, videos, programmes	7	
In-house and bought copyright of programmes	14	
Bought copyright of all channels	3	
Company Capital		
Under NT$ 101 million (35 =US$)	9	31.00
About NT$ 101-200 million	6	20.70
About NT$ 201-300 million	4	13.80
About NT$ 301-400 million	1	3.40
About NT$ 401-500 million	1	3.40
About NT$ 501-600 million	5	17.20
Over NT$ 601 million	3	10.30

N = 29

Business Strategy

In terms of business strategies, the results of frequencies indicate the total business strategies in the satellite channel companies. Overall, the results show that these respondents disagree with (Mode = 2; see Table 10.5) the following statements:

- "Our programmes/channels focus on narrow targets/buyers/ subscribers".
- "Because our programmes/channels focus on narrow targets, we are more competitive, more effective or more efficient".
- "Our programmes/channels focus on a particular geographical market".
- "Our programmes/channels/subscribers focus on particular buyers/ subscribers".
- "Our company's sales policy always focuses on particular buyers/ subscribers".
- "We aim to be the lowest cost producer in our industry; we emphasise competitive prices as part of our marketing strategy".
- "Because we offer very similar programmes/channels/services to our competitors, we try to maintain competitive prices".
- "There is constant pressure here to cut the cost of overheads"

Almost all of the respondents (97.40 %) "make extensive efforts to secure of the cost sources of supply", "carefully monitor operations to keep costs under control" (94.60 %), "place considerable emphasis on the control of operating costs" (94.00 %), and "try hard to maintain the maximum feasible utilisation of capacity/resources (92.00 %)". The results indicate that most respondents tend to control costs.

On the other hand, over half the number of the respondents disagree and strongly disagree that their programmes/channels focus on a particular geographical market (69.30%), or that "their programmes focus on particular buyers/subscribers" (69.30%). The results show that over half the number of respondents do not focus on a particular geographical market nor particular buyers or subscribers. Most respondents tend to promote their channels to wider scopes of markets.

The frequency results only show that overall business strategies are adopted by these satellite channel companies. For further analysis, the model needs to be tested by using other statistics methods in order to classify its dimensions.

Table 10.5: Frequency Results of Business Strategies

Variables	Strong Disagree	Disagree	No Idea	Agree	Strong Agree	Mode	Std. Dev
1. We place considerable emphasis on the control of operating costs	1.30 (1)	4.00 (3)	2.70 (2)	76.00 (57)	16.00 (12)	4	.688
2. There is constant pressure here to cut the cost of overheads	1.30 (1)	53.30 (40)	4.10 (2)	36.00 (27)	5.30 (4)	2	.639
3. We make extensive efforts to secure the cost sources of supply	0.00 (0)	1.30 (1)	1.30 (1)	86.70 (65)	10.70 (8)	4	4.14
4. We try hard to maintain the maximum feasible utilisation of our capacity/resources	0.00 (0)	4.00 (3)	4.00 (3)	80.00 (60)	12.00 (9)	4	.570
5. We emphasise competitive prices in our marketing strategy	2.70 (2)	45.00 (34)	8.00 (6)	40.00 (30)	4.00 (3)	2	1.045
6. We carefully monitor operations to help us keep costs under control	1.30 (1)	2.70 (2)	1.30 (1)	85.30 (64)	9.30 (7)	4	.581
7. As our customers are very price sensitive, we devote considerable time and effort into improving our efficiency	1.30 (1)	14.90 (11)	6.80 (5)	67.60 (50)	9.50 (7)	4	.890
8. We aim to be the lowest cost producer in our industry	5.40 (4)	58.10 (43)	5.40 (4)	29.70 (22)	1.40 (1)	2	1.015
9. Because we offer very similar programmes/ channels/ services to our competitors, we try to maintain competitive price	6.70 (5)	56.00 (42)	14.70 (11)	21.30 (15)	1.30 (1)	2	.949

Table 5 Continued Variables	Strong Disagree	Disagree	No Idea	Agree	Strong Agree	Mode	Std. Dev
10. We emphasise our distinctive programmes/channels/ image in our marketing campaigns	0.00 (0)	2.70 (2)	8.10 (6)	71.60 (53)	17.60 (13)	4	.607
11. We regularly develop new channels or significantly change the line of channels/ service we offer	1.30 (0)	13.30 (10)	9.30 (7)	69.30 (53)	6.70 (5)	4	.844
12.We try to offer unique programmes/channels /services enabling us to charge premium prices	0.00 (0)	16.00 (12)	8.00 (6)	63.50 (47)	12.20 (9)	4	.844
13. We give the development of new programmes/channels/ service top priority	0.00 (0)	14.90 (11)	12.20 (9)	62.20 (46)	10.80 (8)	4	.859
14. Our line of programmes/ channels/services seldom change in a substantive manner	2.70 (2)	44.00 (33)	4.00 (3)	45.00 (34)	4.00 (3)	4	1.084
15. Information about sales performance is considered to be more important than cost control information	0.00 (0)	21.60 (16)	12.20 (9)	58.10 (43)	8.10 (6)	4	.925
16. We aim to offer superior programmes/channels/services to those of our competitors	1.30 (1)	5.30 (4)	6.70 (5)	64.00 (48)	22.70 (17)	4	.797
17. Our programmes/channels are focus on particular geographical market	9.30	60.00	5.30	24.00	1.30	2	1.005
18. Our programmes/channels focus on particular buyers/ subscribers	5.30 (4)	50.70 (38)	4.00 (3)	34.70 (26)	5.30 (4)	2	1.128
19. Our company's sales policy always focuses on particular buyers/ subscribers	5.30	58.70	9.30	28.00	4.00	2	1.060
20. Our programmes/channels are focus on narrow targets/ buyers / subscribers	9.30	60.00	5.30	24.00	1.30	2	1.005
21. Because our programme focuses on narrow target, we are more competitive, more effective or more efficient	12.00	51.40	13.50	20.30	2.70	2	1.037

N = 75, % (Person)

Company Size

One-way ANOVA is utilised to examine whether the companies of different sizes tend to adopt different strategies. The results demonstrate that companies of different sizes tend to adopt different strategies and the results are shown here (see Table 10.6):

Table 10.6: Company Size and Business Strategies

Strategy	Company Size (No. of staff)	Mean Difference	Standard Error	Sig.
Concentrated/	1 – 40	3.578	1.526	*
Focus	41- 80	-3.578	1.526	*
	81-120	-4.111	1.792	*
	121+	-4.694	1.417	***
Distinctive	1 – 40	-1.743	.609	**
	41- 80	1.743	.609	**
	81-120	.778	.709	--
	121+	1.652	.559	**
Cost-control	1 – 40	1.116	.447	*
	41- 80	-1.116	.447	*
	81-120	.894	.447	*
	121+	-.694	.414	--
Competitive-price	1 – 40	.744	.878	--
	41- 80	-.744	.878	--
	81-120	2.083	.815	*
	121+	-2.083	.815	*
Constant	1 – 40	-1.000	.499	*
	41- 80	.417	.425	--
	81-120	1.000	.499	*
	121+	.856	.393	*

* = $P < 0.05$, ** = $P < 0.01$, ***= < 0.001

Companies with 1-40 staff: The "concentrated/focus" (Mean difference = 3.578, Std. Error = 1.527, $P < 0.05$), "cost-control" (Mean difference = 1.116, Std. Error = .447, $P < 0.05$), "distinctive" (Mean difference = 1.743, Std. Error = .609, $P < 0.01$) and "constant" strategies (Mean difference = -1.000, Std. Error = .499, $P < 0.05$) are significantly different for companies of different sizes. This indicates that companies with 1–40 staff tend to adopt "cost-control", "concentrated/focus" and "distinctive" strategies, but not "constant strategies".

Companies with 41-80 staff: these companies have significantly different strategies from others in terms of "concentrated/focus" (Mean difference = -

3.578, Std. Error = 1.526, P < 0.05), "cost-control" (Mean difference = -1.116, Std. Error = .447, P < 0.05), and "distinctive" (Mean difference = 1.743, Std. Error = 0.609, P < 0.01). This indicates that companies with 41–80 staff tend to adopt "distinctive strategies", but not "concentrated/focus" or "cost-control strategies".

Companies with 81–120 staff: These companies adopt "concentrated/focus" (Mean difference = -4.111, Std. Error = 1.792, P < 0.05), "cost-control" (Mean difference = .894, Std. Error = .447, P < 0.05), "competitive-price" (Mean difference = 2.083, Std. Error = .815, P < 0.05), and "constant" (Mean difference = 1.000, Std. Error = .499, P<0.05) strategies significantly differently from other companies. They tend to adopt "cost-control", "competitive-price", and "constant strategies", but not "concentrated/focus strategies".

Companies with more than 121 staff: These firms adopt "concentrated/focus" (Mean difference = -4.694, Std. Error = 1.417, P < 0.001), "distinctive" (Mean difference = 1.652, Std. Error = .559, P < 0.01), "competitive-price" (Mean difference = -2.083, Std. Error = .815, P < 0.05), and "constant" strategies (Mean difference = .856, Std. Error = .393, P < 0.05) significantly differently from other companies. They tend to adopt "distinctive" and "constant strategies", but not "concentrated/focus" or "competitive-price strategies".

Consequently, hypothesis 1, which states that companies of different sizes have different business strategies, can be accepted.

Operational Types

Hypothesis 2 states that companies with different operational types have different business strategies. This is tested using one-way ANOVA, and the significant results are shown in Table 10.7.

Table 10.7: Different Operational Types and Business Strategies

Factors	Operation types	Mean Std. Difference Error	Significance
Concentrated Strategy	Single	3.927 1.868	*
	Multiple	2.007 0.938	*
	MSO	-3.923 1.868	*

N = 75, *P < 0.05; **P < 0.01; ***P < 0.001

Only the "concentrated/focus strategy" is significantly different within single, multiple channels and MSO companies compared with other types of strategy (Mean difference = 3.927, Std. Error = 0.868, P < 0.05; Mean difference = 2.007, Std. Error = 0.938, P < 0.05 and Mean difference = -3.923, Std. Error =1.868, P < 0.05 respectively). Therefore there is insufficient evidence to support hypothesis 2, which states that companies with different operational types have different business strategies.

Ownership Structure

The results of the differences between different ownership structures and business strategies are shown in Table 10.8.

Table 1o.8: Ownership Structures and Business Strategies

Factors	Ownership Type	Mean Difference	Std. Error	Significance
Competitive-price Strategy	Family	-0.465	1.034	--
	Multinational	0.465	1.034	--
	Diversified	-2.008	0.782	*
	Singleton	0.775	1.048	--
	Foreign	2.008	0.782	*
Constant Strategy	Family	0.900	0.442	**
	Multinational	-0.900	0.442	**
	Diversified	-1.365	0.337	**
	Singleton	1.262	0.451	**
	Foreign	1.125	0.326	**

N = 75, *P < 0.05; **P < 0.01; ***P < 0.001

Family ownership structure Only "constant strategy" (Mean difference = 0.900, Std. Error = 0.442, P < 0.01) in the family-owned companies is significantly different from other ownership structures. This indicates that the companies with family ownership tend to adopt "constant strategies".

Multinational ownership structure Only "constant strategy" (Mean difference = -0.900, Std. Error = 0.442, P < 0.01) in multinational-type companies is significantly different from companies with other ownership structures. This indicates that multinationals are less likely to adopt "constant strategies".

Diversified ownership structure Two business strategies, "competitive-price strategy" (Mean difference = -2.008, Std. Error = 0.782, P < 0.05) and "constant strategy" (Mean difference = -1.365, Std. Error = 0.337, P < 0.01) are significantly different in diversified companies compared to other types of companies. This indicates that diversified companies are less likely to adopt "competitive-price" and "constant strategies".

Singleton ownership structure Only "competitive-price strategy" (Mean difference = 1.262, Std. Error = 0.451, P < 0.01) is significantly different in single companies compared with other companies. Companies with the singleton type of ownership tend to adopt "competitive strategies" as opposed to diversified companies.

Foreign ownership structure "Competitive-price strategy" (Mean difference = 2.008, Std. Error = 0.782, P < 0.05) and "constant strategy" (Mean difference = 1.125, Std. Error = 0.326, P < 0.01) are significantly different among foreign companies. The results indicate that foreign companies tend to adopt "competitive-price" and "constant strategies".

The results presented in Tables 10.8 show that companies with differing ownership structures adopt different business strategies. This does not apply to all, however, so there is no strong evidence to support hypothesis 3: companies with different ownership structures have significantly different business strategies.

DISCUSSION

The results show that Porter's model of three generic strategies can be classified into seven different strategies. It means that Porter's model cannot fit well into these Taiwanese satellite channel companies. Although the new classification is closer to the business strategies of these companies, it still has its constraints in reflecting the actual strategies of these companies. This may be the result of the model which is based on the western perspectives—in a way, lack of the eastern consideration. Moreover, the results of this research may be a general or aggregated result from the interviewees' responses, so some Taiwanese aspects and industrial characteristics may not have been reflected in the statistical results. This indicates that there is a need to build up a strategic model that is suitable for measuring business strategies of the Taiwanese media companies. This research suggests that adopting an in-depth interview approach and taking into account Taiwanese perspectives of strategic adoptions could establish a new strategic model that would have higher validity and reliability and be closer to the real conditions of these companies.

The results show that most respondents (over 90%) tend to control costs. The reasons could include several points: firstly, because of the Taiwan is facing economic recessions and intense satellite market competition. For them, it is difficult to estimate returns and profits, therefore, most respondents adopt the cost control strategy in response to the trends of the merger and consolidation. Secondly, some Taiwanese companies are less likely to adopt definite strategies than western ones (Huang, 1999), and tend to invest in business conservatively, thus, undoubtedly they generally adopt cost control strategies. The results indicate that confronting with changeable investing environments, most Taiwanese entrepreneurs tend to adopt cost control strategies.

However, most respondents tend to control costs that would affect their strategic formulations. This research must emphasise that cost control is not only choices. Most successful strategies can give a firm unique position in the market, or can strengthen the competitive advantages (Haberberg & Rieple, 2001: 32), suggesting that entrepreneurs and respondents would attach importance to strategic planning and estimate the advantages and disadvantages of strategies, using defensive or offensive strategy, not only seeking to control costs.

The hypothesis that companies of different sizes have different business strategies, could be accepted (H1). In comparison, the results of this research are efficient in supporting hypotheses 2 and 3, that companies with different operational types have different strategies and companies with different ownership structures have different strategies. The results demonstrate that company sizes are the most important in affecting business strategies among these factors.

This research found that companies of the smallest sizes (1–40 staff) tend to focus on particular subscribers and buyers, or particular geographical viewers, and emphasise costs control (see Table 10.6). These companies usually change their programmes/channels/services in a substantive manner frequently in order to find out better strategies for their companies. In other words, smaller companies tend to focus their resources on achieving particular goals or targeting certain group of viewers, adopting defensive and lower risk strategies. These might be also related to the scale of companies that afford them to be more flexible. On the other hand, companies of the biggest sizes (more than 120 staff) tend to differentiate their channels, maintain their channel characteristics, but not compete on price. These companies tend to adopt long-term strategies and establish their product images. Obviously, companies of the two sizes have significantly different strategies.

In terms of operational types, there are not many significant differences among companies with single, multiple and MSOs types, only the "concentrated/focus" strategy is different (see Table 10.7). Companies with single and multiple channel operational types tend to focus on special viewers, but not MSOs.

Essentially, the MSOs can be seen as multi-product firms. These companies may have broader strategies for their diversified products, and have some advantages, including bigger economies of scope, risk reduction, and complementary demand, compared to single-product firms (Hanly & Cheung, 1998). Similarly, a single-channel operational company can be seen as a single-product firm. They normally concentrate more on their single product, and adopt a specialised or concentrated strategy in response to their competitors. The results show significant differences between the two different operational types: companies with the single-channel operational type tend to adopt concentrated/focus strategies, unlike MSOs, which adopt various strategies.

In Taiwan, not only large firms are able to provide multiple products; small and medium firms can also do so in different geographical markets (Aw & Batra, 1998), e.g. adopting concentrated/focus strategies. It is noteworthy that the multi-system operators (MSOs, owning stations and channels) adopt offensive strategies. In contrast to the other types of companies, MSOs have much more resources than either multi- or single-channel operators, although there may be other different business strategies, which have not been found by using statistical analyses. This research suggests that utilising a qualitative approach might explore more differences.

With respect to ownership structure, companies with the family type of ownership tend to adopt the "constant strategy" (see Table 10.8). Harris and Ogbonna (1999) found that a structured process of strategic formulation does not occur in family-owned companies, with the strategic direction largely being determined by the present chief executive officer. Other members of management find it difficult to participate in the strategic decision-making process. A reason could be that these companies tend to adopt "constant strategies", and "seldom change their programmes or channels in a substantive manner". Adversely, multinationals and diversified companies usually have hierarchical structures of organisations, and might have more members in the TMTs. Thus, they are less likely to adopt "constant strategies". Foreign companies tend to compete prices, which could be an efficient strategy for new entries and easier to get into the market. Moreover, foreign companies may have to do more marketing research and invest more to understand the Taiwanese market. If they only adopt competitive-price strategies, they may be able to distribute their products (channels) universally in a short term.

This research suggests that companies with the family and singleton types of ownership could apply more strategies in responses the market. For a long-term plan, foreign companies could not only compete prices, but also do more research for understanding the local market.

CONCLUSION

A strategic model can help entrepreneurs to rethink their strategic formulation. However, Porter's model cannot fit into Taiwanese satellite companies; there is a need to establish a new strategic model with eastern business organisations. This research suggests that to adopt a qualitative approach and consider the industrial characteristics and business environment to build up a strategic model for understanding the Taiwanese satellite businesses.

This research found that company size is the most influential factor of business strategies compared to the factors of operational types and ownership structures. The investigation is valuable for professionals who can forecast their competitors' strategies. Although there are few different strategies adopted by the companies with different operational types and ownership structures, there might be some strategies that have not been explored by statistical analyses, suggesting that professionals still cannot ignore the two factors.

The findings are meaningful for both academics and professionals for understanding strategic adoptions of the satellite channel companies in Taiwan. In particular for professionals, the results are helpful for forecasting their competitors' business strategies. For future research, in order to have different perspectives to examine and understand the media operations, the issues and topics of competitive positions, performances, business cultures, and decision-making should be considered in the research.

REFERENCES

Aw, B.Y., & Batra, G. (1998) Firm size and the pattern of diversification. *International Journal of Industrial Organisation*, Vol. 16 (3), p313-331.

Bailey, A., & Johnson, G. (1992) How strategy develop in organisations. In Faulkner, D., & Johnson, G (ed.) *The challenge of strategic management*. P84 – 96. London: Kogan Page Ltd.

Bauer, C., & Colgan, J. (2001) Planning for electronic commerce Strategy: An explanatory study from the financial services sector. *Logistics Information Management*, Vol. 14 (1/2), p 24-32.

Bennett, R. (1996) *Corporate strategy and business planning*. London: Pitman Publishing.

Bowmman, C., & Ambrosini, V. (1997) Perceptions of strategic priorities, consensus and firm performance. *Journal of Management Studies*, Vol. 34 (2), p241-258.

Bowman, C. (1990) *The essence of strategic management*. London: Prentice Hall International Limited.

Bowman, C. (1992) Interpreting competitive strategy. In Faulkner, D., and Johnson, G. (ed.) *The challenge of strategic management*. P84-96. London: Kogan Page Ltd.

Chan-Olmsted, S., & Jamison, M.A. (2000) Rivalry through alliances: Competitive strategy in the global telecommunications market. Time and Media Markets Conference, Pamplona, Spain, 4-5th May.

Chandler, A. D. (1962) *Strategy and structure: Chapters in history of the industry enterprise*. London: MIT Press.

Child, J. (1972) Organisational structure, environment, and performance: The role of strategic choice. *Sociology*, Vol. 6, p1-22.

China Time Express (1990), 24th of September. P3.

Chisnall, M.P. (1995) *Strategic business marketing*. Hertfordshire: Prentice Hall International.

Das, T.K., & Teng, B.S. (1999) Cognitive biases and strategic decision processes: An integrative perspective. *Journal of Management Studies*, Vol. 36 (6), p757-778.

Dobson, P., & Starkety, K. (1993) *The strategic management blueprint*. Oxford: Blackwell Publishers.

Dubrin, A.J., & Ireland, R.D. (1993) *Management & organisation*. Ohio: South-Western Publishing Co.

Faulkner, D., & Johnson, G. (ed.) (1992). Introduction. *The challenge of strategic management*, p17-22. London: Kogan Page Ltd.

Feng, C. (1998) *Big media*. Taiwan: Meta Media International Co. Ltd.

Fitzsimmons, J.A., & Fitzsimmons, M.J. (1994) *Service management for competitive advantage*. McGraw-Hill, Inc.

Greiner, L.E., & Schein, V.E. (1989) *Power and organization development: Mobilizing power to implement change*. USA: Addison-Wesley Publishing Company, Inc.

Gunnigle, P., & Moore, S. (1994) Linking business strategy and human resource management: Issue and implications. *Personnel Review*, Vol. 23 (1), p63-84.

Haberberg, A., & Rieple, A. (2001) *The strategic management of organisations*. England: Pearson Education Limited.

Han, K.C., & Suk, D.Y., (1998) The effect of ownership structure on firm performance: additional evidence. *Review of Financial Economics*, Vol. 7(2), p143-155.

Hanly, D., & Cheung, K.C.K. (1998) Market structure of multi-product firms under free entry. *Economic Letters*, Vol. 61 (2), p159-163.

Harris, L.C., & Ogbonna, E. (1999) The strategic legacy of company founders. *Long Range Planning*, Vol. 32 (3), p333-343.

Helms, M.M., Dibrell, C., & Wright, P. (1997) Competitive strategies and business performance: Evidence from the adhesive and sealant industry. *Management Design*, Vol. 35 (9), p689-703.

Hit, M.A., Ireland, R.D., & Hoskisson, R.E. (1997) *Strategic management: Competitiveness and globalisation*. New York: West Publishing Company.

Huang, T.C. (1999) Who shall follow? Factors affecting the adoption of succession plans in Taiwan. *Long Rang Planning*, Vol. 32 (6), p609-616.

Hunt, S.D., & Lambe, C.J. (2000) Marketings contribution to business strategy: Market orienation, relatoinship marketing and resource-advantage theory. *International Journal of Management Review*, Vol. 2(1), p17-43.

Kawahara, Y., & Speece, M. (1994) Strategies of japanese supermarkets in Hong Kong. *International Journal of Retail & Distribution Management*, Vol.22 (8),

Kay, J. (1993) *Foundations of corporate success*. Oxford: Oxford University Press.

Liu, S. (1996) *Satellite operational strategy and promotions in Taiwan*. Taipei: Chinese Culture University, Master degree thesis.

Liu, Y.L. (1997) *Multiple channel television and viewer*. Taipei: Shi-Yin Publishing Inc.

Lorange, P., & Vancil, R.F. (1976) How to design a strategic planning system. *Harvard Business Review*, Vol. 54, p75-81.

Lynch, R. (2000) *Corporate ctrategy*. Second Edition. Edinburgh: Pearson Education Limited.

MacMillam, K. (1998) Strategy and organisation. *Manager Update*. Vol.1, (3), Spring. P1-13.

Mansfield, R. (1984) Formal and informal structure. In Gruneberg, M. and Wall, T. (Ed.) *Social psychology and organisational behaviour*, p119-147. Scotland: John Wiley and Sons Ltd.

McCarthy, D.J., Markides, C., & Mintzberg, H. (2000) View from the top: Henry Mintzberg on strategy and management/commentary/response. *Academy of Management Executive*, Vol. 14 (3), p30-42.

McGrath-Champ, S. (1999) Strategy and industrial restructing, *Progress in Human Geography*, Vol. 23 (2), 236-252.

Mintzberg, H. (1978) Patterns in strategy formation. *Management Science*, Vol. 24, p934-48.

Mintzberg, H. (1987) The strategy concept I: Five Ps for strategy. *California Management Review*, Vol.30, p 11-24.

Mintzberg, H. (1994) *The rise and fall of strategic planning*. New York: Prentice Hall.

Mintzberg, H., & Frances, W. (2000) Sustaining the institutional environment. *Organisation Studies*, Vol. (21), p71-94.

Owers, J., Carveth, R., & Alexander, A. (1993) An introduction to media economic theory and practice. In Alexander, A., Owers, J., & Carveth, R. (Eds.) *Media economics: theory and practice*, pp. 3-46. New Jersey: Lawrence Erlbaum Associates.

Picard, R.G., & Rimmer, T. (1999) Weathering a recession: Effects of size and diversification on newspaper companies. *The Journal of Media Economics*, Vol. 12 (1), p1-18.

Porter, M.E. (1980) *Competitive strategy*. New York: Macmillan Publishing Co., Inc.

Pruet, M., & Howard, T. (1996) Thinking about quality and its links with strategic management. *European management*, Vol. 14(1), p37-46.

Ralph, D.S. (2000) *Strategic management & organisational dynamics*. 3rd edition. Edinburgh: Person Education Limited.

Segal-Horn, S. (1992) How strategy develops in organisations. In Faulkner, D., and Johnson, G. (ed.) *The challenge of strategic management*. P84-96. London: Kogan Page Ltd.

Silva, G., Lisboa, J., & Yasin, M. (2000) Effectiveness of business strategies in the Portuguese culture: An empirical investigation. *Cross Cultural Management*, Vol. 7 (4), p 33-40.

Smith, G.D., Arnold, D.R. & Bizzell, B.G. (1991) *Business strategy and policy*. Third edition. Boston: Houghton Mifflin Company.

Tayeb, M.H. (1988) *Organisations and national culture: A comparative analysis*. London: SAGE Publication, Inc.

Thompson, J. (1993) *Strategic management: Awareness and change*. London: Chapman & Hall.

Taiwan Daily (1999) 16th of January. P2.

Tsaur, C.J. (1995) Competition of satellite TV and CATV. Taipei: *The China Times*, 19th April.

Yang, C.H., Kwan, C.Z., & Mai, L.C. (1996) The feasibility ofrRunning a CATV by China Times Press Corporation within the electronic media. Taipei: China Time Press Corporation.

Chapter 11
An Assessment of the
Broadband Media Strategies
of Western European Telecoms

David H. Goff
University of Southern Mississippi

This analysis examines the broadband strategies of the four major Western European telecommunication service providers: British Telecom (BT), Deutsche Telekom (DT), France Télécom (FT), and Telefónica. According to Goff (2000b), new income from Internet-related services offset revenue lost to telecoms due to deregulation and subsequent price competition in such core areas as long distance and international connections, former profit centres that had partially subsidised the cost of providing local service. Broadband Internet access is considered to be the key to unleashing the Internet's full potential and a critical core business for incumbent telecoms. Telecoms had been offering broadband access to business customers for many years before the emergence of the public Internet. Unlike the earlier forms of premium-priced access that required special lines, telecoms now offer ADSL (asymmetric digital subscriber line) mass-market broadband access at flat rates via their existing copper wire network. Broadband connections are fast, "always on," and theoretically enable the Internet to deliver a wide range of media services (e.g., interactive games and digital video entertainment content, including video-on-demand as well as video conferencing) while also meeting the data needs of small-to-medium size enterprises (SMEs). Broadband connections encourage longer online sessions that lead to higher levels of e-commerce activity. According to Virtel (2001), "the race is on in Europe to become the first country to develop a large-scale broadband infrastructure and hence—and this is what it's all about—to attract call centres, Internet and other technology companies (p. 2)." Broadband access in Europe has been largely controlled by the incumbent telecoms. These firms have been methodically deploying broadband technology, but have been extremely slow to open their networks to competitors. Consumers in most markets have few, if any, choices. Despite these factors, though, consumer uptake of broadband services gained momentum in 2001. Jupiter MMXI asserts that critical mass for broadband in Europe will be achieved when market penetration reaches 15% of all households. This level is not expected until 2006 (Jupiter MMXI, 2001).

As former national monopolies, the four firms analysed in this study enjoy significant economic advantages in wireline telephony, Internet access, and the provision of data services to business; they also compete as major players in domestic and regional wireless communication. Despite their position of privilege, the four companies have experienced rapid and significant change driven by the primary forces of the ongoing convergence of communications technologies and industries: technology, privatisation, deregulation, and competition. While sharing some common characteristics and objectives, each firm has developed somewhat different convergence strategies, appropriate to the specific economic and political conditions within each home nation, but responsive to the pan-European directives and initiatives of the European Union (Laffont & Tirole, 2001). Analysis of these strategies begins with a brief overview of each firm, covering its primary lines of business and organisational structure, and progresses to an assessment of the firm's overall convergence strategies. The primary analysis follows, focusing upon the broadband strategies of each company, addressing the rollout of broadband access services, the actions of competitors, and consumer response. Broadband serves several functions, including data exchange by small-to-medium sized enterprises (SMEs) and the delivery of information content to businesses and consumers. Therefore, the study also examines the efforts of these telecoms to both compete and partner with traditional and new media in the creation and delivery of information and entertainment content.

A SHORT HISTORY OF
WESTERN EUROPEAN TELECOMS

Worldwide, telephone services operated as monopoly enterprises throughout most of the 20th century. In the United States the dominant firm (AT&T) was privately owned, but in most countries telephony was combined with telegraphy and postal services under a PTT (Postal, Telephone, and Telegraph) model. By the 1980s a worldwide re-evaluation of national telecoms was in progress. As a result of the post-WWII shift to an information-based economy and the diffusion of computer (digital) technology, telecommunications systems carried increasing amounts of data in addition to voice traffic. It had become evident that national monopolies were heavily vested in legacy copper wire technologies and inefficient at adapting to change. New firms emerged and clamoured to introduce new high-capacity digital network technologies designed to serve the changing needs of the information-intensive business sector. Starting with the formation of British Telecom in the United Kingdom in 1981, European governments began first to separate telecommunications operations from the PTT structure, and then to authorise limited competition with the government-owned firms (Harper, 1997; Noam, 2001). A decade later national and pan-national (European Union and International Telecommunications Union) policymakers had recognised the developing global information society and were calling for increased competitiveness in the telecommunication sector (Goff, 2000a).

From the mid-1980s onward, national monopoly telecoms were privatised throughout Western Europe. The Internet emerged from the private sector, and its Internet Protocol (IP) quickly became the network technology of choice for the growing number of companies recently licensed to unleash the forces of competition in the telecoms sector of the economy. Wireless mobile services proliferated throughout the region. Cable television firms were licensed to provide competing local telephone services to residences and businesses and soon added Internet access. During this decade, telecommunications services evolved from providers of local and long distance telephony to become full-service integrated communications networks, and from national systems to an interconnected "network of networks," (Noam, 2001, p. 1).

At the beginning of the 21st century the tripartite forces of convergence (technology, economics, and politics) created a set of conditions generally shared by the former national telecoms of Western Europe. In economic terms, telecoms have been forced to adjust to the new competitive landscape. This required substantial investment in new technologies and a realignment of lines of business, changes that impacted the earnings of each firm. The former national telecoms have been forced to offer new services while protecting their legacy core lines of business (Zerdick et al., 2000). These core activities and competencies are significant. In each country the former national monopolist telecom connects the vast majority of telephony and data communications users to the rest of the world. This ownership of the local loop, the so-called "last mile" of the network, is vitally important to the dominant telecoms and to their competitors and regulators. Because of their longevity, the dominant telecoms have evolved long-standing business relationships with their customers, an extensive array of international business alliances, and a strong reputation for customer service, network reliability, and network security. As former components of national government (generally still owned in part by governments), these firms retain considerable political influence. Building new or rebuilding old network infrastructure to 21st century standards is a costly undertaking, and the former national telecoms enjoy distinct advantages over their rivals in their financial resources and access to financial markets (Zerdick et al., 2000).

The competitive advantages of these firms is at the heart of regulatory and policy initiatives in the region. For meaningful competition to exist in telecommunications new firms must connect their networks to customer premises. This can only happen if the new competitors either build their own "last mile" access or "rent" the last mile access from a former national telecom. The European Union (EU) ordered that domestic telephone monopolies would cease on January 1, 1998. Despite the EU mandate, the record of progress in each country is different, and as a general rule, the former national telecoms have been slow to "unbundle" the local loop. In November 2001, Reinhardt reported that no phone lines has been made available to competitors in France, Spain, Greece, or Ireland and that the limited competition in the broadband market caused the price of access in Europe to be 20% higher than in the U.S.

Worldwide, the entire telecommunications industry experienced a devastating economic downturn beginning in 2000, when the European telecoms services sector valuation fell 48% between March and the end of the year (Hurst, 2001). Industry expansion following 1996 had been highly leveraged and European telecoms had acquired $415 billion in syndicated loans, $415 billion in bonded indebtedness, and another $500 billion from the stock market and private sources (Roberts, 2001a). Despite increased competition and falling prices in voice telephone services, "nearly half of European bank lending in 1999 was to telecoms" (Roberts, 2001a, p. 2). Much of this money was spent by newer telecommunications providers on infrastructure built to support an expected upsurge in bandwidth intensive (broadband) uses: undersea cables, vast amounts of optical fiber, and new licenses for third generation (3G) mobile telephony services. Firms bid $99.3 billion for the technology that would bring broadband Internet access to the mobile phone ("Running for the Exit," 2001). These high prices added significantly to the debt load of the successful bidders, and the combined effects of the 2000–2001 downturn are reflected in the strategic actions of telecom firms as firms have begun to restructure and industry segments have experienced consolidation. Despite these negative considerations, the market for mobile phone services continues to grow in the region, and in the first half of 2001 demand for broadband in Europe nearly doubled (Reinhardt, 2001).

THE TELECOMS OF WESTERN EUROPE
AT THE TURN OF THE CENTURY

This chapter focuses on developments of four major telecoms based in the United Kingdom, France, Germany, and Spain.

United Kingdom

British Telecommunications plc (BT) is a wholly owned subsidiary of BT Group plc and the primary provider of telephony services in the United Kingdom. In late 2001 BT operated with six divisions. BTopenworld provides Internet access (including broadband) and Internet-related services. BT Retail markets the firm's products and services to domestic business and residential customer segments. BT Ignite offers data services and consultation to businesses throughout Europe. BT Wholesale provides network services to other BT units and to competing telecoms that must use the BT network to connect to customers. BT Affinitis is a management and information consultantcy service. BTexact Technologies (formerly BT Laboratories) is BT's research and development unit ("BT annual report," 2001).

Debt reduction has been the over-arching strategy of BT since 2000. In March 2001 the company responded to indebtedness of nearly $40.48 billion by selling its Yell directories division for $3.1 billion and liquidating real estate holdings for $3.47 billion ("BT annual report," 2001; "BT Announces, 2001). In October 2001 BT announced the end of Concert, an unprofitable joint venture with AT&T ("British Telecom, AT&T," 2001). More importantly, in November 2001 BT demerged its money-losing wireless assets by creating a new company, mmO2. Prior to the demerger, the BTWireless unit had controlled the Genie wireless portal and a set of wireless operations in the UK (BTCellnet), Germany, the Netherlands, Ireland, and the Isle of Mann ("BT Wireless to Adopt," 2001). BT Group believes that uniting wireless assets under single brand name will improve chances of success in the UK and other European markets. At the same time, the formation of mmO2 effectively separated the potentially profitable but highly competitive and risky mobile telephony business from the other BT lines of business.

Broadband services figure prominently in the strategic plans of BT, although consumers in the UK have been slow to acquire broadband access. While BT's ADSL enabled lines passed 13 million UK households, only 40,000 residential customers had signed up by October 2001 ("Who's Who," 2001). A new marketing campaign was aimed at residential consumers; the price of broadband installation was cut in half, the monthly subscription charge was reduced by £5, and the rate of new connections nearly doubled as a result ("BT Sees Broadband Demand," 2001). Slow demand for broadband coupled with BT's overall financial woes caused an additional strategic shift related to the provision of content to broadband subscribers. BTopenworld initially planned to be a major provider of broadband content to its subscribers. Those plans were scaled back during the economic downturn as BT concentrated on its broadband network build-out. Rather than planning a wide assortment of content offerings, BT has concentrated recently on interactive games and music (Gibson, 2001).

BT is required by the British government to make its access lines available to competitors, and has tasked the BT Wholesale unit to comply with this mandate. However, like other former national monopoly telecoms in the region, BT has been notoriously slow in this phase of unbundling its local loop. Firms wishing to provide competing DSL service have two options. One is to lease DSL-enabled lines directly from BT Wholesale. The other is for competitors to connect their own DSL technology to an unbundled local loop. Critics contend that BT has stymied both approaches in what appears to be a strategic delaying tactic. Requests for wholesale access have met with long delays (Wray, 2001a). Firms that wish to install their own DSL equipment complain that BT is slow to unbundle the access circuits. When unbundled lines are available, competitors then face very high costs to locate their expensive DSL equipment. Essentially, they must either lease physical space within BT-owned structures, or locate their equipment in nearby buildings, aboveground cabinets, or belowground installations. One competitor reported that BT was charging £36,000 to £95,000 to build a room for competitor equipment within a BT facility and then charging a low price of £264 for planned business-hours physical access to the room to as much as £792 for unscheduled after-hours access. Additional charges are collected by BT for the connection from the DSL room to the main exchange where the phone lines terminate (Shillingford, 2001).

In 2000, some 50 firms announced their intention to enter the DSL broadband access competition in the UK, but the economic downturn coupled with delays in gaining local loop access caused all but five to fold (Wray, 2001a). While others may yet emerge as conditions improve, the consolidation in this sector has clearly benefited BT. The company's recent marketing efforts and broadband price reductions, coupled with new "plug and play" technology that allows new DSL subscribers to connect without a visit from a technician, should enable BTopenworld to add substantially to its market share, lessening further the chances of competitors to gain a foothold.

BTopenworld does face competition in broadband access from cable operators as well as satellite broadcaster BSkyB. In fact, as of November 2001, 70% of Britain's broadband-enabled homes have cable-delivered access ("100,000 Broadband Customers for NTL," 2001). Policy-makers and investors once thought that cable would become a key competitor in the UK telecoms market, but cable developed slowly and the 27 franchises in this sector are now owned by only two firms. The largest, NTL, has 2.9 million residential customers including 100,000 broadband subscribers ("NTL Incorporated Announces," 2001). The number two firm is Telewest with 1.74 million customer households, of which 70,000 subscribe to broadband ("Telewest," 2001). Cable telecoms have the advantage of being able to deliver telephony, Internet access, and video through a single connection. However, like BTopenworld, NTL has scaled back earlier plans to produce an array of broadband content, focusing instead on interactive games. As is evident from the sector consolidation, cable growth has been slow, but by late 2001 subscriptions were increasing rapidly. NTL has been rumoured to have an interest in acquiring Telewest. Cable telecoms lack the residential and business reach of BT, and the cable sector in general has a poorer record of customer service, one of BT's strengths. Telecommunications analysts also observe that without a mobile telephony presence, cable telecoms cannot become full service providers. NTL plans to offer virtual mobile network services through an arrangement with Orange, a mobile brand operated by France Télécom, owner of a 22% stake in NTL (Moran, 2001).

While BT has changed direction on creating its own content, the firm still intends to be a force in the provision of digital video. BT plans to offer enhanced VDSL (Very High Speed DSL) service with potential download speed 14 times faster than present day ADSL (Schofield, 2001). In November 2001 BT filed an application with Britain's Independent Television Commission for a license to provide television services using its DSL-enabled fixed network. BT is also evaluating partnerships with terrestrial digital television broadcasters and BSkyB (Wray, 2001b).

France

France Télécom (FT) is a diversified full service telecommunications firm operating lines of business in local, long distance, and international wireline telephony; local, regional, and international data network services; wireless telephony; Internet access; cable and satellite television; media production; and telecommunications-related services to businesses. FT has been only partially privatised; the French government still owns 54% (Milner, 2001). As the former national monopoly operator of the legacy network, France Télécom dominates the country's fixed-line telephone access market. However, deregulation-induced competition is cutting into FT's domestic fixed-line revenues (Matlack & Reed, 2001). In its 2000 Annual Report, France Télécom stated its intention to concentrate its efforts in the areas of wireless telephony, data services, and fixed line services—including Internet access (France Télécom, 2001a). France Télécom is intent on maintaining its market leadership in France while enhancing its competitive position in the rest of Europe, a posture enhanced by recent strategic moves.

Already the top wireless provider in France, FT became the second largest wireless operator in Europe (behind Vodaphone) with the acquisition of UK-based Orange in 2000. Operating generally under the Orange name, France Télécom has wireless interests in 20 countries. In 2001 France Télécom became the number two Internet service provider in Europe following the purchase of UK-based ISP, Freeserve. Combined with France Télécom's ISP subsidiary Wanadoo, FT now operates in the Internet access markets of six European countries as well as Senegal, Morocco, Slovakia, and Lebanon. These two acquisitions have greatly improved FT's competitive position with respect to regional competitors Deutsche Telekom, Telefónica, and British Telecom (Matlack & Reed, 2001).

The $53 billion spent on the Orange and Freeserve acquisitions and 3G licenses added significantly to the indebtedness of France Télécom at a time when telecoms in general were experiencing declining economic fortunes. In February 2001, FT initiated an IPO of 15% of Orange for $790 million, far below expectations. France Télécom was subsequently able to raise $14 billion from the bond market (Baker, 2001). The firm has also been disposing of investments in Sprint FON and Sprint PCS acquired in a joint venture with Deutsche Telekom. FT is also disposing of holdings in a microelectronics firm and is considering the sale of surplus property (Milner, 2001). While both Orange and Wanadoo posted net losses for 2000, Orange experienced 82% revenue growth while the ISP's revenue increased 37%. The number of subscribers of FT-owned firms rose from 55 million to 77 million ("France Télécom, 2001b).

France Télécom is also in the digital television business through ownership of production companies, cable systems in 14 French cities, and satellite distribution. These operations are linked with the Wanadoo Internet access subsidiary and the level of integration should increase as FT's broadband network grows. Wanadoo began as a narrowband ISP and portal service and has evolved into a provider of ADSL broadband. France Télécom also delivers broadband though its FT Cable operation. Current plans call for using FT's content production assets to develop material for broadband Internet delivery, and Wanadoo has acquired a company that produces and markets video games and will use this asset to develop interactive game content for its broadband services (France Télécom 2001a).

Like Britain, the broadband market in France has developed slowly. The regional leader, Germany, has over 2 million ADSL-enabled lines. With only

500,000 ADSL lines in place, France Télécom announced in November 2001 that it would spend $351.5 million to extend the availability of its ADSL service to 80% of the French population by 2004. Competing firms wishing to provide competing ADSL services have encountered many obstacles in dealing with France Télécom. Vivendi's Cegetel subsidiary complained that FT's wholesale fee structure exceeded the European average and temporarily suspended efforts to establish ADSL service, hoping for government intervention. In January 2001, the French government threatened France Télécom with fines and price controls if it continued to delay unbundling of the local loop (Hazan, 2001). Cable broadband access is significant in France. At the end of 2000 there were over twice as many subscribers to cable than DSL users (Pastore, 2001).

Germany

Deutsche Telecom AG is the largest telecom in Europe, due in part to the size and scope of the German economy. The firm is seeking to consolidate its dominant domestic position in the face of competition while positioning itself as a major European and international player. And, like other European telecoms, DT has experienced the travails of the economic decline in the technology sector of the economy and faces a daunting level of indebtedness from bidding on 3G mobile licenses. Deutsche Telekom has organised its operations into four divisions. T-Com provides network services for the residential, business, and international markets. T-Systems offers integrated IT, telecommunications, and e-commerce services to major business customers. T-Mobile International AG controls the consolidated mobile telephony businesses with operations in Germany, Austria, the United States, Britain, and the Czech Republic. Finally, T-Online International AG operates Europe's largest online service provider/portal. T-Online has participated aggressively in the consolidation of the European Internet access market by establishing or acquiring ISPs in Austria, France, Switzerland, Spain, and Portugal in addition to Germany (Deutsche Telekom, 2001a).

Deutsche Telekom is generally regarded as a strong national firm that has been slow to expand into other markets. The company's fixed services network is the most highly developed in Western Europe with over 8 million ISDN lines and more ADSL access lines than are found in Britain, France, or Spain. At the same time Germany leads these countries in the deregulation of the telecoms sector (Purton, 2001). In the area of fixed services, Deutsche Telekom has been forced to engage in price competition and to provide other incentives to retain market share ("The World Beyond," 2000). While most of the competitors seeking access to Deutsche Telekom's network have been relatively small firms, the threat remains that a national telecom from another country may see

Germany's open market as an opportunity to expand its European territory (Purton, 2001).

While most Western European telecoms actively pursued pan-European and international opportunities for expansion, Deutsche Telekom achieved a slow start in this important area of strategic activity. After forging an early relationship with France Télécom and Sprint, Deutsche Telekom unsuccessfully pursued a merger with Telecom Italia and U.S.-based firms, including Sprint and Qwest, only to be trumped by more aggressive competitors (Cantwell, 2000). When Vodaphone-AirTouch acquired the German firm Mannesmann in 2000, Deutsche Telekom's present and future wireless interests were threatened. Vodaphone-AirTouch, now owned by German, British, and American interests, was the largest mobile phone operator in Europe, including Germany (Ewing, 2000).

By early 2001 T-Mobile had passed Vodaphone-AirTouch in the German market and Deutsche Telekom, desperate for an American presence, moved to acquire VoiceStream Wireless and a smaller firm, Powertel, in the United States. While VoiceStream was not a large player in the U.S., the firm is one of the few in that market using the same GSM wireless standard found in Europe. Like other Western European telecoms, DT bid large sums on 3G mobile licenses in Germany, Britain, and the Netherlands (Ryan, 2001). In addition, the economic downturn in Europe forced Deutsche Telekom to write down the asset value of its real estate holdings, losing $1.4 billion from its balance sheet (Ewing, 2001). In order to reduce debt, Deutsche Telekom sold its regional cable television networks and its shares of Sprint FON and Sprint PCS (Deutsche Telekom, 2001a). In April 2000, DT listed T-Online International AG with a Frankfurt stock exchange for the purpose of financing acquisitions with shares. A general IPO of about 9% of T-Mobile was planned for 2001, but the sluggish economy delayed this move (Ryan, 2001). Deutsche Telekom enjoyed a record business year in 2000 with a 15% increase in revenue (Deutsche Telekom, 2001b). Solid growth continued into 2001. At the end of the third quarter of 2001, T-Mobile had added 3.7 million new customers and experienced a 40% increase in revenue over the same time the previous year while T-Online revenue increased 33% (Deutsche Telekom, 2001a).

Despite deregulatory pressure, Deutsche Telekom has remained dominant in broadband access. The firm has promoted broadband aggressively and ended 2001 with 98% of the domestic ADSL market. DT's success in broadband is due in part to its proactive approach to building a modern network infrastructure, outspending its European counterparts by a wide margin during the 1990s, and the firm now benefits from one of the lowest line costs in Europe. Competitors find that they cannot offer ADSL service in DT's price range and generate enough profit to succeed. One analysis determined that nearly half of competitors' revenues are paid to Deutsche Telecom (McClune, 2001b). The potential exists for significant competition from cable television providers. U.S.-based firms Callahan Associates and Liberty Media are selectively acquiring cable properties in Germany (including several purchased from Deutsche Telekom) and elsewhere in Western Europe. However, Cahners In-Stat Group estimated that only 1,000 German households had cable broadband access at the end of 2000, compared to 400,000 DSL subscribers (Pastore, 2001).

Spain

Telefónica, S.A. operates the Telefónica Group, a diversified firm providing fixed and mobile telephony, data services and consultation to businesses, Internet services, and the production and distribution of media content through multiple channels, including the Internet. While Telefónica has a growing set of global interests, its primary activities are centred in Spain, Portugal, and Latin America. The company is organised into ten lines of business. Telefónica de España manages domestic fixed telephony, while Latin American operations fall under Telefónica Latinoamericana. The mobile telephony line operates globally under Telefónica Móviles. Internet operations are controlled Terra Lycos. Telefónica Media is the media content production and distribution division. Telefónica Publicidad e Información (TPI) publishes and markets directories and guides. Telefónica DataCorp provides data and corporate services, and the parent firm has separate units for customer relations management (Atento) and business-to-business commerce (Telefónica B2B). A recent addition, Emergia, develops and operates broadband network services in Latin America (Telefónica, 2001b).

Telefónica enjoys distinct advantages in comparison to the telecoms of other European nations. The firm has a history of using equity financing for its acquisitions, having issued IPOs for its original Terra Internet division and TPI in 1999 (Peterson, 2000; Telefónica, 2001a). Like other telecoms in the region, Telefónica has enjoyed strong growth from its mobile division. In order to generate capital for future developments, Telefónica Móviles was also floated as an IPO in 2000. This enabled the firm to bid successfully for 3G licenses in Spain, Germany, Austria, Italy, and Switzerland without incurring the level of indebtedness experienced by other European telecoms. As of mid-2001, the firm carried less than half of the debt load of France Télécom and Deutsche Telekom (Schmidt, 2001).

Telefónica operates in virtually every Spanish-speaking country as well as in Portugal and Portuguese-language nations. While European fixed line revenues are generally in decline, the Latin American market is growing. In addition, Telefónica's combination of content and Internet assets positions the company to be a major force in both legacy and new media in the Spanish-speaking world. The firm's Internet division, Terra, was formed in 1999 to take over Internet services in the company's fixed line service areas. Terra quickly acquired the other significant ISPs in Spain and Latin America, building scale and market share (Telefónica, 2001c). Terra became the leading Spanish ISP and Internet portal and was further strengthened in October 2000 through the acquisition of Lycos, the third largest U.S. Internet portal and the subsequent IPO issued for Terra Lycos ("Portal Plays," 2000).

Lycos was already a recognised Internet brand and its Lycos Europe subsidiary included a partnership with German media conglomerate Bertelsmann, providing access to Bertelsmann-owned content. Bertelsmann also agreed to buy $1 billion worth of advertising and other services from Terra Lycos over a 5-year period ("Portal Plays," 2000; Telefónica, 2001a). Combining the portal service with Internet access dominance in Spain and Latin America has enabled Terra Lycos to gain substantial market share. Revenue has increased and the company projected that the firm would break even by mid-2002 (Shook, 2001). Terra Lycos' combination of content and distribution assets has been compared to that of AOL-Time Warner, especially in its significance in the Spanish-speaking world. Terra Lycos has established a wide range of partnerships with Web content providers, many compatible with narrowband access. When broadband access is more widely available Telefónica will be in an excellent position to leverage its media holdings from the Telefónica Media division and its Terra Lycos partners to create attractive digital content offerings to broadband subscribers. Telefónica Media pursues an aggressive convergence strategy and develops content for broadcast and pay-per-view television and the Internet. The division is developing interactive content that will be able to exploit digital broadcast transmission as well wired or wireless broadband delivery. Terra Networks partnered with Telefónica Móviles S.A. to establish Terra Mobile in July 2000 to offer a global mobile portal to Telefónica's wireless customers. Initially configured to work with second generation technologies like WAP (wireless application protocol), Terra Mobile offers the foundation on which to build a true 3G portal (Telefónica, 2001c).

Telefónica de España operates Telefónica's broadband infrastructure. Historically, the firm provided ISDN services to businesses and later made ISDN lines available to others seeking faster Internet access. As demand for enhanced Internet services has grown, Telefónica de España has been installing ADSL capability. The rollout of ADSL topped 80% of Telefónica's lines by the summer of 2001, with more than 100,000 digital broadband lines available (Telefónica, 2001d). Broadband access in Spain is marketed by Terra at three levels of service and speed and prices that start at approximately $40 per month for typical residential service and top out at nearly $150 for the premium service marketed to businesses ("Terra ADSL Plus," 2001). As is the case across Europe, competition in telecommunications services has been slow to develop and Telefónica has been accused of using its market dominance to thwart competitive efforts. At the end of 1999, Telefónica controlled 99.5% of the local calling market and dial-up access to the Internet had led to a 14% growth in local call revenues for the year. The firm pursued a methodical rollout of ADSL capabilities, but like the others set wholesale tariffs too high to enable competitors to succeed. In October 2001 the government intervened, ordering a 26% reduction in Telefónica's tariffs and a 43% difference between wholesale and retail charges (Donegan, 2001).

DISCUSSION

Convergence

The forces of convergence have shaped the strategies of the former national telecoms of Western Europe. All have invested heavily in mobile services and Internet access, including broadband. Each firm seeks to be the dominant provider of these services in its home country and a significant player both regionally and internationally. In mobile services incumbent telecoms enjoyed few advantages over new competitors, enabling a firm like Vodaphone to achieve regional dominance. However, while the mobile sector has experienced tremendous growth, it has been subject to substantial consolidation. During consolidation the financial resources of the incumbent telecoms emerged, enabling such moves as the acquisition of Orange by France Télécom and Telefónica's expansion in the Latin American markets.

Mobile Telephony

Both France Télécom and Telefónica are well positioned for success in the mobile sector. FT has a broad European presence with Orange, and Telefónica controls the Spanish-speaking markets. Telefónica has genuine advantage in the 3G stakes due to its lower level of indebtedness and its practice of funding future ventures in the equity markets. Deutsche Telekom is successful in its home market, but has not developed as a regional or international force in mobile telephony. British Telecom has departed from the European norm entirely by spinning off its wireless assets. Because mmO2 is small it is subject to a takeover bid by another national telecom (like Telefónica) seeking to expand its European stake. The demerger enables BT to focus on enhanced fixed network services, but by narrowing the scope of its operations the firm has chosen a different path from the others. Despite the slow rollout of 3G, massive interest remains and 3G projects will move forward quickly as economic conditions improve. However, the level of consumer demand and subsequent diffusion of 3G enabled devices remains unclear.

Competition

Major barriers to entry exist in the Internet access markets of Western Europe. Dominance by the incumbent telecoms in Internet access has been assured due to the lack of competition from other forms of access (e.g., cable) and the firms' ownership of the telecommunications infrastructure. The former monopoly telecoms are under national and European Union mandates to unbundle their local loops, but the incumbents are still in control. The impact of delays imposed on would-be competitors was amplified by an economic downturn, thinning the ranks of competitors and allowing the dominant telecoms to consolidate their positions of strength using price incentives to build market share and potential lock-in effects, especially with respect to broadband services. However, if competing providers of DSL service manage to gain significant access to domestic networks, consumers should experience low switching costs and competitors may experience the same kinds of churn problems faced earlier by the free ISPs in Europe. Switching costs are higher when a shift between ADSL and cable modem access is contemplated.

If broadband access becomes competitive, market share will depend on far more than mere availability of broadband service or price. Demand has been price elastic as the upsurge in demand following recent price reductions shows. Telecoms are starting to offer ADSL packages differentiated by price and speed, usually taking a three-tiered approach. The low price service is designed to appeal to budget conscious residential customers while the costlier higher speed package caters to business users.

Broadband Media Content

Content and value added services are expected to play a key role when broadband becomes more prevalent. France Télécom and Telefónica are configured with significant content assets, but Telefónica holds the stronger position. British Telecom and Deutsche Telekom are largely in the position of partnering with other parties for content provision. This approach affords the benefit of flexibility. However, both the telecoms and the content providers have the ability to change partners. Digital television is growing rapidly in Europe and is delivered by terrestrial broadcast, satellite, and cable. DSL is expected to become a fourth digital delivery platform by using DSL phone lines connected to set top boxes. Strategy Analytics (2001) predicted that DSL delivery of DTV services worldwide will increase from 1% in 2001 to 11% by 2008. McClune (2001a) reports that by 2005 televisions connected to the Internet will account for 13% of the total in France and 11% in Spain. The percentages that will be using ADSL and cable are not specified. At present, cable is generally superior to ADSL in bandwidth and speed, but newer DSL technologies like VDSL (Very High Speed Digital Subscriber Line) are expected by the end of 2002, increasing the potential of broadband to become the fourth DTV platform. However, for telecoms there is a dark side to digital television (Schofield, 2001).

One estimate suggests that the percentage of digital television households in Europe will triple from 28 million to 84 million by 2004. No matter how it is provided to the home, digital television has the capability of delivering all manner of digital signals: audio, video, video-on-demand, interactive content, etc. Terrestrial and satellite broadcasters and cable television operators have far more experience in the production, acquisition, and marketing of compelling content than do telecoms. Therefore, some analysts are advising telecoms to follow British Telecom's lead and leave the content to experienced partners (McClune, 2001a). Of the four telecoms analysed, Telefónica appears to have the strongest set of assets for competition in a broadband future dominated by digital television. Forrester Research raised another broadband content issue in late 2001, contending that the owners of superior content will bypass familiar and established portals like AOL and Yahoo! because content firms are already adept at multichannel content distribution. Forrester predicts that firms like Terra Lycos and AOL will succeed because they own both portals and content (Forrester Research, 2001). Most other portals will simply be used to find the Internet sites of major content producers.

Issues related to broadband services and content also intersect with the plans of mobile telephony providers. The large players have gambled by bidding aggressively for third generation licenses across the continent of Europe. The motivation behind 3G is the provision of Internet content to the handheld device. The term *broadband* is used in connection with 3G mobile services but few expect the reality to match the hype, at least in the near term. Nonetheless, a simple extrapolation of well-established technology trajectories leads to a mobile wireless broadband future. Incumbent telecoms and other mobile players face the same issues as wired broadband service providers about the provision of content.

At the end of 2000 the Western European telecoms and their competitors await improved economic conditions as they aggressively market their broadband connections and build critical mass. The harsh economic trends of 2000–2001 winnowed out the weak players and forced the survivors to streamline their plans for broadband. The market for broadband access is growing at an increasing rate, and digital television continues to develop rapidly. The stage is set both for competition and cooperation between telecoms and digital broadcasters, mirroring earlier relations between cable operators and satellite providers. Where broadband media are concerned, the means of delivery are developing nicely. However, the business model for the financially viable broadband content delivery involving telecoms remains unclear.

REFERENCES

100,000 Broadband Customers for NTL. (2001, November 19). NTL Group Ltd. Press Release. Retrieved October 21, 2001 from http://www.ntl.com/ locales/gb/en/media/ press/ display.asp?id=506

Baker, S. (2001, April 9). Feast of the telecoms titans. *Business Week* International Edition, Business Week Online. Retrieved December 9, 2001 from http://www.businessweek.com/ magazine/content/01_15/b3727149.htm

British Telecom, AT&T announce breakup of Concert joint venture. (2001, October 16). *Wall Street Journal* Interactive Edition. Retrieved Ocober 17, 2001 from http://interactive.wsj.com/archive/retrieve.cgi?id=SB100318347697634 9000.djm

BT announces closure of the sale of Yell. (2001, June 25). BT Group, plc. Press release. Retrieved December 9, 2001 from http://www.groupbt.com/ Media%20centre/ Archive%20news%20releases/2001/nr0137.htm

BT annual report. (2001, March 31). London: BT Group, plc. Retrieved October 21, 2001 from http://www.groupbt.com/report/pdf_index.htm

BT sees broadband demand nearly double after price cuts. (2001, Nov. 29). *Wall Street Journal* Interactive Edition. Retrieved December 9, 2001 from http:// interactive.wsj.com/archive/ retrieve.cgi?id=DI-CO-20011129-004505.djm

BT wireless to adopt new brand, O2. (2001, September 3). BT Group, plc. Press release. Retrieved September 30, 2001 from http://www.groupbt.com/ Media%20centre/Archive%20news%20releases/2001/pr0101.htm

Cantwell, R. (2000, March 13). Deutsche Telekom: Trip, stagger & roll. *Inter@ctive Week*, 7 (10), 11-13.

Deutsche Telekom AG (2001a, November). Deutsche Telekom Group Report: January 1 to September 30, 2001. Deutsche Telekom AG Group Communications. Retrieved November 10, 2001 from http://www.dtag.de/ english/company/ inv_rel/ gesch_zahlen/index.htm

Deutsche Telekom AG (2001b, May 29). Most successful year in Deutsche Telekoms history. Press Release. Retrieved November 10, 2001 from the World Wide Web: http://www.telekom.de/dtag/presse/artikel/0,1018,x1228,00.html

Donegan, M. (2001, October 8). News analysis: Broadband access in Spain -- Telefonica contests unbundling measures. Communications Week International. CWI Online. Retrieved November 25, 2001 from http://www.totaltele.com/ view.asp?ArticleID=44540&Pub= CWI&CategoryID=705

Ewing, J. (2000, February 14). Deutsche Telekom gets a "kick in the pants." Business Week International Edition. Business Week Online. Retrieved December 16, 2001 from http://www.businessweek.com/bwdaily/dnflash/ feb2000/nf00214c.htm

Ewing, J. (2001, March 12). Commentary: Firing the boss won't fix Deutsche Telekom. Business Week International Edition. Business Week Online. Retrieved December 16, 2001 from http://www.businessweek.com/magazine/ content/ 01_11/b3723162.htm

Forrester Research (2001, December 19). Broadband Will Squeeze Europe's Generalist Portals As Media Producers Grab Customers And Revenues, Forrester Warns. Forrester Research, Inc. Press Release. Retrieved December 19, 2001 from http://www.forrester.com/ER/Press/ Release/0,1769,658,00.html

France Telecom (2001a). Annual report. France Telecom ADS. Retrieved November 25, 2001 from http://www.francetelecom.com/vanglais/ who_we_are/ f_report.html

France Telecom (2001b, February 13). France Telecom's consolidated operating revenues up 23.7 percent for 2000. France Telecom ADS. Retrieved December 9, 2001 from http://www.francetelecom.com/vanglais/finances/actualite/ f_actualite.html

Gibson, O. (2001, October 22). BT Openworld abandons TV-style content. Guardian Unlimited. [Electronic version]. Retrieved Nov. 30, 2001 from http://www.guardian.co.uk/Archive/Article/0,4273,4260704,00.html

Goff, D.H. (2000a). Issues of Internet infrastructure. In A. B. Albarran and D. H. Goff (Eds.), *Understanding the web: Social, political, and economic dimensions of the Internet*, 239-265. Ames, IA: Iowa State University Press.

Goff, D.H. (2000b). Online, Time is Money: Internet Growth and the Cost of Access in the UK and Europe. Paper presented at the 2000 Conference on Time and Media Markets, Pamplona, Spain.

Harper, J. (1997). *Monopoly and competition in British telecommunications: the past, the present, and the future*. London: Pinter.

Hazan, A. (2001, February 21). La bataille de l'accès à la boucle locale. *Le Monde* Interactif. Retrieved December 16, 2001 from http://interactif. lemonde.fr/article/ 0,5611,2857--148960-0,FF.html

Hurst, T. 2001, Telecoms services companies - will they ever return? In C. Sharman (Ed.), *International Telecoms Review*, 2001, 11-18. Essex, UK: Euromoney Publications, PLC.

Jupiter MMXI (2001, December 18). The ones to watch on the European Internet in 2002, Jupiter MMXI UK. Press Release. Retrieved December 19, 2001 from http://uk.jupitermmxi.com/xp/uk/press/releases/pr_121801.xml

Laffont, J. & Tirole, J. (2001). *Competition in telecommunications*. Cambridge, MA: MIT Press.

Matlack, C. & Reed, S. (2001, January 8). France Telecom's $53 billion burden. *Business Week* International Edition. Business Week Online. Retrieved Dece,ber 16, 2001 from http://www.businessweek.com/2001/01_02/b3714249.htm

McClune, E. (2001a, August 1). Digital television: No place like home. EMAP Digital, ci-online. Retrieved November 25, 2001 from http://totaltele.com/ view.asp? ArticleID=42430&pub=ci

McClune, E. (2001b, November 12). News Analysis: French and German DSL - what it takes to win with DSL. *Communications Week International*. CWI Online. Retrieved November 25, 2001 from http://www.totaltele.com/ view.asp?Target= top&ArticleID=45680&Pub=cwi

Milner, M. (2001, July 27). Putting on a poker face. *Guardian* Unlimited. [Electronic version]. Retrieved Nov. 30, 2001 from http://www.guardian.co.uk/ Archive/ Article/ 0,4273,4229080,00.html

Moran, N. (2001, May 14). NTL. *Financial Times* [Electronic version]. Retrieved October 21, 2001 from http://specials.ft.com/fttelc/may2001/ FT3W924YOMC.html

Noam, E. M. (2001). *Interconnecting the network of networks.* Cambridge, MA: MIT Press.

NTL Incorporated announces results for three months and nine months ended September 30, 2001. (2001, November 7). NTL Group Ltd. Press Release. Retrieved October 25, 2001 from http://www.ntl.com/locales/ gb/en/media/ press/ display.asp?id=502

Pastore, M. (2001, June 12). Europe remains behind in broadband game. INT Media Group: Internet.com. Retrieved December 19, 2001 from http:// cyberatlas.internet.com/markets/broadband/article/0,1323,10099_783401,00.htm l

Peterson, M. (2000, October). Telefonica convinces the doubters. *Euromoney*, 378, 28.

Portal plays. (2000, May 20). *The Economist*, 355 (8171), 76-77.

Purton, P. (2001, January 15). Germany: Consolidation may temper incumbents' advantages. *Financial Times* [Electronic version]. Retrieved October 21, 2001 from the World Wide Web: http://specials.ft.com/telecoms/january2001/ FT3IMMGA0IC.html

Reinhardt, A. (2001, November 12). Burning rubber on the infobahn. *Business Week* International Edition. Business Week Online. Retrieved December 16, 2001 from http:www.businessweek.com/magazine/content/01_46/b3757131.htm

Roberts, D. (2001a, Sept 4). Glorious hopes on a trillion-dollar scrapheap. *Financial Times* [Electronic version] Retrieved December 9, 2001 from http:// g lobalarchive.ft.com/globalarchive/articles.html?print=true&id= 010905001143
Roberts, D. (2001b, Sept 4). How the world caught third-generation fever. *Financial Times* [Electronic version]. Retrieved December 9, 2001 from http:// globalarchive.ft.com/globalarchive/articles.html?print=true&id= 010906002890

Running for the exit. (2001, August 18) *The Economist*, 360 (8235), 50.

Ryan, V. (2001, March 3). A giant struggle. *Telephony*, 240 (11), 46-47.

Schmidt, P. (2001, June 25). The wrong call on Telefonica? *Business Week Online*. Retrieved December 16, 2001 from http://www.businessweek.com/ bwdaily/dnflash/ jun2001/nf20010625_429.htm

Schofield, J. (2001, December 6). How to stay above the rest. *Guardian Unlimited*. [Electronic version] Retrieved December 12, 2001 from http://www.guardian.co.uk/ Archive/Article/0,4273,4313961,00.html

Shillingford, J. (2001, January 15). Locations will not come cheaply. *Financial Times* [Electronic version]. Retrieved October 21, 2001 from the World Wide Web: http://specials.ft.com/telecoms/january2001/FT3RW9460IC.html

Shook, D. (2001, August 24). Not just any portal in the storm. *Business Week Online*. Retrieved December 16, 2001 from http://www.businessweek.com/ bwdaily/ dnflash/aug2001/ nf20010824_028.htm

Strategy Analytics, Inc. (2001, September 25). DSL digital tv to reach 46 million homes. Strategy Analytics, Inc. Press Release. Retrieved November 25, 2001 from http://www.strategyanalytics.com/press/PRDM031.htm

Telefónica, S. A. (2001a). Annual Report 2000. Telefónica S.A. Department of Institutional Relations. Retrieved December 16, 2001 from http://www.telefonica.es/ memoria/ingles/memoria2000/pdfs/MemoriaAnual.pd

Telefónica, S.A. (2001b). Who we are: About Telefónica. Telefónica, S.A. corporate web site. Retrieved December 16, 2001 from http://www.telefonica.com/quienes_english/index.html

Telefónica, S.A. (2001c). Who we are: Terra Lycos. Telefónica, S.A. corporate web site. Retrieved December 17, 2001 from http://www.telefonica.com/ quienes_english/lineas/negocios/terra_nw.html

Telefónica, S.A. (2001d, April 23). Telefónica installs over 100,000 ADSL lines in Spain. Telefónica, S.A. Press Release. Retrieved December 17, 2001 from http://www.telefonica.es/cgi-bin/telefonica/relac/ora?PROC=inoticia.muestra('A AAIk7AAQAAACfHAAA')

Telewest Communications plc (2001, November 15). Telewest Communications plc 3rd quarter results 2001. Retrieved November 25, 2001 from http://www.telewest.co.uk/pdfs/ urcompany/2001_q3.pdf

Terra ADSL Plus - Precio (2001). Terra Networks, S.A. Retrieved December 18, 2001 from http://www.terra.es/adsl/img/tit_precios.gif

Virtel, M. (2001, April 17). Fast internet -- so what? *Financial Times* [Electronic version] Retrieved October 21, 2001 from http://specials.ft.com/connectis/april2001/FT36J0HTKLC.html]

Who's who in broadband Britain. (2001, Oct. 1). *Guardian* Unlimited. [Electronic version] Retrieved Nov. 30, 2001 from http://www.guardian.co.uk/ Archive/Article/0, 4273,4264983,00.html

The world beyond Deutsche Telekom. (2000, April 15). *The Economist* 355, (8166), 61-3.

Wray, R. (2001a, November 8). BT and the failed revolution. *Guardian* Unlimited. [Electronic version] Retrieved Nov. 30, 2001 from http://www.guardian.co.uk/ Archive/Article/0,4273,4294434,00.html

Wray, R. (2001b, November 8). BT seeks licence to transmit TV content. *Guardian* Unlimited. [Electronic version] Retrieved Nov. 30, 2001 from http://www.guardian.co.uk/ Archive/Article/0,4273,4291249,00.html

Zerdick, A. Picot A., Schrape, K. Artope, A., Goldhammer, K., Lange, U. T., Vierkant, E., Lopez-Escobar, E., & Silverstone, R. (2000). *E-conomics: strategies for the digital marketplace.* Berlin: Springer - Verlag.

Chapter 12
Measurement of the Productivity and Quality of Journalistic Work on the Internet

Aldo van Weezel
University of the Andes

The objectives that the executives of a company establish are primordial in the attainment of their goals. A media company, the same as any other company, has the goal of generating utilities for their owners. However, the fact of being exactly that—a media company—also forces it to have the goal of helping with the development of people in an integral way, promoting values and attitudes that society considers valuable. In order to achieve both goals, economic profitability and social service, the executives of a media company should hold generating products of high quality as one of their high-priority objectives.

The problem resides in how to put the objective of the quality into practice. To achieve that, the first thing is to be clear on the fact that the media companies are highly intensive in intellectual work, which is usually carried out by journalists. It is mostly they who are responsible for products that the company delivers, being their performance and the result of their work, elements that affect the survival and prosperity of the company. Therefore, the task of generating products of high quality belongs to the journalists.

In order to carry out an efficient and effective management of persons and resources, having tools that allow measurements of quality and productivity of the journalistic work becomes a necessity for the executives of a media company.

OBJECTIVES AND SCOPE OF THE RESEARCH

This work seeks, in an introductory way, to study the relationship between quality and productivity within the media companies at the present, concentrating specifically on the news sites on the Internet. Not knowing what the economic future of those companies providing contents on the Internet will bring also justifies this investigation.

First of all, the concept of quality is approached, revising its meaning inside the service companies and then relating this concept to the journalistic theory. As a way of bringing the concept of quality closer to the reality, the results of 14 in-depth interviews to the editors of the most important online media in Chile are presented. The bibliography on productivity and how the concepts seen there can be applied to journalistic work are also revised. All this will allow us to relate both concepts, quality and productivity, in order to generate management policies that will help to improve the quality of the informative products of the company, and the productivity of the employees. Finally, the conclusions of the work are stated.

The Search of Quality

Quality can be defined as "to produce and to provide clients, without error and waste, superior values in products and services that each consumer wants and needs" (Christopher & Thor, 1998). However, there are numerous other definitions of quality, and in the last decades remarkable authors that have written about it have arisen. All their contributions helped with the evolution of the theory of quality management that began as a simple control of the elaborated products through quality inspections to the philosophy of Total Quality Management (TQM) used currently (James, 1996). A review of the most outstanding authors is next.

Juran (1964) defined quality as "fitness for use," and he was known for his trilogy of quality: planning of quality, quality control and improvement of quality. In 1974, Juran pointed out five characteristics of quality: technological, psychological, time oriented, contractual and ethics. Deming (1982), on the other hand, defined quality as "fitness for purpose," and specified 14 points to guide the search for quality, where he pointed out that an organisation should: be driven towards quality, look for the problems to solve them, constantly worry about improving the production systems and the training of its employees, and not be based on numeric production quotas. Crosby (1979) refers to quality as conformance to requirements and pointed out that the only standard of performance is the one that produces zero defects. He argued also that it is always cheaper to do the work right the first time. Feigenbaum (1991) contributes various ideas to the theory of TQM by means of his theory of the Total Quality Control. Ishikawa (1985) popularised the ideas of Juran, Deming and Feigenbaum, and created the concept of Quality Circles. Finally, Taguchi (1988) centred his works in the quality of design methods.

It is also important to mention the ideas and concepts of Garvin (1988) about quality. According to him, it has eight dimensions: performance, features, reliability, conformance, durability, serviceability, aesthetics and perceived quality. It has also five bases or focuses: transcendental, based on the product, based on the user, based on the manufacturing, and based on value.

Therefore, the centre of attention of quality management has passed from the product to people. The TQM philosophy, a result of all the contributions pointed out above, does not only concern the products and the processes involved in its elaboration, but it should also influence mainly the organisational culture, communications inside the company, the education of employees, and the managerial responsibility; and in the external environment, it should consider the clients and the suppliers very much. This way, in order to achieve the goal of the TQM philosophy, a cultural change is necessary to improve the human relationships inside the company (James, 1996).

Within this evolution of quality management, in particular what is related to the service companies, quality has become as important an element as getting scale economies for a manufacturing company. It is desired that services companies adjust to the dynamic changes of clients' expectations, so that the focus of the quality management moves from "zero defects" to "zero desertions of clients". This happens because it is more expensive to get new clients than to retain the existing ones (Prahalad & Krishnan, 1999). This saving in the costs from keeping clients has been designated *loyalty economies* (Reichheld, 1996).

Quality does not only generate a greater loyalty of the clients, but also a smaller sensibility toward the price (Porter, 1980); it also makes a company more competitive (Ivancevich, Lorenzi, Skinner, & Crosby, 1996), and gives it a differentiation strategy, a specially relevant when not reaching production levels that allow a strategy of cost leadership (Litman, 1988).

Quality of Media

Although definitions of quality and theories on managing them are plentiful in the bibliography about service and manufacturing companies, getting to the current TQM philosophy, it is not possible to say the same for the bibliography on media management. Quality in media is not only a desirable objective within the management, but also an indispensable element to reach the social, political and cultural goals that democratic societies imposes on journalism (Picard, 2000). A synthesis of the authors that have treated this problem of quality in media companies is developed next.

Nieto and Iglesias (2000) affirmed that quality of information begins with its truthfulness; with the adaptation among the product that the media company offers and the reality that it tries to reflect; and with the coherence among the promise of information supply made in its moment by the company and the informative contents that it really delivers. In the same line, Sánchez-Tabernero (2000) affirmed that quality consists in the search of a balance between the fidelity to the signs of identity of the media and the capacity of adaptation to the demands of the public; between the information of the public's desires and the implicit demands sensed by the media managers; and between what the public is willing to pay for and its cost. In this last balance, Sánchez-Tabernero stresses the fact that we should not think in short terms, but that managers should rather think of the permanency of the company in the long term. Even more, he affirms that the quality supposes to destine the biggest quantity in available resources to get the best possible elaboration of the informative and entertainment products. The work of Lacy (2000) confirms Sánchez-Tabernero's statement, also specifying that money is not enough to assure quality, but that in order for a media to produce high quality content consistently over time, it is crucial that it counts with enough financial supports. This support would come, according to Lacy, of the financial commitment that would generate an intense competition in the market.

Picard (2000) affirmed that journalism quality tends to be defined not by its presence, but for its absence, due to the practical impossibility to articulate the elements composing it. Bogart (1981) made a quite successful intent of discovering these elements in the press. His research took him to establish that directors of competitive and not competitive, big and small newspapers, agree on three characteristics associated to the quality: accuracy, impartiality and investigative spirit. The surveys of Bogart (1981), applied to managers of written media, delivered as a result that the five most important elements of quality are: a high proportion of writing material with regard to that of agency; the total quantity of contained advertising; a high proportion of interpretative material; the quantity of letters to the director in numbers; and the diversity of the political columnists. The interests of the readers, however, coincided only with one of those mentioned: in the number of letters to the director; the other four elements of interest for the readers would be: the presence of an action column; a high proportion of sport information and features with regard to the total content of the information; the presence of a summary of news; and a high proportion of illustrations. Another empiric study with readers corresponds to the Journalism Credibility Project that was carried out by the American Society of Newspaper Editors (ASNE) in 1999. In this study, the public's attitudes are studied in the face of the credibility of the media, trying to look for the deep causes of disconnection between the journalists and their public. The study detected six fundamental reasons for which the media have a low credibility: too many grammar and factual errors; little respect for the readers and their communities; prejudices of the journalists when covering a story (as much in the selection as in the reporting); too much attention to the sensationalist stories; prevalence of work methods that go against the values of the readers (sacrifice of accuracy for speed, indifference in the face of information that can cause damage, etc.); and finally, those who have participated in a journalistic process are the most critical in the credibility of the media.

The elements of quality that Bogart (1981) mentions and the report of the ASNE (1999) belong to what Sánchez-Tabernero (2000) denominates *subjective elements*. According to him, quality depends on objective and subjective elements. The first ones have to do with raw materials, defects of the products, post-sale services, available technology, etc. The subjective elements refer to the quality perceived by the clients, and even though they are more important, they are not so easily measurable.

As well as Sánchez-Tabernero (2000) distinguished two types of elements in the quality, Nieto and Iglesias (2000) went beyond contents and support, and they included the audience and the advertisers. Quality, according to them, is the sum of qualities: quality of people's work, quality of the informative offer that makes the company in the beginning, quality of the informative necessity present in the market, quality of the contents and support of the informative product, quality of the audience, and the advertisers' quality that insert its announcements in the product.

On the other hand, Nieto and Iglesias (2000) affirm that the economic value attributed to the product is frequently an indicator of quality. Picard (2000) agrees with this, explaining that the concept of quality involves providing enough value for the time or money that the consumers spend when obtaining and using a product or service. This is easy to check in the successful media that offer economic information, like the *Wall Street Journal*, Bloomberg and CNN Financial News, among others. The information that they provide, probably because it is specialised and directed to those who make decisions that involve large amounts of money, is very valuable for their public and therefore they are more willing to pay a high price for it. Salaverría (2000) has studied the factors that have taken Spanish newspapers to success on the Internet: the improvement of the informative update, the proliferation of documentary resources, the interactivity with the users, and the personalisation of contents.

Now, the quality, according to Sánchez-Tabernero (2000) is a comparative concept, since a product has quality if it overcomes its competitors in those aspects that the public considers more valuable. This is tremendously important to generate any type of evaluation, since it allows the scale of measurement not to be rigid, but relative, simplifying the process of analysis of quality.

Productivity of Journalistic Work

It was stated earlier in this chapter that in the area of quality management there is a wide bibliography related to services and manufacturing companies, but not for media companies; the same happens with the management of productivity.

Peter F. Drucker, in his book *The Practice of Management* (1961), mentions productivity as one of the objectives that every company should have for its performance and results. He defines it as the "balance" among all the production factors required to generate the biggest quantity in product with the smallest effort. Of course, it is possible to specify this definition further and to say that productivity worries about the efficiency and the effectiveness with which the goods and services are made (Sumanth, 1998). On one hand, the efficiency is the ratio between the actual inputs and standard inputs. The effectiveness, on the other hand, is the degree of the reach of goals or objectives. Hence, the efficiency is necessary, but not enough to improve the productivity. In a newsroom, it is possible to translate it this way: If you want to be productive you have to be efficient and deliver a quality product. Reaching quality automatically implies reaching the objective of helping the development of people and society, and the survival and profitability of the company in the long term. It is possible then to speak indistinctly about quality and effectiveness in this case. The problem that arises now is what it means for a journalist to be efficient.

The separation of these two elements that compose the productivity is only with the purpose of a theoretical analysis that allows the formulation of plans for the management of people and resources, since in practice, the efficiency frequently helps to obtain a better quality.

Picard (1998) proposed the measurement of the productivity of the journalists by means of the analysis of their activities. The reasoning that Picard uses is based on the fact that a journalist who shows high activity levels has the potential and necessary understanding to produce materials of high quality. The categories of use of time that he specifies are seven: personal or phone interviews; phone calls; attendance at events (conferences, meetings, etc.) pertaining to the stories about which they write; attendance at staff and training meetings; reading of newspapers, magazines, etc.; thinking, organising, and waiting for information; and finally, transfers, taking of pictures, and others.

Apparently more studies about the productivity of the journalistic work do not exist.

RESEARCH OF CHILEAN ONLINE MEDIA

Up to now, the concepts of quality and productivity have been described in a general way, and an attempt has been made to refer to these concepts in the existent bibliography on media management. Before relating these concepts and suggesting management politics applicable to the media, we have to revise the results of 14 in-depth interviews with editors of Chilean online media.

The selected media are among the most noted in Chile, and they include newspapers, magazines, financial newspapers, television channels, radios, and news sites that publish on the Internet exclusively.[1] The list is not exhaustive, since not all the media have their web pages. As for the results, these cannot be extrapolated to all the countries, although they could be comparable to countries with emergent economies that have an Internet penetration rate similar to the Chilean, that already reached 20% at the beginning of 2001. This rate is still far from the rates of penetration in developed countries that are over the 50% mark (CNTV, 2001). It is also necessary to add that since it is an interview and not a survey with closed questions, the answers are very diverse. The questions were directed towards understanding which is the concept of journalistic quality that editors have; what they do to measure and to control it; what importance they give to it; how they try to improve it; the disposition, by the company, to invest in it; the existent relationship between quality and productivity; the motivation level of the journalists in charge; how they control productivity; what they need to achieve a work of superior quality; and if they consider that their competition is of superior or inferior quality.

The answers, since the questions were open, present numerous shades. Grouping those that were similar, it is possible to extract the following information:

---

[1] The most prestigious online media in Chile are about 16. The following is the list of the 14 media that are considered in the research. Internet news sites (no paper copy): El Área (http://www.elarea.cl), El Mostrador (http://www.elmostrador.cl), Primera Línea (http://www.primeralinea.cl), Terra (http://www.terra.cl). Newspapers: Emol (http://www.emol.cl), El Mercurio de Valparaíso (http://www.elmercuriovalparaiso.cl), El Sur (http://www.elsur.cl), La Segunda (http://www.lasegunda.cl), La Tercera (http://www.latercera.cl). Financial newspapers: El Diario (http://www.eldiario.cl), Estrategia (http://www.estrategia.cl). Magazine: Qué Pasa (http://www.quepasa.cl). Radio: Radio Chilena (http://www.radiochilena.cl). Television: Corporación de Televisión de la Universidad Católica (http://www.canal13.cl).

- Most of the editors pointed out that quality resides within the contents: they should be reliable, trustworthy and truthful besides being presented quickly on the site once the news has happened.
- Less than half of the editors agreed that quality implies that the information delivered should be complete and deep and that it also has to be well edited, without spelling lacks and in an appropriate language for the public.
- Very few editors pointed out the importance of: using good sources; the information should be selected and presented according to their importance; the media should have their own agenda; the texts should be brief; and the journalistic ethics should be respected.
- All agreed that it is possible to measure the quality of the journalistic work, independent of the difficulty it could bring. Regarding how to do it, the opinions were diverse. Also, many agreed that the quality should be measured by means of the interactivity with the readers (e.g., e-mails), the visit counters and the quantity of news hits that it achieves.
- Only half of the editors recognised that there is a lot of concern about the quality in companies; and the same quantity of editors affirmed that there are politics within media heading towards the improvement of the quality.
- Half of the editors confirmed that they have formation programs for the journalists in their company. The most frequent answers point towards, on the one hand, the training for using technological tools, and on the other hand the explanation that specialisation does not exist due to the small size of the team of journalists. Two editors also said that the journalists are formed mainly by means of the experience that they acquire when working on the streets.
- The controls of quality are exercised mainly by the editors who apply their personal approaches. Only one of the media in the research has a copy editor.
- Little more than half of the editors believe that their company would be willing to invest in quality. The main reasons for not doing it yet is the recent investment made to begin with the news site and the difficult economic situation of the country.
- Many editors recognise that there is a relationship between quality and productivity. When explaining this relationship half of them pointed out that more quality means more productivity. According to what we saw in the preceding sections, this is not necessarily true, because productivity requires efficiency also.
- More than two thirds of the editors believe that the journalists that work for them are motivated to achieve a quality product, and this mainly

because of the prestige of the media and the journalists' sense of belonging to it.

- More than half of the editors recognise that the reaction of the journalists in sight of a productivity and/or quality measurement would be one of distrust confronted to the control and fear of being discharged. Some of the editors recognised that the measurements would make no sense.
- Regarding the question of what resources the editors believe are lacking that would increase the productivity of their employees, the most frequent answer was to have a bigger team. This answer is contradictory in relation to the meaning of the asked concept. Again, this answer of the editors demonstrates that they do not understand the concept of productivity discussed earlier in this work.
- When asked about the necessary resources to achieve a work with better quality, the most frequent answer was the necessity of getting more time, which reflects what was said in the previous point, regarding how reduced the teams of journalists working online are. Other remarkable answers relate to the motivation of the employees, for example recognition stimuli or economic retributions.
- Almost half of the editors affirm that their competition is of inferior quality, and the others consider that it is similar or that it is not direct competition. Only one of the 14 editors recognised that their competition is of superior quality.

QUALITY AND PRODUCTIVITY MANAGEMENT OF A MEDIA COMPANY

Deming said that quality does not come from the inspection, but from the improvement of the processes (James, 1996). In the case of media companies, these processes are not only limited to those described by Picard (1998), which were enumerated in the above. The processes should have standards of excellence to guide them toward a better quality. Giles (1991), for example, picks up standards that are applicable to journalists and organises them in four categories: accuracy, reporting, writing and communication. For example, in the category of accuracy, all the requirements for writing a story are stated, giving form to the process by means of such indications as following the style manual, show a complete context that includes all the points of view in a fair and complete way, verification of identities and addresses, etc. Determining the standards is a complex process that requires a lot of work and the cooperation of the journalists that will take it to the practice. It becomes necessary to have in mind what has been revised in the preceding sections about quality and productivity to structure a coherent and appropriate standard of quality to the journalistic practice, and that it should offer the media the base of their differentiation strategy. Many traditional media companies have, actually, standards of excellence that reflect, also, their editorial line.

The final stage is to take these standards to appraisal systems that allow to see how much these standard statements have been reached—effectivity—and what has been the cost of reaching them—efficiency. In other words, evaluate the productivity of the journalistic work.

The next goal is an appropriate communication of the standards and procedures to measure them by the managers toward the employees. These evaluation procedures should encourage teamwork and innovation. It is necessary to break the barriers between different areas or sections if these disturb the effective improvement of the quality. In the media, therefore, experts should be in "topics" and not in "areas". This will promote teamwork and innovation in an effective way.

CONCLUSIONS

The media companies that participate in competitive markets are not far from the search of utilities to stay in the business, and therefore, their executives require improving the techniques and management tools they use, continually. Before devoting to the management, it is necessary to recognise that there is an intensive intellectual work in media companies and that it is exercised mainly by journalists. The journalistic work thus becomes the main input of media companies, but it presents two problems at the moment of directing it. On the one hand, the nature of the intellectual work of journalists because of the creativity it requires loses its structure, and on the other hand, the product generated by a journalist has the capacity to influence people and institutions directly. Then, quality becomes the main guide to a good management and a differentiation strategy that allows the company to obtain the goals of profitability as well as those related with the roll of a media in a democratic society.

Quality is part of the search of the productivity, which consists in being efficient and effective. The efficiency resides in the good management of the resources, and the effectiveness in reaching the goal or objectives that in the case of the media belong to reaching the maximum quality.

The TQM theory could help greatly to reach the quality in the newsroom, with the necessary adaptations to the reality of the journalists themselves. TQM implies an active commitment of the whole company and full participation of the employees; all that should be summed up by means of the elaboration of an excellence standard that should be known by all the employees. In order for journalists to participate in the TQM philosophy and to assume the commitment of quality with society and with the very company, the motivation should play a preponderant roll. The journalists should also realise that an increase of the productivity in its company will help to make it more valuable, and as a consequence, they will be more and more irreplaceable.

From the results of the survey of online media editors, it is possible to conclude that there is still a lot to advance regarding management of the newsroom in these media. None of them has formal standards of excellence that indicate the level of quality that they are aiming at; they trust too much in the single approach of the editors, which in turn have been formed mainly through their own experience.

Of the characteristics associated with the quality of the interviewed editors, the only one that would be characteristic of an online media corresponds to the speed and instantaneous publication of the news. The other ones are traditional characteristics of the quality journalism. There is no (or very little) reference to the use of multimedia capacities that the web sites offer today. The scarce attention given to this can be attributed to the following factors mentioned by the editors: a very reduced team, and lack of technical means because it is a recent investment in a business that does not yet show its profitability.

The training and specialisation programs are fundamental in the TQM philosophy. Regrettably, they are not well considered by the editors, given the widespread belief that experience teaches everything, reinforced by the small size of the newsroom team that gives them neither the time nor the space to train and to specialise.

What a media company should finally look for, is productivity. Its components are quality and efficiency. Therefore, the management politics should point to the management of the productivity in order to solve the problems of quality. And, as seen in this work, it is compelling to continue the research about the productivity in online media, especially in order to establish guidelines on how to generate excellence standards.

REFERENCES

ASNE – American Society of Newspaper Editors (1999). *Examining our credibility: Perspectives of the public and the press.*

Bogart, L. (1981). *Press and the Public.* Mahweh, N.J.: Lawrence Erlbaum Associates.

Christopher, W., & Thor, C. (1998). *World-class quality and productivity.* Menlo Park: Crisp Publications.

CNTV – Consejo Nacional de Televisión de Chile (2001). *Estudios de audiencia y consumo televisivo.*

Crosby, P.B. (1979). *Quality is free: the art of making quality certain.* New York: McGraw-Hill.

Deming, E. (1982). *Quality, productivity, and competitive position.* Cambridge: MIT Center for Advances Engineering Study.

Drucker, P. F. (1961). *The practice of management.* London: Mercury Books.

Feigenbaum, A. (1991). *Total quality control* (3rd ed.). New York: McGraw Hill.

Garvin, D. (1988). *Managing quality: the strategic and competitive edge.* Free Press.

Giles, R. (1991). *Newsroom management.* Detroit: Media Management Books

Ivancevich, J., & Lorenzi, P., & Skinner, S., & Crosby, P. (1996). *Gestión, calidad y competitividad.* Madrid: Irwin.

Ishikawa, K. (1985). *What is total quality control? The Japanese way.* Productivity Press.

James, P. (1996). *Total quality management.* London: Prentice Hall.

Juran, J. M. (1964). *Managerial breakthrough.* New York: McGraw-Hill.

Juran, J. M. (1974). *Quality control handbook.* New York: McGraw-Hill.

Lacy, S. (2000). Commitment of financial resources as a measure of quality. In R. G. Picard (Ed.), *Measuring media content, quality, and diversity* (pp. 25-50). Turku: Turku School of Economics and Business Administration, Business Research and Development Centre, Media Group.

Litman, B. (1988). Microeconomic foundations. In R. G. Picard, J. P. Winter, M. E. McCombs & S. Lacy (Eds.), *Press concentration and monopoly* (3-34). Norwood, NJ: Ablex Publishing Corporation.

Nieto, A., & Iglesias, F. (2000). *La empresa informativa* (2da. ed.). Barcelona: Ariel.

Picard, R. G. (1998). Measuring and interpreting productivity of journalists. *Newspaper Research Journal*, Vol. 19, No. 4, 71-84.

Picard, R. G. (2000). Measuring quality by journalistic activity. In R. G. Picard (Ed.), *Measuring media content, quality, and diversity* (97-103). Turku: Turku School of Economics and Business Administration, Business Research and Development Centre, Media Group.

Porter, M. (1980). *Competitive strategy*. NJ: The Free Press.

Prahalad, C. K., & Krishnan, M. S. (1999). The new meaning of quality in the information age. *Harvard Business Review*, Vol. 77, N° 5, 109-118.

Reichheld, F. (1996). *El efecto de la lealtad*. Bogotá: Editorial Norma.

Salaverría, R. (2000). Claves del éxito de los diarios económicos en Internet. *El profesional de la información*, Vol. 9, N° 1-2, 26-30.

Sánchez-Tabernero, A. (2000). *Dirección estratégica de empresas de comunicación*. Madrid: Cátedra.

Sumanth, D. J. (1998). *Total productivity management*. Boca Raton: St. Lucie Press.

Taguchi, G. (1988). *Introduction to quality engineering: Designing quality into products and processes*. Tokyo: Asian Productivity Organization.

Chapter 13
The Influence of the Human Factors on the Performance of Media Enterprise: Case Studies on Cross-Media Publishing in Greek Media Enterprises

Anastasios E. Politis
Royal Institute of Technology and Politis Research

Media enterprises and the publishing industry face significant structural changes that affect the organisational and the administration structure of the enterprises. The implications for the enterprises are related to new requirements, concerning mainly the ability to function in the new publishing environment and the changing market of communications and information industries (Hancock, 1998). In particular, these changes affect the structure, workflow and working environment of the enterprises that are operating in the publishing sector. Keyword of this development is the application of cross-media publishing concepts (Crossmedia – Die Druckindustrie '98, 1999).

Traditionally, competence of human capital within the publishing process was based on print media qualifications and skills offered by the traditional education and training oriented within these fields (Komblinger, 1996). The application of new working tools and technologies like XML, Internet publishing and the new requirements for publishing both for print and for electronic media, need to be administrated by human capital with new competence (GOC, 2000). More specifically, the following aspects need to be investigated:

- Orientation of new skills
- Competence of human capital for cross-media publishing

The main research question that needs to be answered is whether media enterprises, and in particular those activated in the publishing, pre-media and prepress processes, as well as their employees, are prepared for the application of new technologies emerging in these fields. These new processes and technologies form the cross-media publishing production concepts. Their main characteristics are the following:

- Application of new workflows based on the common processing of data for both print and electronic media.
- Development of asset and content management software.
- Increasing applications of new processing technologies for publishing based on XML (eXtensible markup language).
- Development of new standards and formats for production management and workflow in publishing (CIP 4, Job ticket).
- The potential replacement or co-existence in new environments of traditional processes like graphic design, page and document layout made today by software applications like Quarkxpress, Indesign and Illustrator.
- The fact that in new technologies, applied, computer and programming skills are considered important and necessary for the successful employment of existing and potential personnel, but they need to be further defined (Danielson, Ericsson & Estmer, 1995).

The main research objective that needs to be explored is the competence characteristics of human capital employed or to be recruited within a media enterprise. The new competence is related with the technologies mentioned previously and the implications on structure, organisational and technical orientation of the media enterprises and, in particular, of these enterprises operating within the pre-media and pre-press fields of the graphic arts and media sector.

METHODS

The research method is based on literature study consisting principally of industry studies, analyses and scientific conferences on cross-media publishing (Comprint, 1998; Engelbach, Fahnlick, & van Hoof, 1999; GATF, 2000; CIP4, 2001; XML, 2001). Furthermore, literature studies were carried out on the human capital performance in the media sector (Andersen & Fagerberg, 1997; Mediengestalter/in für Digital..., 1998; Komblinger, 1998; Crossmedia–Die Druckindustrie '98, 1999; Koenig, 1999; COMES, 2000; NRW, 2000.

The research method also included interviews with media enterprises. Interviews were conducted through the distribution of a questionnaire at Greek publishing, graphic arts and media enterprises. Research was carried out between October and December, 2001. The selection of the enterprises has been made according to their orientation in prepress and publishing production and processes.

Questionnaires were sent out to 70 enterprises. Twenty-five questionnaires were sent out by e-mail and 35 by fax. Answers were obtained by 34 enterprises, which is almost 50% of the distributed questionnaires. Reminders to the enterprises took place through telephone. At least 10 of the questionnaires were answered through personal interviews with the owners of the enterprises. Following this procedure, interesting remarks and comments were also obtained. It is interesting that, although information of the enterprises was not requested, almost all enterprises provided their data, such as name, address, telephone, fax and e-mail.

The development of the questionnaire was based on the following structure: The first section consisted of two questions requesting the number of employees and the main activity of the enterprise. The second section consisted of three questions where feedback was requested on the familiarity degree on cross-media publishing technologies and processes, the usage of postscript or PDF and the percentage of Internet use for exchanging jobs' documents.

The third section consisted of two questions addressing issues on competence and skills requirements and characteristics and their degree of importance for the enterprise. The fourth section included eight questions regarding the role and performance of human capital within the enterprise environment.

The results of the survey were analysed and combined with the literature research in order to obtain the research conclusions.

CROSS-MEDIA PUBLISHING BACKGROUND

According to a study published by the German federation of printing and media industries (BVDM), print, publishing and Web run together and create new forms of communication. Computer–to–technologies, media independent data handling, cross-media production, database printing, CD-ROM, Internet and Intranet are the elements of communication of today (Crossmedia – Die Druckindustrie '98, 1999).

Cross-media publishing has been developed rapidly in recent years, especially after the spectacular development of technologies used for the publishing process, like digital prepress and new applications of traditional working tools (PIRA, 2000). As an example, Photoshop originally was used for the image digital processing in prepress production for print media. Now, the same software is widely used for web and multimedia applications.

Cross-media publishing is characterising this new process, being a rather new term to the publishing sector. It first appeared in research studies and surveys, international exhibitions and suppliers descriptions (Comprint, 1998; Engelbach et al, 1999; GATF, 2000). It defines the production workflow and process for publishing both print and electronic media. Another term that is used is *pre-media*. Pre-media has been introduced as a keyword at printing and media exhibitions (IMPRINTA 1997, IPEX 1998, DRUPA 2000). Regarding this interpretation, pre-media stands for content and information processing before the specification of the output media is defined (Crossmedia — Die Druckindustrie '98, 1999).

According to Karttunen and Nikulin (1999), printed and web media often use the same content. Then we talk about cross-media publishing or about information trade in selected parallel media. In services and trade, documents need to be produced, output printed and distributed. The distribution may be physical, e.g., remote printing, or virtual, such as e-mail, web-distributed documents, logical documents and databases, from which linking takes what is needed at any one moment. The data management issues of media production are central, and updated process definitions are needed for the workflow, new formats and cross-media publishing channels. There are many standards, and new specifications are derived from various simultaneous and urgent needs (Karttunen & Nikulin, 1999).

Another approach in cross-media publishing is the UPAS concept (universal printing application server), which has been introduced by Karttunen and Nikulin (1999). UPAS is defined as a concept to be integrated into future publishing systems to complement the existing production systems, mainly to bring matadata benefits. Regarding Karttunen and Nikulin, UPAS server collects the XML documents, linking their element files (e.g., PDF) to the final output-ready XML documents. The modelled product data is then organised as the linking elements in a resource repository, easily accessible and linkable over the web for later reuse. The UPAS server may also process metadata files facilitating costing and production management systems (Karttunen & Nikulin, 1999).

Dreyer introduced another issue on cross-media publishing interpretation. He argued that the application of integrated electronic workflow production systems at print media processing cannot be realised without XML-based jobtickets (Dreyer, 2001). As Dreyer points out, the application of job-ticket format offers new possibilities in print and electronic media automation of the production process; it optimises the workflow and allows the standardised exchange of orders' descriptions.

XML is considered as a milestone on cross-media publishing workflow and production process. According to a description by Arbortext, Epic E-content engine based on XML forms the centrepiece of a web-based single source system to capture, personalise, and publish business-critical content for delivery to the Web, print, wireless devices and other media (Arbortext, 2001).

Furthermore, following a description of cross media concepts stated by Söder (2001), printing on demand and database publishing basic characteristic is the ability to publish the same content in different formats—printed on paper, on CD-ROM or published both on Intra- and Internet. The application of a system based on SGML/XML is a necessity in order to enable the separation of the structure, content and graphic appearance by an automated generation of different output products. A further advantage of these formats (SGML/XML) is that information based on these standards will be reusable well into the future (Söder, 2001).

Regarding the use of XML for the job definition format, Mann (2001) explains that its application is necessary in order to relate processes to resources. Furthermore, on the same subject, Prosi points out that the job definition format (JDF) application uses XML as a database and not as a markup language. The use of the same code structure offers the possibility to create and read data necessary for the efficient JDF application. JDF requires an object "tree" in order to navigate among links and references. C++ is used a lot for this application (Prosi, 2001).

Cross-media publishing trends, especially for newspapers, have been recently presented at the Ifra-Expo 2001 exhibition in Geneva. Based on the reports from the exhibition, five main trends have been defined and are shortly presented below (Cross-Media Publishing…, 2001):

- Merging of suppliers offering publishing systems and components in the publishing process of newspapers.
- Increasing use of web application for running newspapers editing and processing; formation of workplaces on web browser structures and XML editors.
- New developments concerning the application of a layout software; Quarkxpress versus Adobe Indesign is one dimension of the problem. Questions arising on the issue of extending the existing layout software in all newspaper layouts or use new software; Interesting new applications on systems supporting XML.
- Application of artificial intelligence solutions on production workflow and asset management issues (mainly in archive browsing for images and newspapers pages)
- Further development of digital printing applications for newspapers.

EMERGING COMPONENTS OF THE
CROSS-MEDIA PUBLISHING PROCESS

Content management is defined as a concept, which, among others, facilitates processes for editorial and production systems, personalisation and syndication, database publishing, rights management, enhanced customer relationship management, efficient delivery of content and e-commerce applications (Seybold, 2001).

Mathison argues that the primary benefit of digital content management is a solution to the production and reuse of digital media files. But its real value extends far beyond tactical production, to a strategic advantage. Based on this, digital content management delivers a strategic competitive advantage to the publisher through faster product and service development life cycles, implementation of new sales channels on the Internet, higher valuation of the company and significantly improved, secure brand management (Mathison, 1999).

Another argument concerning the new interpretation of content is the following: Content within a cross-media process can be also defined as one of the three dimensions in which a media and communications service can be tailored to individuals or communities; the other two dimensions are presentation and delivery (Turpeinen, 1999). According to this argument, the publishing process can be defined in a new way where each element or production step can be adjusted to fit to each of these dimensions. Presentation is the media itself. Delivery is defined as the process whereby the content reaches its users, readers and target groups through the media.

This interpretation of content stated by Turpeinen seems to be developed according to Compaine's definition where content is one of the three dimensions of the media industry. Together with process and format they form the primary business activities of the media industry (Compaine, 1984).

Another cross-media publishing component is considered asset management or digital asset management. Historically, pre-press houses have stored and maintained their customer's material first as film and then as electronic files. Today, many enterprises are finding that digital asset management, if done properly, can be a profitable revenue source. This statement was the conclusion of a panel discussion focusing on assessing digital management needs, at International Prepress Association (IPA's) 36th annual technical conference (Cross-Media production..., 2001).

According to Sisson, one of the panel participants, benefits of the application of an asset management process have been, among others, centralised product information management, ability to leverage content for multiple uses and increased revenue for the customer (Cross-media production..., 2001).

Digital asset management is described as a management system, which can be either an elegantly proportioned database, or a clever manipulation of the operating system's file management technology. Within these two extremes lie all manner of variations on the database theme. Content or asset management is about using computers to improve the ways in which document elements are shared and used. Once it is possible to control digital content elements proactively, they become potentially valuable assets that can be deployed to the overall benefit of the business (Brunner, 2001).

Regarding the EU-sponsored project "PRINT-IT" main objectives, "printing and publishing industries need to be brought together in-line with currently available and emerging information and communication technologies". According to the project description, a global architecture structure should be created for supporting the "Distributed Publishing—DP" concept (Print-It, 2000). The components of this architecture are connected via ISDN and are networked with a high speed ATM backbone. PRINT-IT components are presented here (as they are described in the project brochure):

- Content providers
- DP (Distributed Publishing) service provider platform
- DP point of access platform
- Document server
- DP EDI platform
- Indigo colour digital printing press

The components of the PRINT-IT project system include a variety of tasks and processes such as document creation, job tickets, soft-proof, job specification and billing, remote access, transaction management and www server administration.

COMPETENCE OF HUMAN CAPITAL FOR CROSS-MEDIA PUBLISHING

"Graphic art and media enterprises are entering into new business fields, something that leads to a new market position. Online publishing, cross-media publishing and digital production technologies are the key words for the above-mentioned development. Within this new market orientation, graphic arts and media enterprises should develop their performance further. One of the important factors for the successful market positioning is the further training of

employees and entrepreneurs into the new media qualifications"
(Mediengestalter/in für Digital..., 1998).

This is the introduction to the documentation for the necessity of
restructuring of training in the German graphic arts and media sector. According
to the new qualification profile that has been established in the German graphic
arts and media industry, traditional qualifications have been combined with new
and are offered since 1998 at the German educational system. The most
important element in this reform is the establishment of the "Media designer for
digital and print Media" qualification profile (Mediengestalter/in) which is
divided into four subqualifications as follows (Mediengestalter/in für Digital...,
1998):

- Media designer
- Media operator
- Media technician
- Media consultant

Measures for restructuring the offered education and training are necessary
in order to face the lack of qualified human capital within the new media
production environment. The survey among some European countries has shown
considerable differences concerning the intensity of measurements for the
development of new courses and the adaptation to the new requirements of the
labour market. For example, Denmark, Germany and Sweden have already
developed new courses for cross-media production (Andersen & Fagerberg,
1997; Mediengestalter/in für Digital..., 1998; Grafiska, 1999). Other countries
are now trying to integrate such processes into their educational and training
systems (Politis, Praeventive Massnahmen...,1999; Politis, The new structure...,
1999).

In another study published in Denmark, the multimedia job profiles and
qualification requirements are described in relationship with 10 responsibility
areas: Sales, administrative project management, creative project management,
concept development and design, 2D graphics, 3D graphics, programme
construction, video and picture treatment, sound and text production. A job
profile can consist of one or more responsibility areas. According to Andersen
and Fagerberg (1997), "When establishing a school environment the student's
personal qualifications should be taken into account and the multimedia
employee's many different educational backgrounds and personal interests
should be included in the planning of the supply of continuous vocational
training"

During a further training action applied through an ADAPT project by the Verbund Strukturwandel GmbH at the Munich region (Germany), the graphic arts and media qualifications were divided in three main categories:

- Print-oriented qualifications
- New media qualifications
- Other qualifications

This classification appears to be the one that combines all useful characteristics of the existing knowledge and experience coming from the traditional graphic arts, the new skills from media qualifications and other new qualifications not directly related to the two sectors but necessary for the complete competence development (Komblinger, 1998).

Hence, cross-media publishing competence requirements go beyond this approach by demanding new elements, software tools and extensive management skills in a new publishing environment where content, databases, layout design and standards are met with the traditional qualifications. As Theiss (1999) states: "The necessary dynamic development of the Media sector is based on new competence profiles."

Another emerging approach in human capital competence characteristics is derived from the progress of the CustomDP project (Customdp, 2001). The project is introducing a publishing process based on metadata, XML-editors, content and asset management. Furthermore, following the project's main objectives to build up a system that supports the creation, management, updating and use of different types of customised training materials, a new approach on content creation and management is developing. According to a classification based on Customdp project progress, the following task profiles for different publishing components has been introduced:

Publishing component:

Task profiles:

Content: Author, content creator and validator, chief editor, content compiler.

System administration: SCO (small content object) importer, XML editor, metadata enhancer, metadata validator.

Based on the Customdp project progress, content creation must be done under the instruction given by a content template. Authors must be registered at the database content type. XML is operating as the "integrator between content creation and publishing system, leading to a structured content creation and publishing process". In addition, content must be processed according to system specifications (Customdp, 2001).

RESULTS

Karttunen and Nikulin conclude that technology and format barriers between web and printed media will be lifted. Data interchange between web applications is essential. If XML documents are used as the storage platform for media content and for the linking elements (metadata) to prepare and validate the output documents, the resulting workflow is improved. This will help the print and cross- media actors, such as Internet service providers (ISPs), publishers, printers, printing brokers, repro houses, advertising agencies and buyers and educational media writers. The vendors of the content management, prepress and press fronted systems need to develop more XML and web-aware systems and do it in small steps towards openness required in the web time.

An emerging issue that has been arising following the statements made by Mann and Prosi is that programming languages are used quite a lot for the development of workflow applications such as JDF. But, this software application is directed for real-world application by printers and in general by humans with expertise in printing, and print media workflow production. The question arising is whether humans that will be the end-users of such applications must be forced to update their competence with new specific computer and programming oriented skills.

Furthermore, in newspaper editing and production the combination of new elements based on cross-media publishing concepts is gaining importance. The new applications are the use of web-based applications, Internet-protocol support, XML functionality, and artificial intelligence applications on workflow production and asset management. According to the report from the Ifra 2001 exhibition, XML is considered as media–neutral editor for print and Internet newspapers editions.

In addition, as it can be derived from the PRINT-IT project description, existing/traditional tasks and qualifications of the publishing and pre-press fields are combined with tasks descriptions requiring skills from the ITC sector. Not only the different tasks but also the whole system structure requires administration based on extended and upgraded competence and skills.

Finally, progress on the Customdp project reveals that new tasks and job profiles are emerging, concerning publishing of educational material, based on XML editors. From the tasks description it can be assumed that new competence is required in order to be someone able to work within this new publishing environment as suggested by the Customdp project documentation.

Results Derived from the Questionnaire

Before entering the main findings from the answers obtained from the 34 enterprises, it might be useful to observe the way that the enterprises were involved in answering the questionnaires: This finding is interesting because it expresses a behaviour which indicates the procedure of the enterprises (and in general the graphic arts and media sector, at least in Greece), regarding the pace of changes that are taking place in the enterprises working environment.

Although 25 out of 70 questionnaires were sent out by e-mail (the rest were sent out by fax), 29 answers were received by fax and only 5 by e-mail. Based on this finding it can be concluded that the vast majority of owners of media enterprises received the e-mails, printed out the questionnaire, they answered and sent it back by fax. They did not use their computers to answer the questionnaires. This behaviour becomes even more interesting if we consider that most of the enterprises are quite familiar with computer systems that are used in daily production. But they do not use the electronic process for communication purposes.

As was already mentioned, 34 answers were obtained out of 70 questionnaires sent out. Results have been rounded up concerning the mapping of percentages for better presentation purposes. The results are summarised as follows.

Regarding the number of employees, 54% of the enterprises have 1 to 9 employees, 26% have 10 to 20 employees and 20% have 21 to 50 employees. This is reflecting the structure of the graphic arts and media enterprises in Greece, consisting of micro and small enterprises. Furthermore, regarding the type of the enterprises, 33% are operating in publishing, and 33% in prepress. Twenty percent of the enterprises are operating in the entire production spectrum (prepress, printing and finishing), whereas 7% of the enterprises declare their main operation in printing and 7% in multimedia (web site and CD-ROM) design and production.

Regarding the type of enterprises, it can be concluded that the majority is operating in fields that are subject to the implications of the cross-media publishing environments and technologies applications.

Interesting are the findings from the second group of questions regarding the degree of familiarity on cross-media publishing technologies and processes, the usage of postscript or PDF and percentage of Internet use for sending and receiving jobs' documents.

The majority of the enterprises are familiar in working with PDF technology (almost 65% of the answers), and relatively familiar with colour management (about 45% of answers). In contradiction, regarding all other technologies, the majority of the enterprises declare that they are either not familiar at all or they have a low degree of familiarity. The percentages range between 65% and 70 % for media asset management, content management, digital networks and workflows (e.g., Apogee, Prinergy) and database management.

Even higher is the percentage of very low familiarity with "Job ticket", and JDF (Job Definition Format) concepts (about 85%), reaching its highest point with XML (eXtensible Markup Language), where only one enterprise answered that it has a rather high degree of familiarity with XML. This enterprise is among those operating in the multimedia production field.

As it concerns the usage of file formats for exchanging digital files of orders and jobs with other enterprises, the majority of the enterprises are using Postscript files, at a percentage of 75%. PDF files are used at a percentage of 15%, whereas other files such as Quarkxpres and Illustrator are used by 10%. Furthermore, regarding the usage of medium for digital communication and exchange of jobs, digital disks such as zip, jazz and CD-ROMs are used at a percentage of 75%. Internet is used at a percentage of about 25%.

Regarding answers on the third section of questions addressing issues on the competence and skills requirements and characteristics and their degree of importance of the enterprise, the research resulted in the following.

Only a few enterprises regard programming skills as important to be part of the skills of human capital employed in the graphic arts and media sector (about 12%). On the other hand, web-internet skills, marketing, customer relationship management and skills in publishing production processing are considered important with percentages ranging between 60% and 70 %.

Furthermore on the issue of importance of flexible working time, distance working, and knowledge management concepts as well as the efficiency of the education and training systems, research resulted in the fact that they are quite important for the future development of the enterprises. Going further into the issue regarding the role and performance of human capital within the enterprise environment the following answers were provided by the questioned enterprises.

Regarding the consideration of the application of human resource management processes in enterprises, according to their size, 50% of the answers regard that they are applicable in large-scale enterprises and 50% in all kinds of enterprises.

On the question of responsibility for personnel matters in the enterprise, 80% answered that the owner carries this responsibility, with the remainder, 20%, to be the responsibility of the personnel manager. As it concerns the question of whether there is an employee within the enterprise that the owner trusts totally, by undertaking all tasks and responsibilities without supervision, negative answers were given by 75% of the owners.

Regarding the issue of running discussions with the employees concerning investments, improvements in production processes and the development strategy of the enterprise, about 80% of the answers were positive. Furthermore, on the question of whether a system for human capital development should be necessary to be applied to the enterprise, positive answers reached an impressive 90%.

Answers on the importance of achievement of good relationships amongst people within the enterprise, as well as trust development among employees, customers, suppliers and other people related to the operation of the enterprise, resulted in percentages of 100%. Finally, the "Investment in people" concept and the effort for the development of human capital are considered an important issue for further progress of the enterprise by all of the enterprises.

DISCUSSION AND CONCLUSIONS

Media enterprises must face the issue of potential shift from the traditional operations, such as graphic design and page layout, to the content management and processing using XML editors, for example. An issue of significance and a further question that can be asked is whether the new cross-media publishing process will eliminate or reduce the importance of skills and expertise of the existing human capital within media enterprises.

Trends on improvements concerning newspaper production systems reveal that new applications based on cross-media publishing elements are introduced. Therefore it can be concluded that certainly, competence requirements need to be updated and new job profiles need to be described for the newspaper editing and production field.

Another critical issue related with this is the implications on education and training concerning the effective employment of human capital in the media enterprise of the future. How employees accustomed to working for years with software tools based on graphical interfaces, will react to being employed using programming skills.

Regarding the issue of development of new workflow applications such as job definition format (JDF), they are also based on programming skills. These formats need to be built up with interfaces familiar to the existing experience and perception that employees possess for print and electronic media production. If JDF is going to be applied as a standard for workflow production, then a graphical interface should be developed that will allow the efficient adaptation of the human capital employed at media enterprises in these new working environments.

As a general conclusion: Human capital in publishing and pre-press enterprises need to enrich competence in order to undertake new tasks, by adapting all necessary knowledge and skills required for efficient performing within the cross-media working environment and the future media enterprise.

Based on the research carried out, the cross-media publishing characteristics can be defined as follows:

- Common processing of content and information for publishing of print and electronic media.
- Development of new software tools formats and production workflow systems.
- Reorientation of existing production systems, processes and tools (colour management systems, scanning, image processing) in the new production environments.
- Content management of any form, format and combination of text, images, graphics, sound and video.

The results reveal that the lack of information is obvious among the questioned enterprises. The enterprises are familiar in operating with PDF and colour management. In contradiction, regarding all other technologies, the majority of the enterprises declare that they are either not familiar at all or they have a low degree of familiarity. Media asset management, content management, digital networks and workflows are subjects that are unknown to the publishing and prepress enterprises.

Even lower is the familiarity with "Job ticket", and JDF (Job Definition Format) concepts. XML, which appears to be the most significant tool for the future publishing concepts is absolutely unknown among enterprises questioned and interviewed.

The enterprises still use Postscript files and exchange data with the use of digital disks such as zip, jazz and CD-ROMs. Internet is used at a low rate for exchanging data for publishing and pre-press production. This finding reveals that most enterprises are confident with tools and software used today in electronic pre-press and publishing. The low rate of Internet-based communications in Greece and in particular the poor infrastructure in high-speed Internet connections in the country, restrict the use of the Internet as a tool for exchanging data for jobs among prepress and publishing enterprises in Greece. Digital disks are distributed through the enterprises with the aid of couriers.

The danger, however, will appear when the new cross-media tools are introduced and applied. Prepress and publishing enterprises should not leave the field for further development with cross-media publishing applications to other players outside the traditional publishing sector. The issue here is how the enterprises will react to this development. Education and training should again be the catalyst for the development of the required competence for employees in publishing and prepress applications.

Concerning the results regarding programming skills, it is important to mention that the enterprises do not seem to be aware of the importance of these skills for human capital. As it can be derived from the interviews, most of the owners consider that they can gain all computers and informatics competence required by employing one person that has these skills.

The issue arising, however, is that the trends concerning cross-media publishing, both on common publishing of print and electronic media and as a workflow application, require specific computer knowledge, based mainly on advanced programming skills. It seems that the pre-press and publishing enterprises make the same mistake with the DTP era (when pre-press enterprises with high-end electronic pre-press systems considered that low-end prepress platforms were not important and they were not competitive to their systems).

Furthermore, Internet skills, marketing, customer relationship management and skills in publishing production processing are considered important from the majority enterprises. This seems to make sense as the transformation from production-oriented, into service providers is becoming essential for publishing and pre-press enterprises.

Flexible working time, distance working, knowledge management and the efficiency of the education and training systems appear to be important for the future development of the enterprises. Interesting comments have arisen from enterprises concerning the establishment of specific structures and applications of these concepts. In other words, knowledge management needs to be further defined and transformed to a certain structured application, so enterprises can see whether there are benefits in their development.

To give an example, these concepts are perceived by enterprises like the ISO 9000 quality assurance system: For an enterprise this is something "good" but they do not touch it unless they are thoroughly informed of the potential advantages, added value and, of course, costs for all these new concepts. Being concerned almost all the time with daily production problems, they do not easily find the opportunity to spend time on strategic issues related to the future development of their enterprise.

In most enterprises, owners take care of personnel matters. Another issue concerning tasks and responsibilities is that the owners' enterprises do not trust, or they do not have, employees who can undertake all tasks and responsibilities without supervision. This has to do mainly with the size of the enterprises, which are registered as micro and small ones.

Enterprise size seems to be the factor that leads enterprise owners to discuss investments, improvements in the production process and the development strategy of the enterprise with their employees. Such subjects can be easier discussed due to the closer relationship of the enterprise owners with the employees in daily operation and running of the business.

In addition, good relationships among people in the enterprise, trust among employees, customers, suppliers and other people related to the operation of the enterprise and the "investment in people" concept are considered important for further progress of the enterprise, by all enterprises. Again it must be mentioned at this point that all these words are nice and the answer given is positive, but these "loose" statements need to be to turned into structured concepts and applications in order to have a meaningful content. Only after this process can they be evaluated by the enterprises concerning their importance to them.

If all previously mentioned parameters are taken into account, then it is easy to define some main characteristics of human capital competence for cross-media publishing. Firstly, all new technologies that are applied must be adapted into the new competence. In addition, a first necessary step for the traditional pre-press and publishing enterprises is to re-orientate the consideration that print and electronic media are processed separately.

Within the new working environment, many operations are performed before the output determination to a certain type of media (e.g., the scanning process for an image that will be published in a magazine and will be used for the Web). Apart from the new or further developed skills that are required in order to function with such a new specific technical task, it is necessary for humans to adapt to a new production workflow, where every process has to be determined according to a cross-media publishing working environment.

The structure of the publishing production workflow is changing rapidly (it is a continuously changing process). In parallel, it is becoming more complex if it will be compared with the traditional workflows either for print or electronic media. New competence is therefore required for the efficient adaptation and performance of human capital employed or to be recruited with the publishing process where cross-media publishing concepts are applied. This new competence should be formed by the combination of the following:

- Print-oriented qualifications
- New media qualifications (multimedia, web design and production)
- Programming skills, clearly defined (e.g. XML, database handling)
- Digital asset – content management qualifications
- New production workflow applications (e.g., JDF, CIP4)

An issue that needs to be further investigated is whether cross-media publishing will replace existing publishing, pre-press and web sites creation or it will be used in parallel with the traditional processes. Further research is also required for the updating of qualification and job profiles description on new concepts and applications of cross-media, distributed and networked publishing.

Furthermore, it is important to explore the future media enterprise competence structure of human capital, which seems to be shaped by merging of graphic arts and media professions and new ICT skills. This question goes beyond previous research outcomes, which conclude that graphic arts and media skills need to be upgraded simply with computer skills. Another interesting aspect related with the previous subject is whether humans from ICT sector will undertake the responsibility to work within cross-media publishing environments and to what extent they will replace employees with traditional expertise in publishing processes.

Further extensive research is required in the fields of the adaptation of educational and training systems in such a way that the competence development of human capital for cross-media working environments is sufficiently supported.

REFERENCES

Arbortext. Epic- E-content Engine (E3), information brochure on XML based Arbortext sofware application, XML Europe 2001 conference and exhibition, May 2001, Berlin Germany.

Brunner, L. Asset tests, *Digital Demand*, issue 5, 2001 Pira International Ltd, Surrey UK, 2001.

CIP4 - the need for a comprehensive system integration in the graphical arts industry, 2001, http://www.cip4.org.

COMES: Coaching Human Resources For Continuous Organisational Learning. EGIN Finland, Helsinki, 2000.

Compaine, B., M. *Understanding New Media: Trends and issues in electronic distribution*. Ballanger, Cambridge, Massachuttes, 1984.

Comprint. "Navigating in the future media markets, Comprint international conference, June 1998, Edinburgh UK.

Crossmedia – die Druckindustrie '98. Bundesverband Druck und Medien BVD, Wiesbaden Germany, 1999.

Customdp: Development of a system for customized training material of digital printing, project run by a concortium of 13 partners. Project leader: VTT Information technology, Espoo, Finland, 2001.

Danielson H., Ericsson, B. E., & Estmer, B. Future needs for competence – 2000. Survey by the Swedish Graphic Industry and Newspaper Branch, Stockholm Sweden, 1995.

Cross-Media-Publishing mit XML und Künstlicher Intelligenz. *Deutscher Drucker*, nr 41, 2.11.2001, pp 7-9.

Andersen, K. B., & Fagerberg, M. Present and future requirements for multimedia qualifications. DTI human resources development report, Denmark 1997.

Dreyer, R.. Cross-Media-Publishing erfordet eine integrierte Produktion. *Deutscher Drucker*, nr 9, 1.3.2001, pp 26-31.

Engelbach, W., Fahnlich, K., & Hoof van, A. *Sustaining development and competitiveness for the European printing industry.* Fraunhofer Institut fuer Arbeitswirtschaft und Organisation, Stuttgart, Germany, 1999.

GATF. *Technology Trends for the New Millennium. GATF 2000 technology forecast*, USA.

GRAFISKA. *The need of competence in the graphic arts sector.* Board for Education in Media and Information Technology, GRAFISKA, Stockholm, 1999.

GOC. *Multimedia: beyond the pioneering stage. Report on multimedia qualifications*, GOC, Veenendaal the Netherlands, 2000.

Hancock, M. Technology in a state of change in the graphical sector. Paper presented at the EGF-AFETT international seminar on New technologies, work organization and collective bargaining in the European Graphical Industry, Florence, Italy, 3 June 1998.

Kartunen S., Nikulin H. Content and metadata management in the media production workflow, *Journal of pre press and printing technology*. Pira international Ltd. Vol. 5. March 1999 pp 3 – 8, Surrey, UK.

Koenig, A. *Selbstgesteuertes Lernen in Kleinbetrieben*. Universitat Stuttgart, March 1999, Stuttgart Germany.

Komblinger, D. *Strukturwandel in der Druckindustrie - Arbeitsmarkt und Weiterbildungsbedarf.* Verbund Struktur Wandel (VSW) GMBH, 1998, Munich, Germany.

Mann, G. XML schema for job definition format. Paper presented at the XML-Europe 2001 conference, May 2001, Berlin Germany.

Mathison M. Digital Content Management: A place to begin, *GATFWORLD*, May / June 1999 pp19 –24, USA

Mediengestalter/in für Digital – und Printmedien. Bundesinstitut für Berufsausdildung, Ausgabe Mai 1998, Berlin Germany.

NRW. Qualifizierung in Medienberufen. NRW, Ministerium für Schule und Weiterbildung, Wissenschaft und Forschung des Landes Nordrhein – Westfalen, 2000, Germany.

Politis, A. Praeventive Massnahmen im Rahmen von Beschaeftigungsgesell schaften – Beispiele aus Griechenland, Paper presented at the European conference Brücken zur Arbeit, 13 September 1999, Hannover, Germany (in German) organised by the Landesregierung Niederschachsen..

Politis, A. The new structure of the education and training for the Graphic Arts sector. Report on the necessity for the establishment of new Media qualifications into the Greek vocational – post secondary training system. – Athens, November 1999 (in Greek).

PIRA, *The Future of Print*. Pira International and Prima corporation, Pira International, April 2000, Surrey UK

PRINT-IT, 2000: Publishers re-usable integrated network toolkit for information technologies. European Commission DGXIII sponsored project brochure.

Cross-media production and the networking publishing challenge, *Prepress bulletin*, vol.91 no.2, July/August 2001 pp 20-36, South Holland, IL, USA.

Prosi, R. The open source JDF parser project. Paper presented at the XMLEurope 2001 conference, May 2001, Berlin Germany.

Seybold publications inc. On line registration for attending seminars on the Internet, 2001. http://www.seyboldseminars.com. .

Söder information brochure on content management suite for XML/SGML objects, XML Europe 2001 conference and exhibition, May 2001, Berlin Germany.

Theiss B. *Medienkompetenz resultiert aus zuverlaessigem Aendendungswissen in Bundesverband Druck und Medien report Crossmedia – die Druckindustrie '98,* BVDM 1999, Wiesbaden Germany.

Turpeinen M.: News and learning in network environments in Enabling network – based learning, conference proceedings. Espoo Finland 1999, pp. 338 – 341.

XML. Going vertical and beyond: How XML powers industry applications. XML Europe 2001 conference and exhibition, May 2001, Berlin Germany.

Chapter 14
Customer Satisfaction, Price and Financial Performance: A Study of Finnish Printing Industry Companies

Mikko Grönlund
Turku School of Economics and Business Administration

The recession of the early 1990s brought along an exceptional decline for the graphic industry in Finland. After a long period of growth, turnover, number of employees, and profitability sank to an unprecedented low. In the second half of the 1990s, the economic situation of the printing industry showed a positive trend. The printing industry has not, however, been able to regain its former strong economic growth. The positive development shows itself mainly in the increased turnover. Equity ratio has not shown any improvement. Companies are as indebted as they were during the recession years. This has led to a search for other means of improving the conditions of the graphic arts companies.

Intensifying competition, rapid deregulation, and heightened consumer expectations for quality have led businesses throughout the world to focus on customer satisfaction. Corporate managers now routinely strive to understand customer wants and needs by measuring customer satisfaction levels and determining the product attributes critical to satisfaction formation. Underlying these efforts is a belief that customer satisfaction has important consequences for customer loyalty and, ultimately, corporate financial success (Anderson, Fornell, & Lehmann, 1994; Bolton, & Drew, 1991; Buzzell & Gale, 1987; Fornell & Wernerfelt, 1987). In an effort to improve company performance, Finnish graphic arts industry companies are increasingly focusing attention on issues of service quality and customer satisfaction.

Grönlund, Jacobs, and Picard (2001) carried out a study of customers of Finnish printing companies that explored relations among importance ratings, performance ratings, and problem experiences in different determinants of service quality. The research was based on data gathered through an extensive questionnaire administered to 2,239 customers of 66 printing firms in Finland. For that study, the aggregate data was analysed to produce descriptive statistics of importance and performance ratings. These were then subjected to gap analysis. Descriptive statistics were also calculated for problem experiences. Correlation and factor analyses were conducted of customers' performance ratings with customers' assessments of overall quality of firms. Regression analyses were also used to produce key drivers of satisfaction.

According to Grönlund et al. (2001) there are several important criteria that the customers of printing companies use when selecting the service provider. Nine out of ten customers felt that keeping the agreed schedules, appropriate quality of the actual end product and flawless service process are very important criteria. The great majority of customers also felt that the quality of entire service process and the expertise of customer liaison are very important criteria. Despite the fact that Grönlund et al. (2001) found differences between customer and print service provider groups, one conclusion was clear. Price is not a primary selection criteria.

This article continues the ongoing line of research into issues of service quality and customer satisfaction and is based on telephone interviews of 1,637 customers of 55 Finnish printing companies. The data was gathered through a questionnaire that was designed to explore importance ratings, performance ratings and problem experiences. In the first section of the questionnaire the respondents were asked to assess the importance of various factors when selecting a printing company. The respondents were then asked to grade their print service provider. In the third part the respondents were asked to assess the number and severity of problem situations in the service process. The respondents were also asked to evaluate the effect of the possible problems on customer relationships with their business.

Some past researches (Bitner & Tetreault, 1990; Parasuraman, Zeithaml, & Berry, 1985) have focused on identifying key service dimensions. For this chapter the original statements and evaluations in all three parts of the questionnaire were combined into ten and five service attributes or dimensions presented by Parasuraman, Zeithaml, and Berry (1985, 1988). Price level was handled as a separate indicator. These indicators were then used to produce evidence about service quality and customer satisfaction. These are important because they influence consumers' willingness to purchase from specific companies and thus the demand for other products and services. These were then considered with issues such as price to determine relationship between customer expectations, service delivered, and price.

Some concern has been expressed about the heavy emphasis on customer satisfaction and whether or not it relates to the bottom-line performance (Zeithaml, Parasuraman, & Berry, 1990). Whereas customer satisfaction has received significant attention in marketing literature, and such related areas as service quality, this attention has not focused on modelling the impact of these constructs on profits or other performance measures (Bernhardt, Donthu & Kennett, 2000; Zahorik & Rust, 1992).

In order to get some evidence about the link between customer satisfaction and financial performance, the second data set that was used in this study was the financial statements of companies. Several measures of performance for each printing company was examined including turnover, profitability, solidity, liquidity, and productivity. This was done because so far only few researches (Anderson & al., 1994; Boulding, Kalra, Staelin, & Zeithaml, 1993; Rust, Zahorik, & Keiningham, 1995) have examined the relationship between customer satisfaction and company's financial performance. The final step of this study was to examine the link between overall customer satisfaction and performance measures, and different dimensions of customer satisfaction and performance measures. In earlier studies (Nelson et al., 1992; Schneider, 1991) mixed results have been found for the relationship between customer satisfaction and profitability in any given time period (Bernhardt et al., 2000).

THE CONCEPT OF CUSTOMER SATISFACTION

Hunt (1977) defines satisfaction as a customer's post-purchase evaluation of a product or service. A customer is satisfied when a product performs better than expected and dissatisfied when expectations exceed performance. This line of thinking is representative of the dominant expectation-disconfirmation paradigm (Rosen & Surprenant, 1998; Wirtz & Bateson, 1999), which posits that an individual's pre-purchase expectations for performance are either confirmed when a product performs as expected (Parasuraman, Berry, & Zeithaml, 1990), negatively disconfirmed when the product performs more poorly than expected, or positively disconfirmed when a product performs better than expected (Oliver, 1980). Accepted thinking argues that negative disconfirmation results in dissatisfaction and the customer is unlikely to repurchase (Rosen & Surprenant, 1998). Confirmation or positive disconfirmation results in customer satisfaction and an increased likelihood of repurchase.

The Disconfirmation Model

Researchers have considered a variety of potential factors that affect customer satisfaction. Market level characteristics such as industry concentration, distribution breadth, and consumer cost have been examined and found to account for variation in satisfaction across product categories (Fornell & Robinson, 1983; Singh, 1991). Consumer demographics (e.g., age, gender, and education) have also been evaluated to see how satisfaction varies across consumers, but the literature offers weak, inconsistent support for these relationships (Francken & van Raaij, 1985). More importantly, the vast extent of the satisfaction literature focuses on the relationship between pre-purchase expectations for product performance and post-purchase satisfaction, in other words the disconfirmation model.

The studies (Churchill & Suprenant, 1982; Oliver, 1980; Patterson & Johnson, 1993) on customer satisfaction have discovered that disconfirmation is an important intervening factor. Disconfirmation occurs when customer expectations and the properties of the product do not match with each other (Churchill & Suprenant, 1982). In an under-expectation situation, the experiences of the customer exceed his or her expectations. Exceeding the expectations leads to a positive experience by the customer. In the opposite situation the good or service fails to fulfil the customer's expectations. This is called an over-expectation situation. If the expectations and post-purchase experiences match with each other, it is called a balanced situation (Erevelles & Leavitt, 1992). These relationships are illustrated in Figure 14.1.

Figure 14.1. The Relationships between Customer Experiences and Expectations

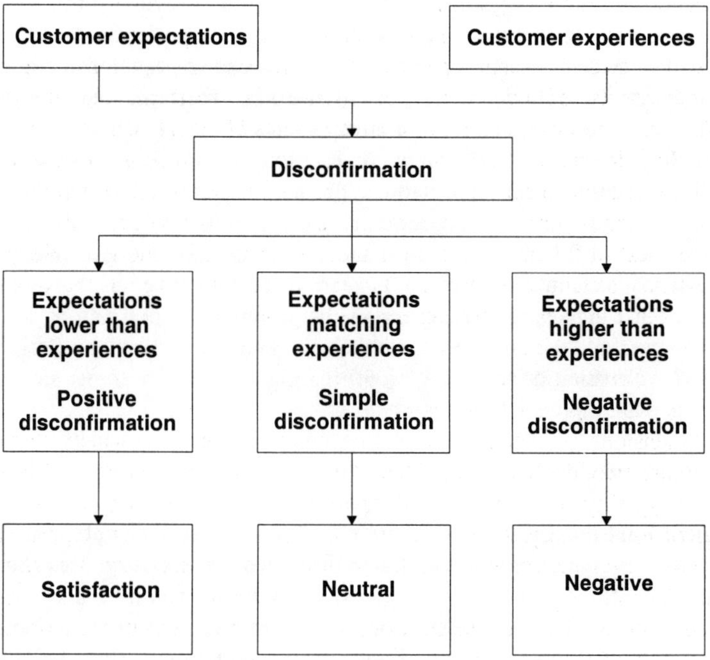

Although the term *expectations* is often used as the comparison standard without differentiating among possible meanings, Miller (1977) has identified a range of potential standards: ideal or desired, expected, minimum tolerable, and deserved or equitable. *Ideal or desired* is the level of performance wished for by the customer. *Expected performance* is what the customer believes it probably will be. *Minimum tolerable performance* is the last level of performance acceptable to the customer. *Deserved or equitable* is what the customer feels performance should be in light of costs such as time and money. These expectation standards have been tested and shown to differ in their ability to explain satisfaction (Tse & Wilton, 1988).

Spreng and Olshavsky (1992) have criticised the disconfirmation model especially for its inability to distinguish between customer's expectations and desires. According to them desires, unlike expectations, include an assessment of how the properties of the product or the benefits it provides fulfil the personal values of the customer. In their own research they reach a conclusion that for the formation of customer satisfaction the customer's desires are equally important to customer's expectations. Spreng, Mackenzie, and Olshavsky (1996) sought to reconcile these comparison standards, and introduce the idea of information satisfaction, by proposing an integrative model of satisfaction formation. The model postulates that the extent to which a product's performance has met or exceeded both desires and expectations (desires and expectations congruency) are antecedents of two types of satisfaction, attribute and information satisfaction. These are, in turn, direct antecedents of overall satisfaction.

Adding desires to the expected comparison standard addresses the illogical possibility of a customer having low expectations for a product and then being satisfied when their low expectations for performance are fulfilled. An empirical test of the model provided support for the hypothesised relationships and extends satisfaction research beyond merely looking at the product to consider other marketing mix elements (e.g., promotion).

Measuri? ? Service Quality

The dimensions of service and service quality have been widely researched during last two decades. The literature on service marketing has begun to approach quality through the concept of experienced service quality and the model of total quality (Grönroos, 1998b). The two best known approaches to service quality research are expectation-disconfirmation or Gap Model and the Nordic School.

The roots of service quality research are in customer satisfaction research, but it has evolved into a distinct research area of its own. Understanding the customers' expectations is a precondition for providing superior service, because the customers compare their observations with their expectations when assessing the service quality of the company (Parasuraman, Berry, & Zeithaml, 1991). The nature and formation of customers' expectations of service quality are still ambiguous factors. The literature has defined customers' expectations in many different ways. The expected service depends upon the previous experiences of the customer, the customer's individual needs and word of mouth communication (Parasuraman, Berry, & Zeithaml, 1991). Also the marketing communication activities of the company have an effect on the customers' expectations. The customers grade the service quality by comparing the experienced quality with the expected quality (Parasuraman et al., 1985). The service quality is therefore the extent to which delivered service matches the customer' s expectations.

The quality experienced by the customer is a result of internal decisions and actions of the company. The management conceptions of customer expectations guide decisions on quality requirements that the company makes during the delivery of the service. The customer experiences two components of quality: the production and delivery process (functional quality) and the technical solution that is created by the service process (technical quality) (Grönroos, 1998a).

Customer expectations are usually reasonable, but they vary depending upon circumstances and experience, and experience with one service provider may influence expectations of others (Lewis, 1995). So in connection with customer expectations, the so-called "zone of tolerance" is often discussed. Parasuraman, Berry and Zeithaml (1991) have stated that the customer expectations of service have two levels: desired and sufficient. The desired level of service quality is the quality the customer wishes to receive. It is a mixture of what the service "can" and " should" be. The adequate service quality is what the customer finds acceptable. Between the desired and adequate service quality is the zone of tolerance (see Figure 14.2). Tolerance zones vary between customers, service aspects and with experience.

Figure 14.2. The Zone of Tolerance

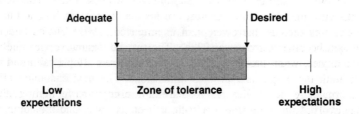

A customer's zone of tolerance may also vary in different dimensions of the service. According to Berry (1995) this means that the boundaries of the tolerance zone may move depending on whether the dimension is connected with the service process or the actual end product. Customers regard reliability as the core of any service and they have higher expectations of the reliability of the service. Therefore customers are reluctant to lower their expectations of the company's reliability. The tolerance area for reliability is probably narrower and the level of sufficient and desired service higher than for some other dimension of the service.

Customer's growing experience is another thing that may cause an increase in the desired level of service quality. Parasuraman, Berry and Zeithaml (1991) carried out a study that showed more experienced customers are more likely to have higher expectations for service quality. More experienced customers are also more likely to be noisy when dissatisfied with service received.

Another important factor that affects a customer's service expectations is the price. The majority of customers believe the more they pay the better the service should be. Despite this assumption, they do not believe that low price is a legitimate excuse for bad service (Parasuraman et al., 1991). In addition, if options (for example number of suitable printing houses) are limited customer desires may not decrease but the tolerance zones/levels may be higher. Conversely, if the customer feels that there are several substitutable service providers, the zone of tolerance is narrower.

Further, customer expectations are higher in emergency situations or when something went wrong the first time. Because reliability of service is such a significant factor of customers' overall assessment of service quality, the company must prove itself reliable when delivering the first service. If the company performs reliably and without defects on the first encounter, it gains also indirect benefits with that customer. The customer doesn't include any "quality compensation" (Blomquist, Dahl, & Haeger, 1993) in the expectations when purchasing the second time. If there are emergency and problem situations in the delivery of the service, it may increase, at least temporarily, the customer's view of a sufficient service quality level. After a failure in a service delivery the customer has a more critical eye for the service quality and his or her tolerance area becomes narrower (Parasuraman et al., 1991). The customer's tolerance area becomes narrower and the sufficient and desired service quality levels rise higher, when the service quality is recovered after a failure. This applies to both the output and process dimensions. The next encounter after failure, normalising of service, is loaded with exceptionally high quality requirements. Those requirements could have been avoided, had the company performed immaculately the first time (Blomquist et al., 1993).

Dimensions of Service Quality

Parasuraman, Berry and Zeithaml Lewis (1995) have presented the most adopted definition of the elements of service. According to their (Parasuraman & al., 1985) definition, service has ten dimensions: reliability, responsiveness, competence, availability, politeness, communication, credibility, assurance, understanding and knowing the customer and tangibles.

Reliability involves consistency of performance and dependability. In other words, it means that the company performs the service right the first time. It also means flawless records.

Responsiveness means the personnel's willingness and capability to serve the customer. It also involves the timeliness of service. For example, whether the company is able to keep the agreed schedule for the print work. It also includes the rapidity of service and customer contacts without delay when necessary.

Competence means mastering the appropriate knowledge and skills. A company's competence consists not only of the contact person's skills and knowledge but also of the knowledge and skills of the organisation as a whole.

Accessibility refers to the availability and easiness to contact the company. This means for example that the service is available by phone, that the waiting time is not too long, and that the service location is easy to access.

Courtesy refers to the attitudes, manners and respect of the company's personnel. This also means neat and flawless service.

Communication means using the customer's "language" and listening to the customer. It may mean that the company has to adjust its language for different customers. It includes giving customer information about price and service. In addition it means convincing the customer of the company's capability to solve problems.

Security means that there are no dangers, risks or doubts. The company's name and reputation are part of this security aspect. The contact personnel's personal properties also influence customers' opinions about company's security.

Understanding and knowing the customer involves making the effort to understand each customer's needs. As the relationship with a customer develops and progresses, the company should learn the customer's specific requirements. This means the regular customer is recognised and is served with some individual attention.

Tangibles contain the physical evidence of the service. This means, for example, the company's facilities and the appearance of the personnel.

In 1988 Parasuraman, Berry and Zeithaml conducted a large quantitative study in which they were able, by factor analysis, to reduce the former ten dimensions into five: tangibles, reliability, responsiveness, assurance, and empathy (Lewis, 1995).

Tangibles include physical facilities, equipment, and appearance of personnel. Reliability refers to the dependable and accurate performance of the service. Responsiveness reflects the firm's willingness to help customers and provide service promptly. Assurance includes employees' knowledge, courtesy, and ability to build trust. And empathy reflects the care and individual attention provided by the firm to its customers.

While reliability is largely concerned with service outcome, tangibles, responsiveness, assurance, and empathy are more concerned with the service process (Parasuraman & al., 1991). Whereas customers judge the accuracy and dependability of the delivered service, they judge the other dimensions as the service is being delivered.

This study considers both the full ten dimensions and the collapsed five dimensions in its analyses.

IMPLEMENTATION OF THE CORRELATION ANALYSIS

Correlation is used to describe the covariance of two variables. Correlation analysis provides a possibility to assess the existence or direction of the factor in the argument.

The significance level can be seen as the probability of making wrong conclusion from the hypothesis. The significance level chosen for this study is .01. A Guilford (1956) five-step model was used to interpret the correlation coefficients: 1) < .20 = low correlation, almost non-existing dependence, 2) .20-.40 = low correlation, certain, but weak dependence, 3) .40-.70 = moderate correlation, significant dependence, 4) .70-.90 = high correlation, evident dependence, 5) > .90 = very high correlation, very reliable dependence.

In the correlation matrix produced for this study there were a high number of low correlations, indicating that variables had weak dependencies. Therefore, the significance level of .40 (moderate correlation) was chosen as the lower control limit.

Correlation Between the Importance of the Selection Criteria

There were several important correlations between the ten dimensions of service quality that are presented in the Figure 14.3. Reliability of service of the printing house was positively correlated with responsiveness (r = .644; sig. > .01), competence (r = .528; sig. > .01), and credibility (r = .506; sig. > .01). Responsiveness was positively correlated with competence (r = .592; sig. > .01), courtesy (r = .461; sig. > .01), and credibility (r = .447; sig. > .01). Knowing and understanding the customer had a clear positive correlation only with the competence (r = .641; sig. > .01).

Figure 14.3. The Importance of Selection Criteria (10 Dimensions of Service Quality)

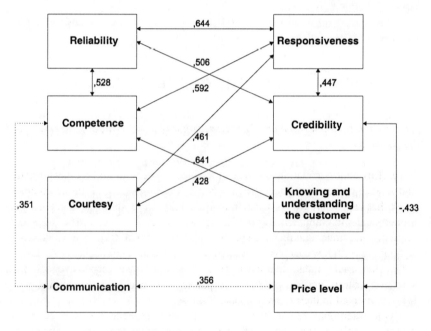

One very interesting negative correlation between the selection criteria was found. It was the negative correlation between price level and credibility (r = - .433; sig > .01). This means that if the customers of the company think that price is a very important selection criterion, they don't see company's credibility as important. So in order to get a lower price they are willing to compromise their credibility expectations.

Reliability of service of the printing house was positively correlated with responsiveness (r = .627; sig > .01) and assurance (r =.594; sig > .01). The correlation between reliability and empathy (r = .386; sig > .01) was very interesting because it was much weaker than the other correlation. Another exceptional finding was that tangibles had no statistically significant correlation with the other four dimensions of service quality (Figure 14.4).

Figure 14.4. The Importance of Selection Criteria (5 Dimensions of Service Quality)

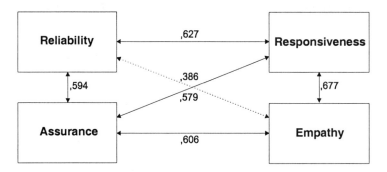

Correlation between Number of Problem Situations and Grades for Service and Performance

Several evident correlations between the selection criteria and the performance and service grades were found (Figure 14.5). If customers of a printing company think that responsiveness is a very important selection criteria, the company gets higher grades in competence (r = .670; sig > .01), reliability (r = .618; sig > .01), knowing and understanding the customer(r = .558; sig > .01), responsiveness (r = .555; sig > .01), security (r = .508; sig > .01), and accessibility (r = .486; sig > .01). This could mean that customers who emphasise responsiveness as a selection criteria choose printing companies that tend to be somewhat more service oriented in their operations and thinking.

One traditional key influence on customers' expectations is price. Many customers believe that the more they pay, the better the service should be, although they do not believe that low price is a legitimate excuse for poor service (Parasuraman & al., 1991). Therefore one interesting finding was the correlation between the importance of price as selection criteria and service and performance grades. If customers of a certain printing company keep the price level as a very important selection criteria, the company gets lower grades in reliability (r = -.509; sig > .01), accessibility (r = -.483; sig > .01), security (r = -.478; sig > .01), and responsiveness (r = -.414; sig > .01). This means that if a customer is only interested in getting the print job at the lowest possible price, they are also likely to get less reliable and responsive service. One might argue that companies that have chosen to compete with price do not invest much in service.

Figure 14.5. Importance of Selection Criteria and Performance and Service Grades (10 Dimensions of Service Quality)

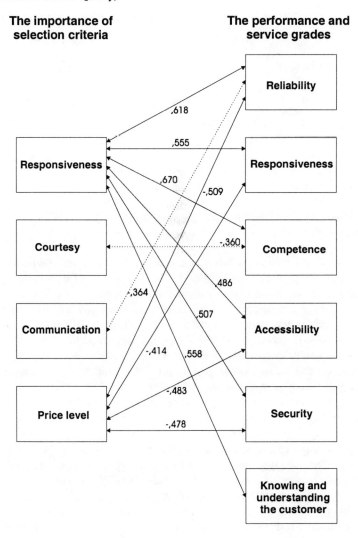

Correlation Between Service and Performance Grades

Several positive strong and evident correlations between the different service and performance grades were found in this study. All the correlations are presented in the Figure 14.6. Company's good grade in reliability of service was very strongly correlated with company's grade in security (r = .871; sig. > .01), responsiveness (r = .854; sig. > .01), and accessibility (r =.823; sig. > .01). Responsiveness was very strongly correlated with accessibility (r = .871; sig. >.01), and security (r = .849; sig. > .01). Knowing and understanding the customer had a strong and clear positive correlation with competence (r = .851; sig. > .01). Companies that received good grade in accessibility got good grades also in security (r = .809; sig. > .01).

Figure 14.6. Performance and Service Grades (10 Dimensions of Service Quality)

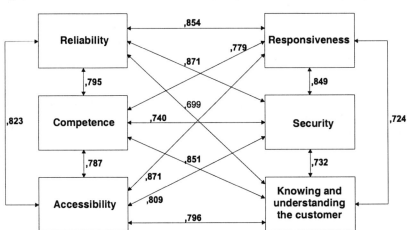

The correlations between different service and performance grades were also evident and strong when using the five dimensions of service quality (Figure 14.7). The strongest relationship was between company's grades in reliability and in responsiveness (r = .868; sig. > .01), and in assurance (r = .850; sig. > .01). Company's grade in responsiveness was strongly correlated with the grade in assurance (r = .848; sig. > .01). Companies receiving good grade in assurance got good grades also in empathy (r = .856; sig. > .01).

Figure 14.7. Performance and Service Grades (5 Dimensions of Service Quality)

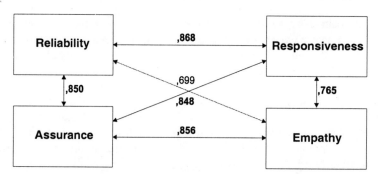

The companies were explored in order to find evaluation of dimensions of the customer service process that correlate with the overall grade given for service. The results of the analysis are presented in Figures 14.8 and 14.9. By paying special attention to areas of the service process that correlate strongly with the grade given for entire service process, the managers of print media firms can make sure that the management, customer liaisons and other staff pay special attention to a successful execution of these functions.

For customers of Finnish printing companies the service dimension that had the highest correlation with overall grade for performance and services received was reliability (r = .919; sig. > .01). No other dimension of service exceeded the .90 level, marking very high correlation. Five other dimensions of service exceeded the .70 level. These involved security, accessibility, competence, responsiveness, and knowing and understanding the customer.

Correlation Between Number of Problem Situations and Grades for Service and Performance

Several correlations between the number of problem situations and grades for service were found in this study. All the correlations are presented in Figure 14.10. Some of correlations were particularly strong and evident. Companies that had problems in reliability got lower grades in responsiveness (r = -.816; sig > .01) and naturally in reliability (r = -.800; sig > .01). Companies having problems in responsiveness got lower grades in responsiveness (r =-.816; sig > .01) and reliability (r = -.730; sig > .01). Problems in courtesy had a strong correlation with the company's grade for responsiveness (r = -.702; sig > .01).

Figure 14.8. Performance and Service Grades and Overall Grade for Services (10 Dimensions of Service Quality)

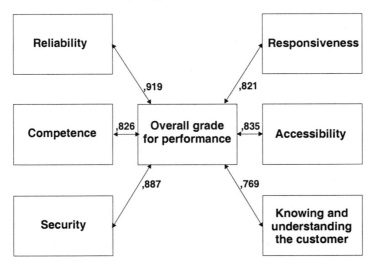

Figure 14. 9. Performance and Service Grades and Overall Grade for Services (5 Dimensions of Service Quality

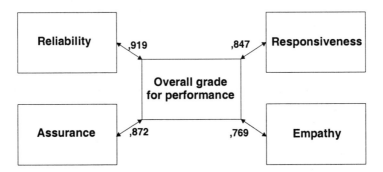

Companies that had problems in reliability got lower grades (see Figure 14.
11) in reliability ($r = -.800$; sig $> .01$), responsiveness ($r = -.704$; sig $> .01$),
assurance ($r = -.699$; sig $> .01$), and empathy ($r = -.588$; sig $> .01$). Companies
that had problems in responsiveness got lower grades in responsiveness ($r = -.732$; sig $> .01$), reliability ($r = -.660$; sig $> .01$), assurance ($r = -.660$; sig $> .01$),
and empathy ($r = -.500$; sig $> .01$).

Problems in assurance leads naturally to lower grades in assurance ($r = -.706$; sig $> .01$), reliability ($r = -.663$; sig $> .01$), responsiveness ($r = -.640$; sig $> .01$), and empathy ($r = -.633$; sig $> .01$). Companies that had problems in
empathy got lower grades in responsiveness ($r = -.673$; sig $> .01$), empathy ($r = -.618$; sig $> .01$), reliability ($r = -.599$; sig $> .01$), and assurance ($r = -.589$; sig $> .01$).

The more a company has problems in the different dimensions of service,
the worse the overall grade for performance and service will be. Problems in
reliability had the highest negative correlation with overall grade (Figure 14.12).
Problems in other dimensions of quality didn't exceed the .70 level, marking
high correlation. The findings of this study are in line with earlier studies
suggesting that reliability is the core of good service. Companies are supposed to
be accurate and dependable and provide the service they promised to provide.
Problems in all dimensions of service had a negative impact on company's
overall grade for services, but the reliability of the company was clearly the
strongest factor of customers' overall assessment of service quality. The more
reliable the company is the better the overall grade for performance and service
will be. Although the reliability is the most important dimension in meeting
customer expectations, the process dimensions (especially assurance,
responsiveness and empathy) are important in exceeding customer expectations.

Figure 14.10. Frequency of the Problem Situation and the Performance and Service Grades (10 Dimensions of Service Quality)

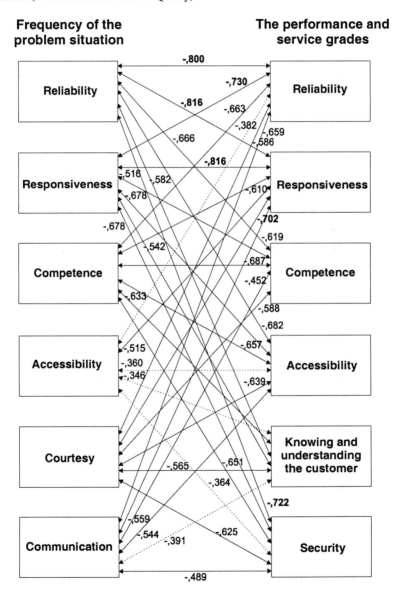

Figure 14.11 Frequency of the Problem Situation and the Performance and Service Grades (5 Dimensions of Service Quality)

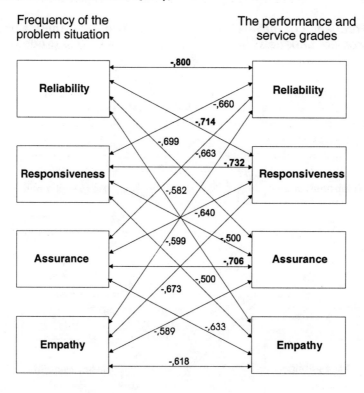

Figure 14.12. Frequency of the Problem Situation and the Overall Grade for Performance and Sevice (5 Dimensions of Service Quality)

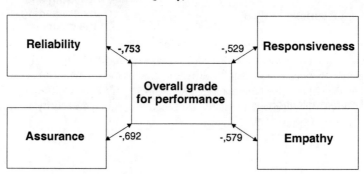

Correlation Between Number of Problem Situations in Different Dimensions of Quality

The customers of Finnish printing companies felt that there were fairly few problems occurring in the customer relationships. Several positive correlations between the number of problem situations were found in this study. All the correlations are presented in Figure 14.13. Reliability proved once again to be the core of service. Companies that had problems in reliability tend to have problems also in competence (r = .744; sig > .01), communication (r = .734; sig > .01), and responsiveness (r = .704; sig > .01).

Companies that had problems in responsiveness had problems also in accessibility (r = .694; sig > .01), courtesy (r = .664; sig > .01), and communication (r = .628; sig > .01). Problems in communication leads to problems in courtesy (r = .601; sig > .01).

Figure 14.13. Frequency of the Problem Situations (10 Dimensions of Service Quality)

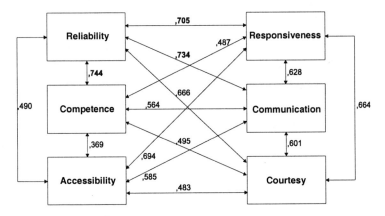

The highest correlation with problem situations between the different dimensions service was reliability and assurance (r = .744; sig > .01). No other correlation between problems in different dimensions of quality exceeded the .70 level, marking high correlation. Three other correlations between problems in different dimensions of quality exceeded the .60 correlation level. These correlations are presented in Figure 14.14.

Figure 14.14. Frequency of the Problem Situations (5 Dimensions of Service Quality)

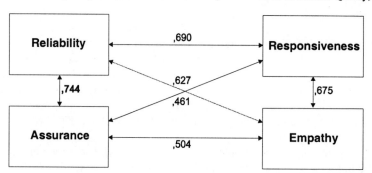

Correlation Between Inconvenience of the Possible Problem Situations in Different Dimensions of Service Quality

According to Grönlund, Jacobs and Picard (2001) printing company customers felt that almost all of the potential problems presented in the original questionnaire were causing at least some inconvenience for them. Inability to meet the agreed deadlines, indifference towards complaints, ambiguity of what was agreed upon and things not proceeding without prompting were problems that were felt to cause great inconvenience. Several positive correlations between the inconvenience of problem situations were found also in this study. All the correlations are presented in Figure 14.15. The highest correlation with inconvenience of the problem situations between the different dimensions service was reliability and responsiveness   (r = .821; sig > .01), and responsiveness and accessibility (r = .821; sig > .01). Five other correlations between the inconvenience of problems in different dimensions of quality exceeded the correlation the .70 level, marking high correlation.

The highest correlation with the inconvenience of the possible problem situations between the different dimensions of service was between reliability and responsiveness   (r = .878; sig > .01). Three other correlations between problems in different dimensions of quality exceeded the correlation the .70 level. These correlations are presented in Figure 14.16.

Figure 14.15. Inconvenience of the Problem Situations (10 Dimensions of Service Quality)

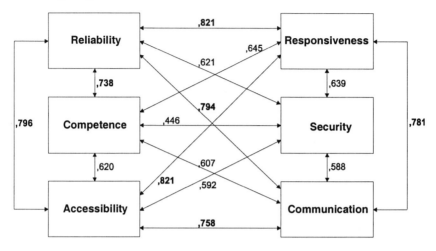

Figure 14.16. Inconvenience of the Problem Situations (5 Dimensions of Service Quality)

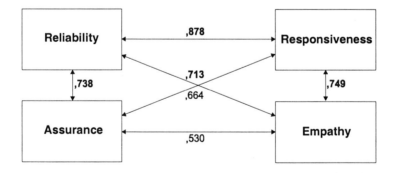

The Inconvenience of the Possible Problem Situation and the Importance of the Selection Criteria

According to Grönlund, Jacobs and Picard (2001), customers of Finnish printing companies' feel that most of the potential problem situations are at least fairly problematic for their business. Despite that view, there were only few correlations between inconvenience of the problem situation and the importance of the selection criteria (Figure 14.17). Customers who felt that poor accessibility is very problematic for their business put less weight on price as a selection criteria (r = -.562; sig. > .01). Price was also a less important selection criterion for customers who felt that poor communication (r = -.437; sig. > .01), and worse responsiveness (r = -.428; sig. > .01) are very inconvenient for their business.

Figure 14.17. Frequency of the Problem Situations (10 Dimensions of Service Quality)

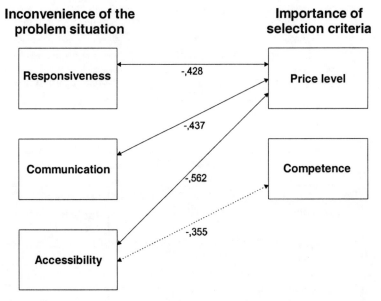

Correlation Between Importance of the Price Level and the Inconvenience of the Possible Problem Situations in the Different Dimensions of Service Quality

Earlier in this chapter we stated that many customers do not believe that low price is a legitimate excuse for poor service. Nevertheless the findings of this study suggest that customers who keep price level as a very important selection criteria are, at least to some extent, indifferent if the company has problems in accessibility (r = -.562; sig > .01), in communication (r = -.437; sig > .01), and in responsiveness (r = -.428; sig > .01). On the other hand, it also means that if the customer is willing to pay more for the print job and service, he also expects more responsive, prompt and individual service from the print company.

Relationship Between Customer Satisfaction and Company's Financial Performance

The final step of this study was to examine the relationships between different dimensions of customer satisfaction and performance measures. The relationship between different dimensions of service quality and several financial performance measures were weak, and only one statistically significant correlation between the performance and service grades and financial key figures were found in this study. The better grade a company got for price level, the lower was the company's value added per employee ($r = -.453$; sig $> .01$). In other words, companies that received good grade in price level had lower productivity. No other correlation between a company's service and performance grades in different dimensions of quality exceeded the .40 level, marking moderate correlation.

DISCUSSION

Intensifying competition, deregulation of the media business and the increasing quality expectations by customers have forced print media companies to concentrate increasingly on customer satisfaction. By regularly assessing the level of satisfaction among their customers, managers of printing companies are able to better understand the wishes and needs of their customers. At the same time it enables the managers to define the primary factors and products that create customer satisfaction.

The measures for customer satisfaction and service quality have, during the past decade, become widely used tools for evaluating company performance. The firms measure service quality and customer satisfaction because they believe these elements to be indicators for other important components of success, such as customer loyalty, profitability, market share and growth. The underlying assumption of that kind of pursuit is that customer satisfaction is a significant contributor to customer loyalty and, eventually, the company's financial success. The logic of this approach originates in the idea presented by Drucker in 1954, that customers are the most important resource for a firm and when customers are happy, it leads to success for the firm.

Previous studies have been able to identify the key service dimensions. For this study questionnaire's statements and evaluations were combined in to ten and five service dimensions to clarify the relationships between different service dimensions. Price level was handled as a separate indicator. These indicators were then used to produce evidence about service quality and customer satisfaction. These are important because they influence consumers' willingness to purchase from specific companies and thus the demand for other products and services. These were then considered with issues such as price to determine relationship between customer expectations, service delivered, and price.

The Finnish printing companies have traditionally been very production driven. In order to be able to meet the new challenges printing companies should move from product orientation to more customer and service orientation. This shift towards service orientation and improved customer satisfaction could create new opportunities and possibilities for printing companies. Some researchers (Jones & Sasser, 1995; Reichheld & Sasser, 1990) have concluded that even in price-driven commodity industries creating complete satisfaction will often lift the product or service beyond the commodity category.

Customers who felt that reliability of the printing company is a very important selection criterion felt also that responsiveness, competence, and credibility are important as well. Responsiveness importance as a selection criterion was positively correlated with competence, courtesy, and credibility. Knowing and understanding the customer had a clear positive relationship with the competence. One very interesting finding was the relationship between price level and credibility as selection criteria. If the customers of a company think that price is a very important selection criteria, they don't see company's credibility as important. So in order to get a lower price they are willing to compromise their credibility expectations.

One traditional key influence on customers' expectations is price. It is said that for many customers low price is not a legitimate excuse for poor service. Therefore one interesting finding was the correlation between the importance of price as a selection criterion and service and performance grades. If customers of a certain printing company keep the price level as a very important selection criterion, the company gets lower grades in reliability, accessibility, security, and responsiveness. This means that if a customer is only interested in getting the print job at the lowest possible price, they are also likely to get less reliable and responsive service. One might argue that companies that have chosen to compete with price do not invest much in service.

One definite conclusion of this study is that the more a company has problems in the different dimensions of service, the worse the overall grade for overall performance and service will be. Problems in reliability had the highest negative correlation with overall grade. The findings of this study are in line with earlier studies suggesting that reliability is the core of good service. Companies are supposed to be accurate and dependable and provide the service they promised to provide. Problems in all dimensions of service had a negative impact on company's overall grade for services, but the reliability of the company was clearly the strongest factor of customers' overall assessment of service quality.

Printing companies should concentrate on the problems in those service dimensions that the customers feel most affect the work of the firm they represent. And if the problems occur on those service dimensions, the company needs to solve them quickly, or it starts losing customers. This research has shown consistently that customers of the Finnish printing companies value reliability above all the other dimensions of service. Companies that do not provide the service core that customers are buying, a print job within an agreed schedule, deceive their customers in the most direct way. And so problems in reliability had the strongest negative impact to company's overall grade for service and performance. Printing companies are supposed to be accurate and dependable and provide the service they promised to provide. The more reliable the company is the better the overall grade for performance and service will be. Although the reliability is the most important dimension in meeting customer expectations, the process dimensions (especially assurance, responsiveness and empathy) are important in exceeding customer expectations.

Findings of this study suggest that customers keeping price level as a very important selection criterion are, at least to some extent, indifferent if the company has problems in some dimensions of service quality. Customers are, in order to get lower price, willing to accept a printing company that is less responsive and harder to access. This means for example that the personnel's willingness and capability to serve the customer are not as good than with some. It also involves the timeliness of service. So by selecting the lowest price they are also willing to accept a longer delivery time for the print job. What this doesn't mean is that even though they are willing to accept a longer distribution time they still want the printing company to keep to agreed schedules.

No strong link between customer satisfaction and company's financial performance was found in this study. This may occur, for example, beccause a company might make a strategic decision that increasing its service quality and customer satisfaction is important, but in doing so, it has spend a lot of money. This could result in high customer satisfaction, but lower incomes. Conversely, internal cost-cutting measures might be taken that will make a company seem more profitable in any given time period, even if customers are not satisfied. Given the fact that many of the actions of the company that are beyond the scope of customer satisfaction have such a huge impact on profits in any give time period, it's not so surprising that this relationship between financial success in a particular time point and customer satisfaction at the same time point might be insignificant.

Only a few researchers have examined the relationship between customer satisfaction and financial performance. Most of those researchers have taken a cross-sectional approach to examining the relationship and subsequently have found inconclusive results. So suggestion is that this relationship should be examined using multiple time frames. The use of longitudinal data sets when examining customer satisfaction and financial performance in the Finnish print industry would give a better picture of the real importance of customer satisfaction to company's financial performance and success.

REFERENCES

Anderson, E., Fornell, C. & Lehmann, R. (1994) Customer satisfaction, market share, and profitability, *Journal of Marketing* Vol. 58 (July): 53-66

Bernhardt, K., Donthu, N. & Kennett, P. (2000) A longitudinal analysis of satisfaction and profitability, *Journal of Business Research* 47, 161-171

Berry, L. (1995) Lessons from a ten-year study for service quality in America. In *Customer satisfaction research*, ed. by Richard Brookes, 7-18

Bitner, M., Booms, B. & Tetreault, M. (1990) The service encounter: Diagnosing favorable and unfavourable incidents, *Journal of Marketing*, 54, 71-84

Blomquist, R., Dahl, J. & Haeger, T. (1993) *Suhdemarkkinointi: Asiakassuhteet strategisena kilpailukeinona.* Weilin+Göös: Jyväskylä

Bolton, R. & Drew, J. (1991) A multistage model of customers' assassments of service quality and value, *Journal of Consumer Research* 17 (March): 375-384

Boulding, B.,Kalra, A.,Staelin, R., & Zeithaml, V. (1993) A Dynamic process model of service quality: From expectations to behavioral intentions, *Journal of Marketing*, Vol. 30, February, 7-27

Buzzell , R. & Gale, B. (1987) *The PIMS principles: Linking strategy to performance.* New York: Free Press.

Churchill, G. & Suprenant, C. (1982) An Investigation into the Determinants of Customer Satisfaction, *Journal of Marketing* Vol. XIX (November 1982): 491-504

Drucker, Peter (1954) *The practice of management.* Harper & Row: New York

Erevelles, S. & Leavitt, C. (1992) A comparison of current models of consumer satisfaction/dissatisfaction, *Journal of Consumer Satisfaction, Dissatisfaction and Complaining Behaviour,* Vol. 5 1992, 104-113

Fornell, C., & Robinson, W. (1983). Industrial organization and consumer satisfaction/dissatisfaction, *Journal of Consumer Research,* 9, 403-411

Fornell, C. & Wernerfelt, B. (1987) Defensive marketing strategy by customer complaint behavior: A theoretical analysis, *Journal of marketing research* 24 (November): 337-346

Francken, D., & van Raaij, W. (1985) Socio-economic and demographic determinants of consumer problem perception, *Journal of Consumer Policy,* 8, 303-314

Grönlund, M., Jacobs, R. & Picard, R. (2001) *Customer satisfaction – elemements and preconditions; expectations and assessments of Finnish printing industry customers.* Series B Research Reports, B 2/2001, Business Research and Development Centre, Turku School of Economics and Business Administration.

Grönroos, C. (1998a) Marketing services: the case of a missing product, *Journal of business and industrial marketing,* Vol. 13, No. 4-5, 322-338

Grönroos, C. (1998b) *Nyt kilpaillaan palveluilla.* Gummerus: Jyväskylä

Guilford, J. P. (1956) *Fundamental statistics in psychology.* New York: McGraw-Hill

Hunt, H. (ed.). (1977) *Conseptulization and measurement of consumer satisfaction and dissatisfaction* (Report No. 77-103). Cambridge, MA: Marketing Science Institute

Jones, T. & Sasser, W. (1995) Why satisfied customers defect, *Harvard Business Review,* 73, 88-101

Lewis, B. (1995) Measuring customer expectations and satisfaction In *Customer satisfaction research,* ed. by Richard Brookes, 57-76

Miller, J.A. (1977) Studying satisfaction, modyfying models, eliciting expectations, posing problems, and making meaningful measurements. In *Conseptulization and measurement of consumer satisfaction and dissatisfaction* (Report No. 77-103). Cambridge, MA: Marketing Science Institute

Nelson, E., Rust, R., Zahorik, A., Rose, R., Batalden, P.& Siemanski, B. (1992) Do patient perceptions of quality relate to hospital financial performance? *Journal of Health Care Marketing* (Decenber 1992), 6-13

Oliver, R. (1980) A Cognitive model of the antecedents and consequenses of satisfaction decisions, *Journal of Marketing Research*, 16, 460-469

Parasuraman, A., Zeithaml, V. & Berry, L. (1985) A Conceptual model of service quality and its implications for future research, *Journal of Marketing*, Vol. 49, 41-50

Parasuraman, A., Zeithaml, V. & Berry, L. (1988) SERVQUAL: A multiple item scale for measuring consumer perceptions of service quality, *Journal of Retailing*, Vol 64 (Spring): 12-40

Parasuraman, A., Berry, L., & Zeithaml, V. (1990) Guidelines for conducting service quality research, *Marketing Research*, 2, 33-44

Parasuraman, A., Berry, L., & Zeithaml, V. (1991a) Refinement and reassessment of the SERVQUAL scale, *Journal of Retailing*, 67, 420-450

Parasuraman, A., Berry, L. & Zeithaml, V. (1991b) Understanding customer expectations of a service, *Sloan Management Review*, Vol. 32 No. 3, 39-48

Patterson, P. & Johnson, L. (1993) Disconfirmation of expectation and the gap model of service quality: an integrated paradigm, *Journal of Consumer Satisfaction, Dissatisfaction and Complaining Behaviour*, Vol. 6 1993, 90-99

Reichheld, F.F. & Sasser, W.E. (1990) Zero defections: Quality comes to services, *Harvard Business Review*, 68, 105-111

Rosen, D. & Surprenant, C. (1998) Evaluating relationships: are satisfaction and quality enough? *International Journal of Service Industry Management*, Vol. 9, No. 2, 103-125

Rust, R. & Zahorik, A. & Keiningham, T. (1995) Return on quality: Making service quality financially accountable, *Journal of Marketing*, 59, 58-70

Schneider, B. (1991) Service quality and profits: Can you have your cake and it too? *Human Resource Planning*, 14, 151-157

Singh, J. (1991) Industry characteristics and consumer dissatisfaction, *Journal of Consumer Affairs*, 25, 19-56

Spreng, R. & Olshavsky, R. (1992). A Desires-as-Standard Model of Consumer Satisfaction: Implications for measuring satisfaction, *Journal of consumer Satisfaction, Dissatisfaction and Complaining Behaviour*, Vol 5 1992, 45-54

Spreng, R., Mackenzie, S., Olshavsky, R. (1996) Re-examination of the determinants of consumer satisfaction, *Journal of Marketing*, Vol 60 (July): 15-32

Tse D.K. & Wilton, P.C (1988) Models of Customer Satisfaction Formation: An Extension, *Journal of Marketing research*, 25: 204-212

Wirtz, J. & Bateson, J. (1999) Introducing uncertain performance expectations models for services, *International Journal of Service Industry Management*, Vol. 10, No. 1, 82-99

Zahorik, A. & Rust, R. (1992) Modelling the impact of service quality on profitability. In *Advances in service marketing and management* ed. David Bowen and Stephen Brown. Greenwich, CT:JAI: 247-276

Zeithaml, V., Parasuraman, A. & Berry, L. (1990) *Delivering quality service.* New York: The Free Press.

Subject Index

Author Index

Contributors

Alan B. Albarran is professor and chair of the Department of Radio, Television and Film at the University of North Texas, United States of America. He is editor of *The Journal of Media Economics* and the author of *Media Economics: Understanding Markets, Industries and Concepts, Management of Electronic Media, Understanding the Web: Social, Political, and Economic Dimensions of the Internet*, and *Global Media Economics: Commercialization and Integration of World Media Markets*.

Angel Arrese Angel Arrese is Associate Dean at the School of Communication at University of Navarra, Spain. He is Assistant Professor of Marketing and has been Director of the Media Management Department (1996-2001). His main research interests are media marketing management and the economic and financial media markets. Among his main works are *La identidad de The Economist* (1995), and *Economic and financial press: from the beginnings to the first oil crisis* (2001). Professor Arrese is a member of the editorial boards of the *Journal of Media Economics* and *Comunicación y Sociedad*.

Piet Bakker is a researcher at the Amsterdam School of Communication, Department of Communication Science, University of Amsterdam, The Netherlands. He studied political science, worked as a journalist, and previously taught mass communication at the Journalism School in Utrecht. His current research concerns are journalism, traditional media, and the Internet.

Allan Brown is senior lecturer in economics and an associate at the Australian Key Centre for Cultural and Media Policy, Griffith University, Australia and the 2002 visiting research fellow at the Media Group, Turku School of Economics and Business Administration, Finland. He is the author of *Commercial Media in Australia: Economics, Ownership, Technology and Regulation* and numerous articles on media policy and economics.

Terje Gaustad is a doctoral fellow at the Norwegian School of Management's Centre for Media Economics. His main research interests are interfirm relations and investments in the entertainment industry as well as economic property rights issues related to entertainment content-production and distribution.

David Goff is director of the School of Mass Communication and Journalism at the University of Southern Mississippi, United States of America. His research interests centre on the convergence of the media and telecommunications industries, especially in Western Europe. Recent publications include *Understanding the Web: Social, Political and Economic Dimensions of the Internet* (with A. B. Albarran, 2000), as well as book chapters examining the Media markets of the United Kingdom and the Internet access market in Western Europe

Mikko Grönlund is research manager at the Media Group, Turku School of Economics and Business Administration, Finland. He is the author and co-author of numerous publications including *Competitiveness of the European Union Publishing Industries, Managing Company Atmosphere: Relations Among Organisational Characteristics and Employee Perceptions,* and *Customer Satisfaction—Elements and Preconditions: Expectations and Assessments of Finnish Printing Industry Customers.* He is responsible for the annual financial and economic statistics of the Finnish graphic arts, advertising, commercial radio, and new media industries.

Jan E. S. Helgesen is a doctoral fellow at the Centre for Media Economics, Norwegian School of Management BI. He did his graduate studies in Economics at the University of Oslo, and he wrote his cand. polit. (M. Phil.) thesis on a junior research project in the Central Bank of Norway. He also holds a BA in Philosophy and Sociology from the University of Oslo.

Li-Chuan (Evelyn) Mai is an associate professor in the School of Communications, Ming Chuan University, Taipei, Taiwan, and has researched the Taiwanese media since 1987. She has worked as a journalist and editor and is a director of the newspaper Media News. She obtained her doctorate from the University of Westminster and specialises in media management.

Mercedes Medina is director of Media Management Department at School of Communication at the University of Navarra, Spain, and teaches audio-visual media economy. She is the author of "The impact of European media groups in the Spanish television market," in *Evolving Media Markets: Effects of Economic and Policy Changes* (1998) and *Valoración publicitaria de los programas de televisión.* She is the co-author of *Estrategias de marketing de las empresas de televisión en España.*

Terry Moellinger is a graduate research assistant in the Department of Radio, Television and Film at the University of North Texas, United States of America, and has been accepted into the doctoral programme at the University of Oklahoma.

Marina Pavlikova is a researcher at the Faculty of Journalism, Moscow State University, Russia. She is lecturer of the Centre for Russian Finnish Studies and coordinator of the Nordica Programme. Her current research focuses on Nordic media system, especially Finnish mass media and culture, new media and the role of information networks in media progress.

Robert G. Picard is VTTS professor of Media Economics and manager of the Media Group, Turku School of Economics and Business Administration, Finland. He is author or editor of 15 books including *The Economics and Financing of Media Companies, Evolving Media Markets: Effects of Economics and Policy Changes; The Newspaper Publishing Industry; Competitiveness of the European Union Publishing Industries, Media Economics: Concepts and Issues*, and *Press Concentration and Monopoly: New Perspectives on Newspaper Ownership and Operation*. He was founding editor of *The Journal of Media Economics*.

Anastasios E. Politis is a member of the research group for Media Technology and Graphic Arts, Department of Numerical Analysis and Computer Science at the Royal Institute of Technology (KTH) Stockholm, Sweden. He holds the position of assistant professor at the Department of Graphic Arts Technology, Athens Technological Educational Institute (TEI) in Greece, where he works since 1981. He has more than 25 years of experience in education and training, projects and studies on the European graphic arts and media sector. He is author of 4 books and over 100 articles and studies.

Richard van der Wurff is an associate professor at the Amsterdam School of Communications Research ASCoR, University of Amsterdam, The Netherlands. His research interests include competition and performance of information markets, innovation and competitive strategies of information providers, and new approaches in communications policy.

Aldo van Weezel is a professor in the School of Journalism at the University of the Andes, Chile. He is an Industrial Engineer, and holds a Master of Science in Engineering. His research interests are in the areas of media management and economics and new media technologies.